IT HAPPENED
THIS WAY

ELLEN COIT ELLIOTT

Very truly yours
Ellen Coit Elliott

IT HAPPENED THIS WAY

American Scene

ELLEN COIT ELLIOTT

STANFORD UNIVERSITY PRESS

Stanford University, California

STANFORD UNIVERSITY PRESS
STANFORD UNIVERSITY, CALIFORNIA

THE BAKER AND TAYLOR COMPANY
55 FIFTH AVENUE, NEW YORK

THE MARUZEN COMPANY
TOKYO, OSAKA, KYOTO, SENDAI

INTRODUCING THE BOOK

THIS BOOK is a slice of American life, veraciously reported, covering some seventy-five years. All the characters are real persons, appearing in their true, unfictionized natures and mostly performing under their own names.

Part I, "Growing up in York State," is the story of a well-born child, rooted in New England ancestry, and brought up in the lovely Lake Region of central New York and the villages and small towns of other parts of the state. Connecticut was our mother, but New York the family adopted as a beloved foster parent about the turn of the eighteenth into the nineteenth century. It is a family chronicle, written in pictured episodes, cinema fashion. To freshen and enlarge my memories (for the child was I) I have had bundles of old letters preserved and added to from generation to generation by a line of articulate and sociable forebears. They march through vanished circumstance, capably carrying on, busy and lighthearted, vivid to the life as when they sat down and wrote.

My aim has not been to trot out for public inspection my personal memoirs (average and unimportant), but through my own experience to show the rich, warm, fruitful life that surrounded and nourished me, and to recall again into reality those elders back of me, native to our country from its beginnings, the like of whom a diluted America shall not see again. This record should inform the reader what New York State people said and thought and how behaved—for instance, how they brought up their children—while the 1860's and 1870's were stepping along, showing in its cinema flashes the life of home and community in

v

those vanished years. If the great stories of this country need to be told—and they do—so do the little domestic ones; for the hero stands on the shoulders of the undistinguished crowd, and the public event vibrates and echoes in the group of every household. That is why I give my childhood account of Lincoln's death—not for its significance in world history, but to show how it actually seemed on that very day to the family in a New York hill village when Peter, running up the road from Watkins, shouted the news over the fence, and Mother (from South Carolina) was found weeping in the woodshed, and Grandma "went around and shut all the window blinds."

As an American for ten generations I have been interested to carry out this aim of intimacy even further back. Having a grandmother given to telling the stories she heard from her elders and a treasure of family documents accumulated and "handed down," I carry back to the Revolution by a living and by a word-of-mouth family tradition to the "Mayflower" and the Great Migration; to the founding of the early settlements and the spread of the new pioneer communities who ventured from the seaboard toward the West. A girl in my teens, I touched my grandmother's hand and thus linked back to Washington; for her father served as a young lieutenant and a staff officer under him, and Grandmother could vividly describe her father so that I saw him plain through her girlish eyes.

Part II is no less typical of the American scene; for, characteristically, this early-colonial family, moving from Massachusetts to Connecticut, then to the city of New York and then into that state's "Western wilds," at last jumped over to the Pacific to have a hand again in a pioneer enterprise, the organizing of Stanford University. Part II, "Transplanted to California," details the beginnings of Stanford in the amazing weeks of the first summer, before the earliest buildings were ready, the President in a corner somewhere with a roll-top desk and a secretary, riotously appointing his faculty and reducing his visions to concrete plans. From the opening, October 1, 1891, the record is here of the informal family and social life of the University community, a tale of half a century, this also being my own story, for we came West with Dr. Jordan three months before the University's opening and have taken our part in the campus life ever since.

My warmest thanks for appreciative help and encouragement go to Miss Margaret Whiting of Deerfield, Massachusetts, and to Mrs. Helen Stirling and Mrs. May Hurlbut Smith of Stanford. I am much indebted also to Mrs. Clarissa Kimber for the extensive use I have made, in my chapter on the war, of her book *The Story of the First Flag.*

E. C. E.

STANFORD UNIVERSITY
  November 1, 1940

CONTENTS

Part One

GROWING UP IN YORK STATE

Part Two

TRANSPLANTED TO CALIFORNIA

ix

CONTENTS

LIST OF ILLUSTRATIONS

Part One

GROWING UP
IN YORK STATE

E. W. B.
M. C. B.

IN GRATITUDE

I

FLOATING MEMORIES

When I was two years old they took me to a Sunday School picnic. It was at the village of West Dresden. I was born there, Father was the minister, and the picnic was on a grassy, tree-shaded point running out from the shores of Seneca Lake. I sat on the grass and my mother sat beside me. A tree which I felt to be enormous towered above me. I fingered smooth, dove-colored, flat stones from the beach; I heard a quiet murmur of talk; I looked up into my mother's smiling face and was happy.

When I was three or four and put to bed upstairs, I waked in the early dusk and knew that I was alone in the house. After listening a while I felt that I must do something about it. I turned on my stomach and dripped my legs out of bed, they would not touch the floor. I waggled them downward, pushing my body toward the edge with my hands. Good! The floor was touched by my toes; soon I was standing entirely independent of the bed. I walked slowly down the stairs, feeling solemn, and was refreshed to see when I entered the kitchen a glowing fire shining through the grate of the cookstove. I sat down on a wooden chair and put my feet up on the hearth toward the blaze. The house was very still, I was quite alone. I thought about the work which had to be done. I undertook it soberly: I felt that I could manage. But the sermons? Could I manage the sermons?

Here my parents came in and were astonished to see me sitting by the kitchen stove instead of in bed and asleep. I told

3

them I was alone, they were gone, I thought I could do the housework but I didn't know about preaching the sermons. They had
just been to prayer meeting next door.

I was with a little girl in our yard with green bushes near us.
We had a small block of red paint from my paint box and we
were quarreling violently. I call the paint "fire-red" and she
says its name is "vermilion."

"It *is* fire-red!" I am hot and prickly and very angry.

"It *isn't*, it's vermilion!"

"It *is* fire-red! Fire-red! Fire-red! Fire-red!" How can
anybody not know the right names for things. *"Fire-red!"*

"It isn't, it's vermilion!"

My mother puts her head out of the window and asks us what
we are quarreling about. I tell her. "It *is* fire-red, isn't it? Not
vermilion, Mother?" She says they mean the same thing.

I visited at Uncle Lounsbury's across the Lake at Ovid. He
was the minister. He had a strawberry patch in the big front
yard and I saw him in it bending over the plants. He wrote his
sermons sitting in a large chair that had one arm made into a
sort of shelf for him to write on, and the shelf was covered with
green cloth. When he was not there, I climbed up in the chair
and wished I knew how to write so that I could do it on the little
shelf. Their house had great double parlors, shaded by green
blinds, flowing white lace curtains at the windows. On the walls
were handsome pictures, such as "The Voyage of Life" and
"Youth and Age." The grand-looking sofa was black horsehair
and slippery, but I loved to sit on it—like a throne. The carpet
was deep-red roses in bunches. Aunt Lounsbury was fat and
jolly. But she liked me to eat my crusts: "Eat your crusts, Nellie.
That'll make your hair curl."

At Ovid I played with the children who lived next door. We
were in a rough horse-shed which had dark brown board walls
and roof and no floor, but muck all over from wall to wall. We
played, going along the beam at the side, holding fast to the wall,

to see if we could go all the way through without falling off. When part way through I fell off into the horrible manure and filth. I am shocked to the soul. I am defiled beyond remedy and can never be clean again. I scramble up and cry loudly. They tell me not to mind: they will scrape me off, it will be all right. I know better. I race home bawling, wiggling through the fence as fast as I can, go in at the best front door between the nice white-painted doorposts, and climb the white stairs. My filthy skirts go swish, swish against the white banisters at every step. I cannot help it, nothing can help it. It is a part of my uncleanness and misery. My heart is bursting with anguish. I cry and howl. "Cousin Ma-a-ary! Cousin Ma-a-ary!" I call—she will help me, she will help me.

Cousin Mary comes along the upper hall in a pink calico dress, walking easily over the flowered carpet. She takes me and cleans me up. I feel better: I had not thought it could be done.

My mother sang,

> Shall we gather at the ri-i-iver
> Where bright angel feet have trod . . . .

She sang,

> My days are gliding swiftly by
> And I a pilgrim stranger . . . .

And,

> We will walk in the light
>   In the light, in the light,
> We will walk in the light,
>   In the light of God.

My grandfather and grandmother live at Burdett. We go to make them a visit. We arrive in the evening and they have not got the letter we wrote. They do not expect us. We go up on the porch in the dark and open the door to the bright sitting room. They are all kneeling down, having family prayers. My grandfather goes on praying; Aunt Lidy and Aunt Louise turn their heads and open their eyes at us, and Grandma rises silently from her knees. They look surprised and pleased. Nobody says anything until Grandpa stops praying, which he does soon.

In the Burdett sitting room is a sewing stand which Aunt Louise and Aunt Lidy have made. It is in the shape of an hourglass, covered with flowered calico, and stands by the window of the stoop. Small puckered bags hang around its upper edge holding spools, buttons, and thimbles. Along the wall by Grandma's bedroom door is a low lounge covered with flowered cloth and with a flounce reaching to the floor. My aunts keep their workbaskets under the lounge and they are hidden by the flounce. I admire this neat arrangement.

I am sleeping with my grandmother in her small bedroom. I wake in the night lying next the wall, find my grandmother sitting propped up with her knees hunched up in front of her, reading by a lighted lamp on the bureau. I am screened behind the hill of her knees. I feel dark and warm and cosy. She does not know I am awake.

Grandma calls her best dress "my bombazine," a nice round word; but I think it odd to call a dress "bombazine." She has her shawls folded in the bottom drawer of the secretary in the sitting room. There are two very little drawers in the upper part of the secretary, for pens and such things. In one of them she always keeps a two-dollar bill: no matter what happens, she will always have a two-dollar bill. She takes her naps in the front parlor where it is cool and still, the green blinds closed. She lies on the long, big, black, mahogany lounge and puts her head on the pillow of worsted-work—a wreath of roses.

In the hall, always dark, is a tall, narrow closet at the side of the front door (always shut), with a brass catch to it. They call it "the depot." In it are shawls and veils and scarfs; they smell nice when the door is opened.

I love the smooth white curving surface of the wall that goes upstairs. As I climb the stairs I touch it along with my fingers. Grandma says not to do that because it will soil it. Another thing she tells me: I sit with my feet on the rungs of the chair. She comes and tells me not to do that because it scratches the rungs. I am astonished. I supposed the rungs were made to put your feet on. Grandma says no, they are made to hold the chair together.

If you open the cellarway door off the kitchen you see the wrong side of the curve of the stairway, all rough lath-and-plaster. There is a string bag hanging up there, and you can always get a piece of string. The cellar steps go down, and if they don't want to bother they set the milk and butter on the top step instead of going all the way down. The cellar floor is black, very hard, smooth earth, moist. There is a swing shelf on account of mice.

The pantry off the kitchen is light from a window, not like other people's pantries. It has a broad shelf painted punkin color. Two silver tablespoons lie on it neatly side by side. In the small low cupboard under the sink in the back entry is a glass jar with raisins in it. They are not very good. In the sink is a wooden soap dish with mottled soap in it, red-and-white.

My grandfather is a doctor, not now practicing; but he once traveled all over the hills of Hector in his buggy and tended the sick; and Grandma says nobody had time to be sick except at night—and he always went, no matter what. He was a good doctor. But he could not collect his bills.

Grandpa goes across the back yard with a tin pail, and gets over the fence by some little steps into the field. The cow stands close to the fence and he milks her. Sometimes the cow is in the yard at the side of the barn instead of in the field. One day I am climbing the fence of the yard, in play. I take off my straw hat and stick it up on a high post of the fence. It is a small round hat with a black ribbon round it. I forget to take it down. The next day we go to get it and it is gone. The cow has eaten it up.

Far beyond the field is the church, and we sometimes go to church across the field instead of by the street. We hear the church bell across the field on Sunday morning. It is a convent bell brought from Spain. It rings first, and that is the first bell. You must get ready then to go to church—your Sunday dress and all your clean underclothes. Afterward it tolls, and that is the last bell. You must be in your place in the pew when it stops. I think "pew" is an odd word; I do not like it.

I like to go to church—anywhere, but specially at Grandpa's in Burdett. Everybody gets ready together, and we go along together in our best clothes, clean and bright, like flowers when it has rained. Sunday clothes even have a sweet smell. Ladies' hats are flowery. Ribbons tie under their chins or under their ears. Gentlemen in black walk along with their families, we children taking hold of hands walking in front of our father and mother. We like to slat the picket fences with a stick as we go, but we must not because it makes a noise—we must not be noisy on Sunday. I am glad we mustn't. It is more peaceful to walk along quietly this way, all the people we know going along the same, and the last bell tolling sweetly. The maple trees shade us greenly; the grass grows at the edge of the path.

My aunts planted the flowers in the yard at Burdett. There are lilies-of-the-valley under the parlor window and myrtle in the three-cornered bed between the front stoop and the side one. There is sometimes a sprig of bleeding-heart, sometimes a plant of coral-colored columbine with little fairy curving horns. And the horns have honey in them; we suck them sometimes. A snowball bush is by the gate, and under Grandma's bedroom window are lemon lilies. There are two pear trees and a black Tartarian cherry, and one evergreen, and a big Virginia creeper that my aunts dug up as a sprout in the woods and brought home long ago—and it has climbed up the cherry and trailed over to all the other trees near by and hangs in festoons all over. There is green grass to walk on. In the fall, Grandpa rakes up the fallen leaves in little piles and goes about burning them. He stirs up the ashes to make the flame come again. He makes a bonfire in the back yard and they all run out to see it—"A bonfire! A bonfire!"

When she was a girl, Grandma made her sampler—a piece of poetry about our sins, a picture of a barn, "Harriett Woodward aged 9," all in black. Her two sisters, Charlotte and Jennet, were older. They made her make it in black though she wanted to have it colored. After she got it finished except for the border, she put that in color, a pretty vine, pink and green (I've seen it). Her sisters scolded and she stopped it right there; she would not finish it, and never did. A little piece of the border is not done and the green silk thread is hanging out of the canvas just as she left it.

It is terrible!—I was in the front yard playing, Grandpa planting two linden trees by the parlor windows. The grass coming up for spring, little leaves on the trees. Dash lay over on his side sprawled in the sun. A man ran up from toward Watkins; he pushed himself against the picket fence. "Dr. Brown! Dr. Brown! They've shot Lincoln! Lincoln's dead!" He ran on. Grandpa had his spade lifted; he did not put it down. He stood stock still. He called, "Peter! Peter! *What did you say?*" But by that time Peter was telling the same thing to Auntie Robinson, at her gate in her blue-check apron.

Everybody began to fly around. Everybody talked at once. Grandma came outdoors. Aunt Lidy and Aunt Louise ran down the gravel walk and out of the gate; Father jumped off the stoop over the steps and ran after them so fast that his coattails flew out behind. Dash leaped up and barked and barked, and the cat scrabbled up the cherry tree.

I ran to find my mother. I could not find her. The house was empty, it was still; the clock ticked; the workbasket sat on the floor beside the little sewing chair, and the spread on the leaf table was a lovely dark pink. I went on. I cried "Mother! Mother!" I found her in the woodshed, crying. "Oh, Mother, what is it?" "Lincoln is dead. Now there will be more war!" she said, crying.

It is terrible. Will Father go to war? He is a minister—

do ministers go to war? Will my mother's brothers have to fight again? She had four brothers and they fought on the wrong side because they lived in South Carolina and had to. It was Mother's home too, before she came North to school and got married to Father. Two of them died in the war. We are abolitionists. But my father is a minister, and so was my mother's.

After a while they all come back into the sitting room. They shut the doors and don't talk much. Father and Mother are on the lounge together. Nobody is thinking about me. I sit on the little cricket and fold my hands and keep quiet. Grandma gets up and goes around closing the window blinds.

I am sick in bed at Grandma's, lying in the spare room with the light-grey flowered paper on the walls. I am worried by some little tiny black creatures that keep jumping around on the ceiling at the angle where it comes against the side of the room. I call my mother and show them to her. She gets a broom and sweeps them all away. "There," she says, "they're gone."

I cannot get to sleep. It is at Grandma's; I have been put to bed. I am afraid I shall break a blood vessel; a lady who was calling talked about a man who broke a blood vessel. I begin to cry. My mother comes to see what ails me. "I am afraid I'm going to break a blood vessel!" But she says little girls never, never do that, and even grown people hardly ever. I am so relieved.

My mother and I are measuring five yards of ribbon; she sits with her skirts flowing out and I stand up in front of her. "O-o-one," says Mother, catching my hands and drawing them out as far as they will go on each side. Our faces come nearer and nearer together as our arms stretch out. When close we kiss; that means one yard. "Two-o-o," she says. We take hold of hands, we stretch our hands apart again as far as they will go. Kiss. Two yards. We giggle and laugh and measure that way five times, five kisses. "Five!" says my mother. "That's enough."

She tosses me on to the lounge and I lie there laughing. I sit up and begin to ask her if I am going to Europe with them. Martha Hubbard says you have to go across the ocean and it is all pitching and tossing; her father went across it to Europe and that's what he says. "Will it be pitching and tossing, Mother? Am I going too? Is Boltie going with us, Mother?"

I heard Father say he would like to take both of the children, but he is sure Nellie is old enough to profit by the trip. Bolton can go to Burdett; the girls are crazy to have him while we are gone. Aunt Anna's husband has died, over in Germany where they went for my cousin's education; and she wants us to go and take a trip with her and my Cousin Henry, to comfort her. She sent the money for initial expenses by Mr. Hanchett—four hundred dollars. Mr. Hanchett must have a great many trunks to carry four hundred dollars. My father has been a colporteur lately, in Jefferson County, and has done a very useful piece of work. But now we are going to Europe.

I am jouncing on the lounge. I am so glad we are going to Europe. "Stop fidgeting," says Mother. We have a book about Fidgetty Skeert; she forgot her own name and fidgeted all the time, and had St. Vitus Dance. She remembered finally, and it was "Italia." Mother says it means Italy. A funny name for a girl. When I fidget she says, "There, Fidgetty Skeert!" I jounce up and down. Jouncity-jounce. *"Nellie!"* says my mother. "Oh, Mother, I'm only jouncing. I'm not talking a bit." (She says I talk too much.) Jouncity-jounce. "It rests me." But my mother says I positively must stop it or she will send me to bed. So I stop. But jouncing rests me more than going to bed.

Hoboken! *Hoboken!* What a funny name! The people crowded and cheered to see us off; but there was no rolling and pitching, for I did not know we had started until the dock began to back away. Every one on the ship went along close together and I began to get much bumped, shut down in the middle of them. . . . . I am bumped now; I can't see a thing except ladies' dresses and gentlemen's legs moving along . . . . moving along . . . .

My father has escaped from me! I had his hand—but he is gone. I cannot see him anywhere among all these thick people and legs. . . . . But he is on this ship, of course. I can walk along with everybody else without him, they are all going the same way. . . . . Here is a man with a cap on, trying to get me out.

"Are you alone, Miss?"

How pleasant to be called "Miss." They don't do it in Watertown.

"No sir. My father was here a minute ago but he seems to have vanished." (I like "vanish." "Gone" is too dark and empty. So I say, "He seems to have vanished.")

"You'd better come with me." He takes my hand, but I withdraw it. He is a stranger to me. Besides, a child that is almost six years old can walk alone without anybody's hand. We come to a sort of big empty dining room with long tables, tablecloths on them but nothing else.

"Sit up and have something to eat!" He bounces me up on a chair before I know it and pushes it up to a table. A woman comes, and then another. Probably hired girls. They are nice and they like me and ask my name and where I came from and where going. I tell them all, and, besides, that my Aunt Anna has lost her husband and has sent for us to go abroad and engage in foreign travel. And about the four hundred dollars sent in Mr. Hanchett's trunks for initial expenses. And Boltie's being left with Grandma and the girls. They laugh, and so do I; they are so nice.

"And what will the little lady have to eat?"

I sit up straight like a little lady. I am not hungry, and I see no food here.

"I will have some kettle tea, if you please."

But they have never heard of such a thing. I have to tell

them—"Milk, and water, and sugar. I have it when grown folks have ordinary tea." So they all go off, the man with a cap, too, to get it. Here I sit alone counting the windows—portholes, I mean. My father explained to me that ships don't have windows and what look like them are portholes. . . . . They come back, but, alas! it is cold instead of hot, and in a tumbler instead of a cup-and-saucer! My father appears at the door.

"There you are. We lost you. Your ma is in the stateroom; I guess she's going to be seasick."

The floor is beginning to roll and pitch. I can hardly stand up when I get down from the chair.

"We'll soon get our sea-legs on," my father cries, jollily. We stagger out on deck.

Sea-legs—sea-legs! How funny! I grab my father's hand to keep myself from falling, and swing it back and forth hard because I like him so. We bump together from the rolling and pitching, and nearly tumble in a heap on the floor. We laugh and lurch along. The wind blows, stinging, in our faces. We giggle in fits and reel up against the rail. My father straightens himself and looks off across the foaming waves. "The ro-o-ollers of the Atlantic!" says he, in a grand pulpit voice.

There is a storm. The ship stands up on its side. I fall down and cut my forehead. I bleed profusely and the ship doctor sews me up. The waves are mountainous. The wind blows the foam off their tops in feathers. Mother is sick abed. I try to take care of her, but I think she prefers the stewardess. Father jokes. He says he saw a man dashing across the deck "spouting like a whale." Mother says, "Edmund, I will give *you* an emetic if you don't stop making fun of us." But he says he is good, and dresses me and takes care of us both. He does. Nobody takes such good care of me as my father.

He is the only minister on board. Germans the other gentlemen are. They are Jews, mostly infidels. Clever. He goes and talks with them. He says they are intelligent and that he means to post up immediately on the authenticity and inspiration of the Scriptures. I myself visit with the gentlemen sometimes. They like me, and I find them very pleasant. They all have a brogue.

Father is reading *Childe Harold* and *The Bible in Spain.* I wish I could read. He loves the Bible better than any other book. He is copying out whatever it says about the ocean. "There goes that great Leviathan. The noise of thy waterspouts. Who covereth thyself with light as with a garment; who stretcheth out the heavens like a curtain; who layeth the beams of his chambers in the waters; who maketh the clouds his chariot; who walketh upon the wings of the wind; who maketh his angels spirits, his ministers a flaming fire."

My father learns them by heart and recites them out on deck in his round, dark voice that seems like flowing waves. I look at him. I listen. I see why the Bible calls ministers a flaming fire.

Cousin Henry wrote not on any account to omit our meals but to eat well. So I do. The meals are long and large; seven times the plates are changed.

Berlin has a Thiergarten, with monkeys. Lots of trees, houses, clocks on the steeples. Lots of soldiers marching past— they've got to have war, but it isn't going to trouble the Americans. Lots of fleas. Outside the window of this Hotel of Russie I see a fountain and a statue on a bridge; and the king's palace next door has a big steeple upon it.

Father preaches as soon as we arrive, on "Growth in Grace." He intends to make some investigations about evangelistic tendencies in Germany. Besides our Bibles for Sunday, when nothing can be done, he brought Longfellow's *Poems* and Byron's *Poems,* and he has bought, here in Berlin, Tauchnitz *Robertson's Sermons.* He wants to get hold of some more of the English poets. I wish I could read.

Governor Wright calls on us and Father tells him all about our sight-seeing.

"Mattie and I stick together like brothers," says he.

Governor Wright looks at my mother sitting there in her new silver-color silk dress. "I don't wonder," says he.

We are called upon by many pleasant friends. Aunt Anna feels just as Mother does about my talking and says, "Your tongue is hung in the middle and runs at both ends." Today she said, "Nellie, some friends of mine are coming to see me this afternoon and I don't want you to monopolize the conversation."

"Monopolize," a lovely word. It hops and then it flies.

The minute we got to Berlin Auntie bought my father a new broadcloth black preaching suit. Then she bought him a steel-grey traveling suit, a grey overcoat, and shiny shoes. Me she bought a wax doll with real hair and open-and-shut eyes—although I brought my china one from home, of course—two new sashes, one blue check, the other pink stripe, with narrower hair ribbons to match. And things for Mother. They wrote us not to bother about clothing but to wear our old things on shipboard that we could throw away afterward and provide a suitable wardrobe when we got here. So we did.

Today I have a cold in my head and a headache. There is a roaring fire behind me and woolens basted under in my white drawers to warm me up. Soon I have to go and see a sick gentleman in the hotel; his niece thinks it will cheer him up.

I am quite a favorite, especially with the gentlemen. Mother says not to be too forward. She and Aunt Anna talked about it, and Mother said she believed the cheerful company of a bright American child was as good as medicine to all these gentlemen here for their health. They have several different kinds of whiskers, some close and dark like Father's, some frisky curly like Cousin Henry's, some that fly out at the sides like wings, some small dabs on the chin like a little butterfly, and many others. Long, grand whiskers that you could brush and comb are called a beard. They run their fingers through them. General Lawrence had mutton-chops. He was my great friend;

once Governor of India, he lost his only son in the war. He liked me. Now he is gone away; we were loath to part.

We went to Dresden (not where I was born, but in Saxony) to see Cousin Ellen North, who married a German named Mr. Banc. We went to Worms where Luther was. I *think* he threw his ink bottle at the Devil there. They don't pronounce the name of their town like angleworms, exactly. Went to Baden-Baden and I asked them why you said it twice.

Mother said, "I'm sure I don't know."

Father said, "Shakespeare never repeats."

Cousin Henry said, "Probably for emphasis."

I suppose it is the German way of saying more than one— "Bath-Bath."

My father has seen the king go by. Cousin Henry saluted; they all saluted. I asked Father if the king saw him. He said he guessed not but he must have seen Henry, and that was just as well. He doesn't think the king would know the difference. We are back just now from our travels. Cousin Henry has gone to buy Father a small knapsack and to find out when Professor Helmholtz lectures and when the next duel comes off. Father posted up on Helmholtz before we left home, about heat, electricity, and modes-of-motion.

We are in Italy by the Mediterranean Sea—not the sea we crossed called the Atlantic, another one entirely. We came by the Mt. Cenis route, probably Hannibal's. We play on the shore with the pebbles. The olive trees, as we come along, blow in the wind like a soft silver—like a brook I've seen over stones.

There are Roman Ruins. In an empty court of one of them I find a good brown marble in a crack of the pavement, and keep it. It makes up for three crystal ones I had in my purple leather bag when I lost it—so it is all right, no matter who it was that lost this marble. It had to be.

We are in Paris. Coming, on the train, we all sat in the compartment, everybody reading. I got a book, too, and held it up open so that they would think I was reading and say "what a smart child to know how to read so young." Across from me was a pretty lady, and she looked at me and smiled. She opened her satchel and took out a pink book and began to read to me— English, though it was *Les Malheurs de Sophie,* and all in French. When the station came and we had to get out she gave it to me to keep! Mother thanked her and so did I, and we never saw her again. I shall never forget her—never.

We got a new word from the Sophie book, *"malheureux."* Now, when things go wrong, instead of saying "for pity sake," or "dear me suz," we say "Oh, *malheureux*"—like Sophie's bonne. It's a good thing Sophie had a bonne, for she had more *malheurs* than anybody I ever heard of. It was because she was naughty. She put her wax doll in a basin of boiling hot water and the legs all melted off in streams, much to her regret. There's a picture of it. She had a fight with her Cousin Paul and shook her fist in his face. (Picture.) She tried to walk on the smooth-looking mortar the masons left there and went in over her shoe tops and screamed in agony, burnt by the lime. Her bonne came running, capstrings flying, and grabbed her out and stripped off her shoes and stockings, and Sophie continued to yell and fling out all four of her legs and arms in every direction. The bonne rescued her generally.

I have a bonne, too, so that they can be free to go and come, and leave me with the bonne. She takes me to the Champs Elysées. Other children are playing around and suddenly there is Punch and Judy getting set up by the path. We run to see it. Funny old Punch, funny Judy, funny little black devil! She takes me to a kind of a school where they pass around plates of chocolate wrapped in white paper for us to eat between meals, which I never saw before. We go to learn French, but the scholars are mostly English and you can't make them talk French every minute. It isn't natural. They teach us to braid mats with

strips of colored paper. I can braid mats easily enough. I'd
rather learn how to read.

I can talk French pretty well anyway. My father and I walk
by the River and come to a bridge with bookstalls. Father
loiters and picks up the books and leafs them over. He finds a
little ragged brown leather one he wants to buy, but he cannot
talk French. He says,

"You ask him how much it is."

"Combien?" I say to the man.

"Dix sous, mademoiselle."

"Dix sous. Ten sous, he says, Father."

"*Bong*," says Father, and pays him from his wallet. We turn
back from the bridge and walk away by the river-side wall
under the trees. He looks down at me proudly; I am proud of
myself.

The French have a brogue through their nose. However, I
like their language. My father has no gift for languages. All
the German he knows is "Nixcomeraus to the Dutchman's
house," and he doesn't know any French at all. He went to
college and wasted seven valuable years of his life studying
Latin, Greek, and Hebrew, preparing for the ministry. He'd
rather read history in the library. But for history all they had
at Yale was to learn pages by heart from the book, and he had
a poor verbal memory; and so he hated that too, but not so
much as the languages. No child of his shall fool away his time
learning dead languages! What are *dead* languages? How can
a language be dead? Well, I suppose I shall not have to fool
away my time at them anyway.

The French for *amiable* is the same word, Mother says,
only they pronounce it *ahm-yabble*. The first part is *ami*,
friend; and in both languages, she says, it means *love*.

We travel some (without the bonne), but there is much to
see in Paris. In the cathedrals there are always statues, and
always the Lady and Baby. I asked Mother who it was. "Oh,

"Mother"

Father climbs an Alp

just a mother and her baby," said she. How nice to put them in the churches. I wish we did it in America. I don't remember any in the Presbyterian Church at Burdett. The picture galleries are full of paintings and notable pieces of sculpture. We get awful cold, even though wrapped up in all the cloaks and shawls and scarfs we've got. We can hardly stand it. Father says it is the cold of the primeval universe before the sun was created. We go to the little shops under a long porch and Aunt Anna continues to buy things. She says we are to be comfortable, and have what we need.

"Oh, Mother, I do so want a new hat with a large white feather on it and ribbons hanging down behind!" But she says, "You cannot *have* everything you *want*."

In America we don't dance. But here I have seen a dance; I have danced!

I was playing in the salon with the French children, on Sunday. I suppose Father and Mother and Aunt Anna and Cousin Henry were sitting around somewhere, reading their Bibles. The children and I talked French together and ran about the room. Suddenly something happened—I did not know what—and they began to race toward the hall. I raced after them. We came to a very large, light place filled with music and people, and they ran on in. I ran after, but stopped near the door. The children melted together among the moving crowd and paired off. What was happening! They whirled away together and the grown people whirled too. They were dancing!

This—is—*The Dance!*

If only I could dance! Patting my feet on the floor—standing still—doesn't do. Why can't I, too! *Why!* A boy who played with me in the salon comes, sees me standing here by myself. He takes me by the hand, draws me away from the wall toward the dancers, urges me in. Oh, I cannot dance, I don't know how .... *Oui, oui,* venez, venez—you can dance—venez! .... I yield in a rush and a whirl. I *can* dance, I *am* dancing. How easy it is! I whirl in an ecstasy. I leap to the ceiling. I run with the boy, skipping and swaying, down the room. We are all dancing together, the music flowing us along .... My father, looking in at the door! Oh, Father, do notice me. Aren't you proud of me, your little girl—see how I can dance! As well as anybody. I don't really shout to him, but I want to. I think it yearningly to him at the door there .... Now he has caught sight of us in our whirl. He crooks his finger for me to come to him.

Alas! I must leave the little boy, I must cease dancing, and go away. Slowly I walk to the door and the boy does not come with me. I am weary and heavy-laden. Father draws me out into the quiet hall and we go and find the others, sitting around reading.

"I found her at the dance, the belle of the ball." Father looks down at me comically and drops my hand. Mother seems surprised, but laughs. Nobody says much, only tell me to get the Sophie book and Cousin Doctor will read to me.

"Oh, Cousin Doctor, find that place with the picture of Sophie in the mortar box, and the lime eating her feet, and she pushed a cry of agony. Read it—will you!"

"Anything you like," says he. "I presume you do require excitement at the moment."

"Oh the delight of glacier water!" my father exclaims. He does like water. In my mind I can see him drinking glacier water from the tiny pool, bright and icy. He takes out his leather cup and unfolds it, bends down and dips it into the spring, lifts it to his lips. He stands straight again, looks off, away, all around at the mountains, and the sky, and at the white, billowy clouds. He drinks .... slowly, with stops between .... "A-a-ah!" he says, drawing in his breath coolly. He turns the empty leather cup upside down and shakes a few bright drops out of it, folds it, puts it in his pocket. .... How much better to climb mountains than to hear about it! Still, I like to hear about it. Father is climbing the Alps. A gentleman has offered to propose him for the Alpine Club, but he will probably never be in Switzerland again and it is not worth while.

Besides this cup, Father carries in his pockets handkerchiefs, a green veil, a jackknife. He takes his little Testament in his knapsack, besides arnica and iodine, one extra pair of socks, three collars. They wear masks with eyeholes to keep the sun on the snowfields from burning them. They wear heavy gloves and enormous boots, caps tied on with handkerchiefs, and *goggles!* Each carries an alpenstock, and they are all tied together eight feet apart along a thick rope, so that if one falls over the precipice the others can drag him back again.

Sometimes they are gone for days. We stay at the hotels and wait, and go for little walks, till they come back. My aunt is afraid Henry will get hurt sooner or later—fall into a crevasse, or get swept off by an avalanche; or a stone will strike him on the head that some one in front of him kicks, or lose his footing on a glacier and roll down into a moraine. She begs him not to be imprudent. My Cousin Henry says, "Mother, you must remember that I am just as much interested in preserving my life as you are." Auntie laughs her all-over laugh. She is fat. Father says, "Fat, fair, and forty, the life of the party." Mother is not afraid of things happening to Father. She thinks he knows how to take care of himself. Besides, there is one guide, sometimes two, for each person on a climb. That's the law. Father told us the young guide fell down and the old one got drunk on his own private brandy after he came home. But they saw eleven chamois moving along in a row not very far off, threw snowballs at them, causing them to turn and go leaping away out of sight.

Once they were in great danger, on the Col du Géant, at a bad snow slope with fifteen hundred feet of immense snowbanks towering above them. Father prayed, as a Christian should, that they might be protected and if anything should happen to them that they might be calm and prepared. So they went on, and the guide began to hurry them. Then, suddenly, they heard and they saw flash down across the path at the place where but three minutes ago they had stood, a flying mass of snow, an avalanche, rushing into the valley to a crevasse in the glacier below. The guide told them he had noticed the loosening of the snow field as they came by—said nothing, only hurried them. Father thought of his prayer and could but notice the connection.

Father took me out on the Grindelwald; he took me so that I could see how it felt to walk on a glacier. We walked, and he held my hand always, and we came to a deep, blue, ice crevasse. We leaned over and looked far down the smooth blue ice sides. The bottom was far below.

He takes me to see everything, pictures in galleries, pieces of statuary—like the statue man I saw eating some statue children. We see statue bears and live bears, and monkeys and churches. I saw a white peak in the highest part of the sky, alone, by itself, far up above the earth. Nowhere did it come down to the ground, for a cloud was underneath it. "What is that?" I asked him. It was strange and wonderful. "That is Mt. Blanc," he said, "the highest mountain in the Alps." So then I always knew about Mt. Blanc.

One time Father got me out of bed, wrapped a cover around me, and I trailed it through the hall after him. We stood at the open door. The sky over the hilltop was softly bright; not a strong shining, but like a spirit, pale and gentle. I asked him in a whisper, "What is it?" "The moonrise," he whispered back. We waited quietly, hand in hand, and all was still. Soon the great silver moon rose from behind the hill and began to go up the sky.

They planned carefully for Monte Rosa. The guide they took, eighty times he had made that ascent. The lesser guide was reliable and spry but not like the old one. My father slept but one hour, he was so excited, and had the honor of waking up the guides themselves at one o'clock at night. They had their breakfast in the dim light of the hotel dining room—the Riffel-haus, highest-up hotel in Switzerland—then got ready, rope tied to them each eight feet apart, alpenstocks in hand, that little leather cup in Father's pocket. Soon they started quietly away. It was starlight. My father followed the guide silently, stepping in his footsteps in the snow. He thought of Burdett and our family there, not yet in bed (the time is different), Bolton in his cradle, family prayers. He thought about stepping around among the stones in Grandpa's barnyard—but down he came off a hummock and wrenched himself and saw he was *not* in the barnyard at home.

They went up a glacier, a precipitous slope. Big stones, crevasses. Two crevasses they crossed on snow bridges, laid their alpenstocks side by side and crawled over them. The guides cut steps with the ice hatchets they had. Their breath began to come hard. Seven hours they climbed like that and then were at the Saddle. They stopped there and it was like being in the moon. Eternal solitude and desolation, eternal snow and ice, no animal or vegetable life, no earth, nothing but plains and slopes of ice, with peaks of rock.

So they sat down under a rock. The guides would not let them stand for fear they would fall off. They ate their lunch, rested half an hour, and then crawled slowly around the rock, arose, and started off again. This now was the *hard* part. There were three *grats*—a *grat* is a thing you go up like the roof of a house, only tipped up much steeper (forty degrees), covered with ice on one side and packed with icy snow on the other. Two feet wide was the edge, and then a precipice of thousands of feet if you slipped and fell down. Father looked up into the sky—you must not look down—and followed up the grat. He balanced in the narrow steps, hung onto his alpenstock, and bored it into each step as he went along.

Suddenly the wind rose in a puff. The next puff stronger, then a furious blast. Now he knew, says my father, his life depended on himself. "You can keep cool and steady,

Edmund," says he, "careful of every movement, or slip and shoot off." But down went the forward guide, all doubled up, and down went the rest. In a moment that blast was over and they going up their razor edge again. Another blast—Father wallowed again. For two or three minutes the wind did tear and pull at them, and in that time he thought of a number of things. He thought nobody would ever catch him up there again, and he would make Mattie and Aunt Anna promise never to allow him to go into such a place again. And he thought he was a fool to come. The wind lulled. "Forward!" shouted the guide tied behind him, and gave my father a punch in the seat. All the way up the three grats this guide shouted "Forward," and every time he shouted he gave a punch in the seat. Ten tottering steps, and the wind again, and down they went. Father lay in a narrow trough about like a cutter track, half full of snow. One leg and arm hung outside over the thousand feet *down*, the other leg and arm gripped the fifteen hundred feet *up*. He shivered and he shook; he buried his face in his straight little bed. Oh, how the wind blew! It blew to blow them off of the grat, but they clung. "Never," he thought, "will I again endanger my life, save for a call of duty." And in the midst of the blast, a long steady one, the guide jumped up crying, "Forward! Forward!" and punched him in the seat. In the wind and blowing ice they crawled on upward. One slip by any, and the four might go down.

The grats climbed, there came three narrow rocky peaks. Up and over and down each one they went. But the third they did not go down, for that was the Top and down was ten thousand feet into an Italian valley. Nearly perpendicular. There they sat. They rested and enjoyed the view, and Henry laughed and laughed to hear about the guide's "forwards" and punches in the seat all through that awful hour. They looked and saw the Alps from Austria to the Gulf of Genoa, and saw Mt. Blanc like a great cathedral set on top of the ice peaks. Everywhere ice peaks. All Europe lay below them, and they were probably the highest persons in Europe just then. They ate their lunch. Father shivered and he shook; they thought he was cold, but he says he knew better—he was greatly scared.

When they came down the wind jerked off their hats, first my father's then Henry's, though they were tied on with hand-kerchiefs, and blew them away. The guide broke an ice axe. They crawled around great rocks, they stood on ledges two inches wide, they swung around cliffs by their arms, crawled over tables of rock in the wind, sat down and hunched along from one ice step to the next. Below, out of the tail of the eye, a vast expanse of air, and the white of the glacier far, far down. When they got down the rocks and down the grats, and to the Saddle, my father was a happy man. No more danger of blowing away through ten thousand feet of air. And they scrambled and ran and slid and finally got home to the Riffelhaus.

Their faces were as red as beets and afterward peeled off. Their eyes would have been blinded by the wind and the snow if it had not been for the goggles. It was the terrible wind; when it began to blow, the landlady had said they would never be able to reach the top.

"I was a fool to go into such a place," said Father. "Mattie, I want you and Aunt Anna to absolutely forbid any more such excursions."

No, he says; he has desired the experience of being in mortal peril, but those three hours have completely satisfied him. "Anyway," says Cousin Henry, "we do not think it right to endanger our lives, except at the call of duty." And my father says that too. So my Aunt Anna looks relieved.

"Good-bye, Captain Buss, good-bye, good-bye!"

I hate to say it. He does too. I was the only child on board coming home, though we had eighteen children going over, and I sat by the Captain at dinner and had raisins. We liked each other all the time, but sometimes he was busy and disappeared.

As soon as we came off the ship he took me—alone—on a ride in a buggy all over Boston. He gave me a golden garnet ring and I have it. Now he is gone. We have his little boy's picture in a pleated white dress, socks, and black shoes, and his yellow hair rolled up in a curl on top.

Captain Buss is a German. His whiskers are mutton-chop, and so his chin shows and has a dimple in it. He parts his hair in the middle and it curls up around his ears.

II

CARTHAGE, NORTH BERGEN, WELLSVILLE

WE HAVE come home to Burdett. Bolton did not know us. He sat on Aunt Lidy's lap and said, "That isn't Boltie's mother. Boltie's mother is out on the ocean sailin'." I saw my mother drop a tear. Gone so long, and now her child does not know her. Mother had a new baby. That was all right, because Grandpa is a doctor. We named her after two aunts Anna Louisa. Father has gone to Carthage where we shall go to live as soon as he gets our house ready for us.

He writes many letters. The Dunants, he says, have eleven children and one at the breast. Poor Mrs. Dunant counts time by her babies—"The year *that* baby was born." The daughter of a minister, intelligent, but what use is intelligence with poverty and eleven children? Mr. Dunant is hard-working but easy. They live down the hill from our house in Carthage. Their home is but a shanty, some beds, some trundle-beds, the baby sleeps in the butter bowl (he says), the next older baby takes the bread tray, and the little fellow like Boltie has the clothesbasket. He says we can occasionally invite them to tea. I hope so. The neighbors all help these poor people; they keep open garden for their fowls and sheep, which latter ate up four little trees on our place. The Dunant hens picked up five shillings' worth of corn sown in his garden by our neighbor, Mr. McCullum. But, my father says, the fowls are going to be shut up, and Mr. Dunant is going to plant the corn over, and the sheep are to be kept in the lower end of the lane, where they alternate between a fine large meadow and a field of spring grain. The lambs are hearty little fellows and we'll always have life in the foreground.

He has cleaned up the yard half a dozen times and slicked up the street in front. The workmen are finishing the house, so boards and stuff lie around. He is making a garden. He can shovel like an Irishman, and his face is getting like tanned leather. "My hands are brawny and tawny," says he, "but I am plump as a partridge. Yesterday I bathed in the shallow of a rock in Black River."

The Black River is broad and deep. Steam and canal boats come down it from out of the woods. We see it from our house, he says, for the house is on the brow of a hill and the yard slopes away down. Beyond the garden and the meadows and the woods, a little to the right, is the river, and beyond it is a sloping hill covered with woods and fields. A tall elm over that way adds to the view.

I think we shall go soon, for the fence is about done, and Father says the Dunant's sheep took their last turn around the lot to bid farewell to their accustomed haunts and then with a rush went over the small portion of unfinished fence to be gone for good. He thinks Mrs. Dunant will one day make him a present of a fleece or a quarter of mutton for what his lot has done toward their keeping. And he has bought some furniture, as Mother sent him a list to do, and it is coming down the river in a canal boat. But the stove is set up. It has taken the premium at four state fairs and bakes charmingly. When your biscuit burns, it burns equally hard and black on every side. Potatoes boil before the kettle gets fairly on, and meat begins to fry as soon as the frying pan leaves the pantry. Seventy-five cords of wood, he says, are stacked in the woodshed.

I have a room of my own in Carthage, the first I've had.

Mother says I may do whatever I like with it because it is my room. Oh, Mother, how good you are! I love you.

One bedroom has to be the study, of course. In it the book-cases and desk. The desk has at each side a cupboard closed with a door, and between them a cubbyhole. Father writes sit-ting at the desk in a black wooden armchair they bought at Pen Yan when they were first married. One day he was writing; Boltie was playing on the floor by his feet. Boltie rose up sud-denly, hit his head on the cupboard door which was swinging wide open, and burst out yelling. Father leaped out of his chair, grabbed up Boltie, and rubbed his head round and round to stop the pain so hard Boltie had to stop crying and pull away from him. "Poor lambie! Poor lambie!" And then he let go of Bolton and turned and wrenched off the door and threw it across the room. Since then the desk has only one door.

This is my father's first charge since we came home, quite a small communion. We receive home mission aid. There is a Catholic church which draws many on Sunday evenings with ample accommodations and good music. We are near Canada, a somewhat Papal country, and some of the better class of people in Carthage are Romanists. Said to be good people, too. My father hopes to build up the congregation and set the women to work, gather in the young, and develop the Sunday School. He is Sunday School superintendent and teaches the Bible class.

Pleasant summertime it is, flowers in the yards and fields and along the grassy roadsides. The garden Father has planted flourishes; he hoes it. His young fruit trees grow.

Loads of tanbark are dumped in front of our house. What do you think for? Winter is coming, winter in this northern clime, and we must bank up the house all round its roots and darken the cellar windows with tanbark heaps to keep out the cold. Double windows we put, and storm doors outside the others. Between are little snug entries where we can shake off the snow without bringing it inside. The big stoves are up. My father goes around with listing and a case-knife and carefully stuffs every crack at the window casings. My mother makes us woolens to wear, and me pretty hoods out of blue flannel lined with red. Mittens we have. They are fastened together by a long crocheted string put through the sleeves of our cloaks, and left dangling so that they won't get lost. We put on leggings whenever we stir out. Everybody has leggings, even if it is only a pair of woolen socks over your shoes, which make good ones and don't slip.

Now the snow and the cold have come, and storm after storm. But we are snug and comfortable. Father has bought us a sled. Boltie and I and Cornie Dunant go sliding down the hill. The snow has banked up on a level with the fences and we walk through the boughs of the trees. They shovel the snow. They bank it up at the side of the street and make a gallery through which I walk to school, with the bank higher than my head.

On the windows of the rooms where no fire is, the frost makes beautiful pictures in the night: Ferns, like lace; thin, small, shining spears of ice lying crossways of each other; pure, velvety puffs of fairy snow at the corners and edges where the frost thickens. There are frost flowers and even tiny trees—perfect, and all pure white or crystalline. If I feel I must look through the window I breathe warmly on one spot of glass till the frostwork grows thin, then put my warm finger on the spot and gently rub and rub. Soon it is a clear peep-hole where I can look to see what is going on outside.

The frost outdoors covers small things like door latches with a thick, white, soft fur. It is a cruel joke to tell somebody to touch the latch with his tongue. It is cruel, for when he does it the frost bites him so quick and sharp that it takes the skin off his tongue or at least makes it sore. I would never do this to anyone, but I have seen the boys do it to a smaller boy who didn't know, or when "double-dasting" one another. I wonder if it always does. I try it, all alone by myself, to see. It does.

My Aunt Julie has come, and right in this stormy winter-time she and Mother both are sick with a bilious attack. Very troublesome to have both ladies who take care of you sick at once. We do the best we can. Boltie hurts his finger and gets up on Mother's bed to sit beside her and cry about it; and just then the doctor comes. Boltie keeps right on.

"Hush, Boltie, don't cry before the doctor," says Mother. He keeps still a minute, then he says, "When will the doctor go away so Boltie can cry?"

"Sh-sh-sh."

Pretty soon, in a plain, clear voice, "I wish the doctor would go away. Boltie wants to cry."

Mother whispers to him, "If you cry after the doctor goes away I am going to spank you." He lies right down beside her and goes to sleep.

He is a smart child, but contrary. The more you fuss over him when he hurts himself the more he bawls; I think he keeps getting more and more sorry for himself. But Father's friend, Mr. Gilbert, thinks something can be made of that chap. The first time Mother took him to church she wanted to take off his hat like other gentlemen and boys. He would not let her.

"Why, Bolton, nobody wears their hat in church!"

But he said, "Bolton Brown wears his hat in church." She had to leave it on.

I think it very strange that Boltie always wants things to go on just the same forever and I want them to be always changing. The same, over and over—ah, how it tires me! I know the word for it—"monotonous." I find lots of use for it. At the present time my brother is worrying because Mother is having some pants made for him and he'd rather stay in his dresses. She makes him a new nightgown, and he cries because it fastens with a button instead of a string like the old one.

"Why, Boltie, a button is ever so much nicer," says Mother. "You know how the string gets tied into a hard knot, a button never does that." (He stops weeping.) "See here, put your hand

up, I will let you push the button through its little hole . . . .
there! Nice shiny little button to hold Boltie's nightgown shut
all night long while he is asleep." So then he lies down quite
contented and thinks the nightgown very fine.

Aunt Julie says she will teach me French. So she begins,
and says, "Now Nellie, you ask me some questions I can't
answer."

I am puzzled. I cannot think of any such questions.

"Oh, just any kind of thing," says she. "Ask me what the
moon is made of."

I laugh, because they always say "green cheese" to that. So
I say, "What is the moon made of?"

"Je ne sais pas," says Aunt Julie.

I am more puzzled than ever. I feel foolish to not know
what she means.

"Well, I told you I would teach you French. That means
'I don't know.' Say it. Je ne sais pas."

"Je ne sais pas. I don't know." How easy French is. But
then, I got a start when I was abroad.

Aunt Julie went to Mlle Rostand's school in New York City.
It was taught in French. She practices on the piano over at
Mr. McCullum's six hours a day; it is right across the road, and
we have no piano. She played the "Hallelujah Chorus" which
we had in a music festival.

My mother went to Miss Brace's school in New Haven and
lived with her grandmother and Aunt Eliza. Her grandmother
was not used to seeing people sit and do nothing, even when
they had nothing to do. Mother was born and brought up in
the South where it is hot and the darkies do the work. So when
she came to live with her grandmother she sat down and rocked
in a rocking-chair, when there was nothing else, with her hands
in her lap. "Haven't you anything to occupy your fingers
with?" says Grandmother North. And in the South they let her
lie down as much as she wanted to; but when she cast herself
upon the sofa at her grandmother's house, she said in surprise,

"Lying down in the daytime! Are you sick!" But they liked each other, and her grandmother gave her a little gold ring to remember her by. I've seen it. She taught my mother how to make up the bed and change the sheets in the proper manner. "Didn't you ever study the uses of a sheet?" says she. Mother never had; the darkies made beds in South Carolina. Of course at her grandmother's they had a hired girl. It was a new one. The girl they had before did their work for ten years right in that same kitchen and at the end of that time she jumped through the window and ran away, raving crazy.

My teacher and I stand together between two schoolrooms. One is my own, the primer room, the scholars sitting there at their desks looking at me. The other is the second grade; I do not know it, it seems strange, and the scholars there sit at their desks and look at me. I am surprised, I do not know what is happening. Another teacher comes and talks with my teacher, about me. Why, goody, goody, I am going into the second grade right now, in the middle of the term, *alone—I have learned to read!* The new teacher seats me down in front. Everyone watches. I feel calm and proud.

Oh, glory, glory, hallelujah! Now I am home and can burst. Bring me all the books now, pile them up around me, let me get at them! Now I will know what is in them. Now I will find out why there are so many of them. Now I shall have words, words, words—and know what they mean. Now people won't have to stop their important work and read to me half an hour and tell me to run away now and look at the pictures, they have to get at their mending. Pictures—pooh! There is a story in Revelations about a man that ate a little book and it was sweet in his mouth but bitter in his stomach. I've eaten things that behaved like that, but not books. I can eat books now, eat them up, and they'll not bother *my* stomach. I have learned to read!

I learn the multiplication table. We sing it all together. I enjoy this singing very much:

Tu-tums *one* is *two*,
Tu-tums *two* is *four*,
Tu-tums *three* is *six*,
Tu-tums *four* is *eight*.

We children have a picnic. On the way we go through a street with iron hitching posts along the edge of the sidewalk. They have horses' heads and seem very elegant. A boy catches hold of them as he goes along, one after the other, and pretends to jump over them. He is very lively. I admire him silently. We take lunch in baskets.

I decide to have a party. I have it Saturday of course. I forget to tell my mother about it. They come all dressed up and she is astonished. I say I am having a party. She says, well, they will have to take what they can get to eat. She seems cross. I am surprised, for she is never cross. Aunt Julie helps us play in the yard—"Drop the Handkerchief," "Simon Says Thumbs Up." I don't worry about the eating. When it is time they call us in and we sit at the table and have canned peaches. The minute I see them on the table I am glad and know it is all right. One girl couldn't come. Her mother wouldn't let her because she did not have a *written invitation!* The idea!

"Mother, Boltie is in the kitchen marking on the wall."

"Tell him to come here," she says. I go tell him.

"*He* doesn't want to. He's marking," Boltie says. He is making pictures all over the wall, boys on sleds, men on horses, "cockadaddles chasin' Nellie." (This is a picture he always makes, a crocodile with big teeth chasing me and me running away.)

"He's marking the wall all up with his chalk and he won't come," I tell my mother. She goes and stands in the door a minute.

"Bolton, you must not mark on the wall," she says. "The wall is not made to mark on."

"He likes to," says Bolton, not turning around from drawing Auntie Robinson's rooster on the pantry door. He keeps on making tail feathers.

Mother gets a basin off the shelf and dips water into it from the pail. She picks up the paint brush, and takes them over to him. "Now," says she, "I want you to take this brush and paint out all the marks on the nice yellow wall. This way" (she shows him). "You can go all over the wall and make it clean, and if a little water gets spilt on the floor you can take the mop and mop it up afterwards." Bolton is as pleased as Cuffy; he loves to do things. He paints and paints and is getting the wall rather clean. We go back in the sitting room and Father comes running from the study. "Edmund, I wish you would fix that child a blackboard," she says to him. "He's been marking all over the kitchen wall with his chalk. I've set him to cleaning it off."

"He has, has he!" Father looks into the kitchen. "You're a scalawag," says he, and pokes Bolton in the ribs. Boltie doubles up and shouts with laughing.

Bolton cries *at* people to get what he wants, but I am just a crybaby. Almost anything sets me off. My mother says if I will try to conquer this bad habit she will reward me for it. She will give me a penny for every day I go without crying. I try hard. When I start to cry they call out, "Take care, you will lose your penny!" After some time I have earned a good many pennies and my father says I had better buy a book. He puts some more to the money I have earned and buys me a beautiful book, *Pilgrim's Progress*. It has a brown-reddish cover and exquisite pictures: The Delectable Mountains, Giant Despair, Greatheart and the others on their journey. Bolton calls it my "*Sprigrom Sprogram.*" I have not read any book, though I have learned to read. I read my *Pilgrim's Progress* all through. I skip the fine print at the bottom of the pages, which don't belong. I am seven years old. This book has many nice long words in it, different from the primer and reader, more pleasing to me. I spell them out. We have a joke about the Pilgrim's always getting into a "lamentable condition." Mother will say, "Well, Nellie, your shoes are in a *lamentable condition!*" Muddy.

We have another baby, "Edmund the Fifth," a good name because there are now five Edmunds in our family. Now there are four of us, two boys and two girls, and I'm the oldest. Louisa has got too big to be the baby; we are much pleased with the new one. His eyes are very big and blue, and he's quite smart though so young. "Where's the baby?" they always say the minute they come into the house, and go and get it and cuddle it or play with it. Or, if it is asleep, we just tiptoe and look quietly at it to see if it smiles in its sleep, and if it does that is lovely. Some say it is an angel's wing brushing over the baby's face, and some say it is wind on the stomach.

We move to North Bergen, I ask them why and they say "Oh, never mind." It is a modest parish and we live in the parsonage, which we do not own. It has a session room at one side with its own door, for prayer meetings, and it's a wonderful place to play in, being empty so. The church is up the street and grey and rather old-looking, with a steeple, and the usual graveyard around it.

Our grassy yard has large and shady trees, garden in the back. A grapevine is trained on a trellis over the back door. We have a well, a pump, and a large Yankee girl who will do anything we ask her to if we will only give her enough to eat— my father says so, I haven't myself noticed. Potatoes are already planted for us when we come, and my father starts all the other vegetables right away. There is a strawberry bed, and everything is flourishing.

Father always makes a garden. He hoes in the garden for exercise. *Jab, jab, jab.* He starts in at one end of the row of beans, *jab, jab, jab,* with the hoe blade turned sidewise so that the sharp corner does it. He goes fast and furious. The soft brown earth bursts up in little spurts around the green plants. His arms work steady, like a machine, and his feet step along quickly. At the far end of the row he stops a moment, turns around and comes up the other side, *jab, jab, jab*, good deep digs, and the earth spurting up at the bright blade. At the stoop he drops the hoe, *clatter, clatter*, flops down on the step, cries: "Goody; how hot I am! Mattie could you bring me a drink of water?" He looks very red and sweaty. She brings him a drink and sits down on the step. They talk about the garden, how well it is doing, and whether there will be new potatoes by the Fourth. My father says, "I must get at it and brush the peas."

We have an eclipse. Father smokes bits of broken glass over the flame of a lamp, round and round, pushing the glass slowly, and the black soot comes softly on to it in little curls. He gives everybody a piece. He tells me it will smut my nose if I hold it wrong side up. We hold up our bits of glass and look at the sun. I have never seen the sun before, only its brightness. I see it now shorn of its beams, red—and small! I would surely think it was bigger than that. Somebody cries, "It's beginning." I hold my breath and look hard. Yes, yes, there it is, a small flat curve cut in the sun's edge, it goes on, very slowly, till it is quite a bite. I get tired tipping my head back; my neck aches; this is a slow old eclipse. "See, Nellie," says my mother, "the chickens think it is time to go to roost." The air is getting darker, the chickens go "cre-e-ew, cre-e-ew," low and gentle, and waver about, not knowing what to do. But they follow one another along, slowly, headed for the hen-house. The birds sing not but twitter, in a low secret way, to each other, and hop about the branches. The air is cool, a little small wind, and the light is dimly tinted with yellow and darkness. The air is magic; it is like the Arabian Nights. Now the shadow begins to slip away off the other side. The day grows lighter, the strange stillness dissolves, a bird bursts into his song. The shadow is gone and is no more, and the sun shines forth in the sky.

We kneel down at family prayers. My father prays that God will overturn, and overturn, till he whose right it is shall rule and reign. I like these words, and many others he uses at family prayers. I do not feel devout, especially. Sometimes I amuse myself sticking my fingers up through the little holes in the wicker weaving of the chair bottom where I am kneeling. I like the Bible. It has splendid words in it. My father reads them in a rich, large voice.

My bedroom is right off the sitting room and they leave the door open at night. Seven o'clock is my bedtime. One night in this bedroom I cannot get to sleep. I am sad. I don't know why. Presently I cry. Father comes in and asks me what is the matter.

"I—don't—know."

"Do you feel sick, Pussy, have you got the leg-ache?"

"No-o."

"What are you crying about?"

I tell him, "I want to be good." "Well," he says, "the way to be good just now is to turn over and go to sleep." A load falls off of me; everything seems all right. My trouble is gone.

"Good-night, Father."

"Good-night, Pussy."

He tucks me up and goes out into the sitting room. He would have stayed and rubbed my legs if it had been leg-ache that was the matter.

Mother's home was in Cheraw, on the Great Pedee in South Carolina, though both her parents came from Connecticut. They had slaves there. She did not know how to do housework at first, but she learned how of Auntie Leach where I was born on a farm when my father preached at West Dresden. So she always could do it. But it was better to have a hired girl. Father gladdens my heart when I hear him say, "Nellie is a good child and quite a help." It is necessary for me to help, for our hired girls will not stay with us, on account of hop-picking, or their sister being took sick, or they drather learn dressmaking, and then Mother tries to do it all and overworks and gets sick abed. So we all turn in. Father sweeps. He says it is good exercise. But it's awful; you wouldn't think there was so much dust in the world. Mother sneezes and sneezes and flees out of the room. I sneeze too, but I stay to watch him. He flies the broom around so fast you can't see it, hardly, and you never know which corner he'll light on next. He does not pay any attention to us or anything, seems to be thinking about his sermon, looking at nothing and sweeping *hard*. Suddenly he is on my side of the room and he sees me. "Oh, come, get out of here before I sweep you out!" says he and flourishes the broom so close to my toes I have to dance to get away. So I go laughing out. The reason he can raise so much dust is that it is there to raise, underneath the pink and green flowered carpet, though you wouldn't think so to look at it. It is in amongst the straw. Nobody else raises it, they sweep differently and let it lie.

In the spring we take the stoves out and put them in the woodshed. Three men are required with an enormous lot of fuss and puffing. We take up the carpet, going all around the edge with the other end of a tack-hammer, and hang it over the clothesline for somebody to beat. All that old straw that's been under the carpet a year and got smashed and broken to bits by walking on it, they sweep up into the clothesbasket and carry it out to the bonfire. And in the straw is lots of dust, and under the straw on the floor is a thick grey layer of dust, and the straw itself is dust. They burn it all up on the bonfire, and wash the boards and scrub them with soapsuds and a brush, and open every window wide, and put up clean summer curtains. It smells so clean, so fresh. We are glad that spring has come. They empty the stovepipes onto the bonfire and beat on the links of the pipe to get it all out. The soot fluffs all over them. Those who do the stoves and stovepipes go with smut on their foreheads and smears on their cheeks and smudges all up their bare arms and hands as black as the pipe itself. They can't touch anything, and go about with their hands stuck out away from themselves till they wash.

Bolton and I can wash dishes together when they put the pan down where we can reach it. We play and play and take our time. One day it is on a board between two chairs and it tips over and goes splash on the floor, dishes and dishwater and all. But there were only two cups and a plate left and they don't break, and Father flies around and swashes up the water with a work apron before it spreads over the entire room. Mother says why didn't he take a cloth or the mop, it was a spandy clean work apron. "My hand fell upon it and I took it," says he. "My policy is to sacrifice everything to the present emergency." If he hadn't grabbed the first thing at hand, dishwater would have been pouring out of the windows by this time.

When Mother gets sick Father gets the breakfast and makes us pop-robin, which is our favorite dish. There is lots of milk on account of the cow. Father milks her. Sometimes he throws the pail at her when she *won't* stand still but goes along away from him as soon as he sits down on the stool—but not very often. We have our strawberry bed, and a cherry tree, and the garden. Then, these kind, good parishioners send us cooked chickens, and sausages, and so on.

Joanna Peters pesters the life out of us telling about where she worked before.

"Joanna, it is time to sprinkle the clothes so they will be ready to iron in the morning."

"Martin Munger's folks always sprinkled the clothes the same day they ironed them."

"Bring me in a pail of water, Joanna."

"At Martin Munger's the man of the house fetched the water. He said 'twan't women's work."

"I will not have her around!" says Mother. But she does— has to.

Then one day in the middle of the dishes Joanna steps on the baby's rubber dog and it squeaks. Off flies Joanna upstairs, mad, and packs up; and when Mother comes in, there she is sitting on the sofa with her best clothes on her and her bonnet on, waiting for her pay. So *she* leaves and Mother finishes the dishes and gets supper and goes on doing the housework, and Father hunts for another girl; and in about a week she is in bed again and Father making pop-robin for breakfast.

Maggie Farrell is finally secured, a slattern, but can cook and is good to the children. We always have to have a girl that can get along with the children. Maggie does not mind if Eddie's playthings are all over the kitchen floor. Like enough she would sit down on the floor right in the middle of getting dinner, she is so good-natured, and build him a clothespin cabin and let the soup boil over and make an awful stench through the house. My father can't bear a stench. If the smell of burnt meat or peas or whatever she lets burn, if it comes floating gently through the hall and upstairs to his study, he leaps up and goes and gets a pan and wobs up paper in it and sets it afire. He goes all through the house waving the burning paper like a torch, and then we have burnt-paper smell instead of burnt peas. Brown paper is best. He does it in a sickroom, too, to purify the air.

My father loses his temper and scolds me harshly. I don't mind it very much. Afterward he comes and begs my pardon— just as though I was grown up. He says he ought not to have spoken so. This makes me uneasy, confused; I don't know what to say. I do not know what to do with the apology. I wish my father had not apologized.

We play together. Louise teases Bolton; she steals up behind him and pulls his hair, but she is little. Mother is the one who has us go to bed at seven. Father rolls on the floor with us at that time and we sit on his stomach. "Get off, get off," he cries. "Who's sitting on my bread-basket!" Mother says, "Edmund, I wish you wouldn't romp so with the children at bedtime; it excites them so." She makes Boltie stop marking the wall, by spanking. The third time she did it, after he went right on marking, he said, "Are you going to spank me every time I mark the wall?" "I certainly am," said she. "Then I'm going to stop," says he. She says, "I guess you better."

There is a big rough boy at school who runs around at recess catching the girls and kissing them. He comes to me and tries to kiss me. I hate him and feel crazy. I snatch a pin which is in my waist and jab it into his cheek with all my might. A round, bright, red drop of blood comes out instantly, like a currant. The boy jerks away his head with his hand to his face and seems very mad.

I have a composition to read in school. I have brought mine from home. It is on a sheet of white paper just plain, but I notice when I get to school that some of the girls have theirs rolled up and tied with pink or blue ribbon. Mine now seems to have no style. I wish I had rolled it up with a ribbon. When I go up in front of the school and read it, there comes a place in it where I think of a better way of saying it, so I read it *that* way instead of as it is written. I tell my mother about it when I get home. "Oh," she says about the new way of saying, "extempore —just like your father!" She says my flat paper was better than to be rolled up with a ribbon. "Extempore" is a nice new word. I am puffed up to be like my father.

I learn another word, "suicide." Bolton and I catch minnies in the brook. Bring them home, and put them in a goblet of water on a table. They swim about livelily. When I come home from school and go to look at the minnies, one of them is gone. Aunt Lidy is there and I ask her where he is. She says, "He committed suicide," and looks sober. I do not know what she means. At first she will not tell me; she says again solemnly, "He committed suicide." At last she says he jumped out of the glass on to the table and is dead. So now I know "suicide."

They send me and Bolton to get two dressed chickens in a basket (but when we look at them we see that they are absolutely naked, like the baby in his bath). It is a long way off on a road and we play along and take a good while getting there. Mother says it does take us a long time to do things, but children's time is not very valuable. The basket makes a good helmet over the head to play soldier with, and we can drag it behind for a cart also, and so on. We get to Cutter's and they give us each a cookie and show us their peacock, and put the two chickens wrapped in a newspaper into the basket and turn us around to go home. Bolton takes hold of the handle on one side and I take hold of it on the other and we carry it along. We carry it along. It is very heavy—the sun hot, this is a long road. We sit down on the bank to rest. Here's a stick, maybe that would help us. So we get up and string the stick through the handle and each of us takes an end of it, we start on. Now it is light as a feather! We prance home. We tell them about it, how we had used the stick. "Oh, yes, that is a principle in physics," they say.

I wish to earn money, so I pick hops. Everybody is picking hops and Mother says I can try it but to come home when I get tired. I never get tired. The vines are in tall green rows; the pretty stems and leaves go winding round and round up the poles. The hops are ready to pick; they hang upon the vines in delicate lovely green tassels. I walk in the green aisles, the poles reaching far above my head. People are here and there picking in front of very large wooden boxes with the hop poles laid across their tops. The man leads me to a box, takes a pole down and lays it across, and leaves me to pick off all the green tassels and drop them in. How pleasant! How pretty the tassels are. I am quite grown up to be picking hops with all the others.

I begin; I pick and pick; you mustn't put leaves in the bin. I lean over and drop the hops in—how many it does take to cover the large, far-away bottom. I pick and pick. The sun shines very bright, though I have my sunbonnet on. I pick and pick. A very hot day, seems as though. I sneeze, have to stop everything and begin wiping my nose. I sneeze, once I begin I keep right on and have to stop and lean on the box and devote myself to it; my eyes run, my nose drizzles. Nobody else sneezes. They busily fill their boxes, pay no attention to me. I pick and pick. I don't see how it will be possible for me to fill this box with these little hop tassels. But I shall stay here till I do it. I go on sneezing, picking, wiping my nose, sneezing, picking. I prickle all over like a gooseberry. At last they stop for noon. I stop, too, though the bin has only a little in the bottom. We all go up to a platform, where is a watering trough and a pump and a man hearing what they tell him and giving pay. I go up. The platform comes up to my shoulders. I tell him my bin is not finished but I guess I will not come back that afternoon. He looks over at me kindly. "Then you will want your pay now?" "Yes, if you please." He hands me five cents, I feel proud and grown-up. I go home, hot, prickly, dirty. When I get to my mother I fear I shall cry. "You poor child!" she says, and lays me down on a bed, puts a cool wet cloth over my eyes, shuts the blinds. She has hay fever, too.

Mr. Chauncy Finch is a friend of our family. He is not married, though old enough, and lives with his mother and sister in their house two miles from the village. Quiet and gentle he is, and the most pious of anybody we know. Of course my father is pious, too, and Mrs. Talcott, my Sunday-school teacher, and many others. You have to show piety if you are a Christian; that is how they know you are one—and, I'll tell you, my father *is* a Christian, a bouncing one. But Mr. Finch is a different kind. No bounce.

Now, Mrs. Talcott has the prettiest dresses in the place; her hair is shiny and brown, bright brown eyes. She can speak to you about anything, anything whatever, and you like to hear her. She is a widow of long standing, and spends a good deal of time taking care of herself, they say, and she is one of our best family friends, too. Yet you wouldn't think of her being a Christian the *first* thing about her. And Father, you always forget he's a Christian and a minister engaged in the Lord's work and responsible for the care of souls. But with Mr. Finch you never think of anything except how pious he is. Doesn't talk much, but sings in the choir. Thin and clear and beautiful his voice, a silvery sound that you hear mingling in with the others like threads of light twisting through darkness.

Aunt Lidy is visiting us, and he comes to see us very often. He sits around. She has a sprightly manner and he sort of likes it, and she likes anybody different, so they get along. Maybe they'll make a match of it.

Aunt Lidy always says her husband was killed in the War. I don't think she had a real husband, though, for she was only a girl at the time. Fifteen is grown-up for a woman, but they needn't get married then. My mother went right on getting her education until she was past eighteen and did not get married until she was nineteen, though I don't know but she would of had she met Father earlier. Aunt Lidy's education was interrupted. Grandma's father went to Yale, and her brothers went to college, and Grandma went to school in New York City, where she lived. But she stopped getting her education early. Why? Because then their father died and they had to all come out to these western wilds on a packet boat and be farmers. She had just got to the Rule of Three. Naturally Grandma wants her children to have an education. She had nine and raised three. So Father went to Yale and Aunt Louisa to Mount Holyoke and Aunt Lidy to the Elmira Female Seminary, for a while. But she got her feet wet standing in the snow at the railroad crossing when an awful long, slow train was passing and caught cold and had inflammation of the lungs and went into a decline. They thought she had consumption, and I do not know whether she did or not; but they had her stay home and lie around doing nothing, and bought her a beautiful buff leather sidesaddle and had her ride horseback. I've seen the sidesaddle.

The War was so long ago I can't remember it. Aunt Lidy says they sent the soldiers pincushions. And scraped lint. I see

some men going around in long blue overcoats, not like anybody else, and those are left over from the War.

Aunt Lidy's hair is as pretty even as Mother's, which is thick
and brown and long and in big waves. Aunt Lidy's is exactly
like fine silk, a dark brown with a shine of reddishness, and it
lies flat on her head in small softly shining ripples. She does it
up the back loose and tumbling down, and it is soft and curly.
She doesn't care. When my Aunt Lidy walks, you think of
young trees bending along; and she sits down like a flower in
her skirts.

Her name is Eliza Lounsbury Brown, after the little girl
Uncle and Aunt Lounsbury had with her hair curling in ring-
lets around her shoulders, and she died at the age of six. They
had a little boy too, who died young. (But three of their children grew up.) Samuel was his name, and his boots hung up
where he left them in the closet for many years, until somebody
who didn't know about it cleaned house and threw them away,
little Samuel's boots.

I make a little visit to the Finch house. His mother is very
old, an invalid, like a picture on the slate almost rubbed out.
There is a woman who takes care of them; she is an albino,
she has not a speck of pigment in her; perfectly white hair (not
like silver or snow, like wool), it does not even curl, white eye-
brows, white eyelashes, white skin like paper. She is deaf as a
post and talks in a whisper and has on a white dress and apron.
But she can make good apple pies.

Miss Ella Finch is kind to me and shows me everything.
They have a big barrel in the yard called a leach, sitting up on
a platform, full of ashes. The rain rains into the barrel and
soaks down through the ashes and out at a place in the bottom
into a keg; and it is *lye*, would you believe it! Lye is awful
strong; you must on no account put your hand in it; and they
use it to make soap. Yet rain is soft and pleasant and ashes are
feathery and clean and pure—how can they together make lye,
a dark angry water that eats you if you touch it?

If it must eat things, they give it something to eat. They save up all the old scraps of fat and pork grease and such kind of things, and once a year they dump this lot of rancid old fat in with the dark strong lye in an enormous iron kettle outdoors over a bonfire. They stir and cook and cook and stir, and after many hours of that it comes out soap. Soft-soap, slick and brown and clean, quivering, with streaks in it like rainbows. They put it in a keg and it is their keg of soft-soap to use all the year for washing and scrubbing. It stands in a shed smelling of shavings, on a carpenter's bench.

The house of the Finches is tall, made of grey stone, grass in the yard, chickens pecking around. No trees; I see no flowers. There isn't any porch either. It does not look like our house at all, or any of the houses in the village. But then, it is far away by itself, and lonely. I hardly know what lonely means, but it is a good word. I can think about it. Perhaps, once in a while, its meaning comes to me.

Mr. Chauncy Finch took a Vow of Silence. It was because the tongue is a little member but set on fire from Hell. He was not very talkative anyway; so it would not be the cross to him it would to me. He held out more than a year, resigned from the choir, and sat in their pew with his sister and made signs whatever he wanted anywhere. Then one Sunday in church they stood up to sing the last hymn:

> There is a fountain filled with blood
> Drawn from Immanuel's veins;
> And sinners plunged beneath that flood
> Lose all their guilty stains.

Mr. Chauncy Finch stood up with the rest, dumb and smiling, as usual. They came to the chorus, which repeats and goes up and down, wavering, over and over; so when that part came, he opened his mouth and joined in—"Lose all their guilty stay-ye-ains, lose all their gi-ul-ty-y sta-ayns; and sin-ners plunged beneath that flood lose all their guilty sta-a-ayns."

Everybody knew his silver voice and knew what had happened. They looked at each other and looked round at him, and his sister could hardly contain herself for joy. Not that she would have made any noise about it if she hadn't contained herself—they're a quiet family. The congregation spoke to him as they went out, "How are you, Chauncy," "How-de-do, Mr. Finch," and he answered them as pleasantly as though he had spoken that way every blessed Sunday for a year: "Very well, thank you," "How-de-do, Tom." But old Deacon Elwood, wrinkled old bald-headed man, passed him and peered up at him and said in his thin cracked voice, "Ye broke yer vow, Chaunce!" Mr. Finch only looked at him smiling, as if he had not heard, and said nothing. Miss Ella Finch was terrified lest he had stopped talking again; but they went on out, and he says, "How pretty the maple trees are in the breeze." How relieved she was, for even before the vow he'd never said as much as that about a maple tree.

We have moved to Wellsville. Father is to be the Presbyterian minister; but the church is a Congregational Church. It is quite a large town on the Genessee River. We have a small creek in our back yard; but our house is bleak, no trees. It is up on a bank near the railroad, a mere temporary shelter.

My father looks out of the window. His blood runs cold: Bolton is dodging under the freight cars, they stand on the track crossing the road, with their engine puffing. Father rushes down, but Bolton is through on the other side. Father can't call him back *that* way nor crawl under himself after him; and if he runs around the end of the train it is about a mile long, so he cannot catch him that way. Oh, Father! He waits, he fumes up and down. The cars start and chankle away. Of course Bolton is nowhere to be seen. Anyhow he has not been run over. Here comes Father rapidly back and goes into his study and begins to write his sermon furiously.

I suppose my mother needed a workbox even when she was

only four years old, though I haven't one yet; for she hemmed a handkerchief by stints and finished it and gave it to her father on her fourth birthday. What an odd way to celebrate your birthday! It was the fashion then to teach little girls to sew every day of their lives. They could not go out to play until they had done their stint. My mother's mother—the pretty young lady in the portrait—died when Mother was two years old, and she does not remember her. But her stepmother was all right enough. Every day before she could play she had to sit down on a stool beside her stepmother and make three inches of stitches, for a stint. If they were too big or if they were scraggly or slanted wrong, she had to rip them out and do them over.

My mother and I are in the big bedroom upstairs taking a nap. Side by side we lie on top of the smooth bed and the window shades are drawn down to make a dimness. My mother says:

"You don't believe the doctors bring the babies in a basket, do you?"

This amuses me. I never heard of such a thing. I do not think about it one way or the other. It is no responsibility of mine.

"Why of course I don't think the doctors bring the babies in a basket!"

My mother tells me how babies are born. She says she is going to have a baby. We take a nap. . . . .

Now we have another baby. Father has named her Gertrude of Wyoming, after a book he read. Not Wyoming, of course; her name is Gertrude North Brown, but he calls her that when he pets and holds her. "Coo-o, coo o," he says, silvery, and strokes her cheek with his forefinger to make her smile, "Gertrude of Wyoming."

Back of our new house runs the River. The church has

bought this house for a parsonage, on the main street, school-house next door—but a hole in the high board fence so that Bolton and I can crawl through instead of going round by the gates. Trees it has, and a lawn in front where the croquet set is, and Father playing with the ladies of the parish.

Father looks out of his study window upstairs—one bed-room always has to be the study—and sees us in the back school-yard, where we go to play out of school hours. He chants it to Mother: "I see Boltie in the schoolyard, walking in the set-ting of the sun," says he, "with red-legged stockings and with a crossbow on his shoulder. And Nellie walks behind him, and now they have disappeared through a board off the fence and down toward the River." We go to play mumble-je-peg on a pounded earthen circle we have made under the willow bushes.

Through that board off the fence runs away my pearl-grey rubber ball Cousin Henry gave me. I like a round thing. Bolton and I play toss-and-catch in the back schoolyard, and the ground slopes down. The ball gets away from us; it runs bounding down the hill; it slips through the gap in the fence. We race after it; we slip through the gap in the fence; the ball is dis-appearing beneath the willows. The River catches it and sweeps it off, and Bolton and I run and run along the bank, dodging through the bushes, faster on the open gravel. We reach out with sticks—almost have it—no, no, it dances away. A little smooth water near the shore, now we shall have it—no, no, it dances away. The River runs faster and whirls, the ball whirls and flies on, far, far out of our reach. It races toward the bridge. We stop. It is no use any more. We stand and watch it, stretching out to look. It grows smaller and smaller, a dancing speck—under the bridge—it is gone. We have lost it forever. Oh the flowing, sparkling waves of the endless River, you have taken my round ball from me and I never shall see it again!

It is dusk and we are bathing in the River. The hired girl is here and we have on our shimmies or a calico dress. We hang onto the drooping willow bushes and wade and paddle by the shore. Out beyond it is rather dark just now. Perhaps a leech will catch your foot, one did mine the other day. I shook it off, but I did not like it. They have them in bottles at the drugstore.

Bolton has a raft and I have a raft; his a regular one he nailed together, mine just a plank. We pole them along on our voyages. If we tumble off it does not matter, the water is shallow, you can wade to the middle of it. But we do not tumble off. When we wade, we wade, taking off our shoes and stockings; and when we raft we raft.

I love to slide down hill. I can steer perfectly, alone or with a sled full. I sit straddle. I can't bear that lying on your stomach and steering with your foot dragging out behind the way the boys do. They tear by, yelling, and look like crocodiles. Sitting up straight I can see. The ropes are tight in my hands. The snow flies up in spurts at my heels. I feel like a charioteer in a race. The wind blows in my face; it tries to keep me back; nothing can keep me back with the glassy slide under the runners and the long hill stretching down. The ropes pull in my hands. Over into the snowbank! Who cares—nobody. We shout and carry-on, tumble up and shake the snow off, and snowball each other. We choose sides and have a snow battle. But as for having my face washed, I will not stand it. I hate it. The boys are always doing it at recess, or any time. A handful of wet snow dashed in my face, rubbed all over me and down my neck—I can't stand it, and I won't. But it is quite the thing. Bertie Baldwin meets me on the street and says, "I'll wash your face!"

"You won't! If you do I'll tell your father on you."

He catches me and laughs and washes my face before I can get away. I am mad. I march straight down to the bank to Mr. Baldwin in his office and tell him Bert washed my face and I think he ought to be punished. Mr. Baldwin likes me; he smiles at me; he says he will attend to Bertie.

Another fire in the night, Father races off to them with his pants over his nightshirt.

"Oh Father, take me, take me!" I *will* go. *Whang*-whang, *whang*-whang, *whang-whang-whang*. Fire bells! I rush to his door, I drag my dress on over my head.

"Get your shoes, get your shoes," he cries, buttoning up.

I run back, put on shoes, button top and middle. Off we go after the glow we see down by Treadwell's, and others all running along from here and there. The flames tear and leap. They eat up Treadwell's store where we buy calico and spools of thread. The fire darts from the windows like bright snakes, curls up the walls like dragons. The roof falls in and millions of sparks and firebrands spray into the black sky. Then columns of smoke roll up.

A fire has burned up Chicago. I write a piece about it and show it to my father. At the end is: "Well may we look out at those slain at our very gates and be thankful." (Thankful *we* have not been slain, I mean.) He reads it over carefully, hands it back to me respectfully. He says the word "slain" is generally used only for those who lose their lives in battle. Oh! I am glad to know about the word "slain." I can just as well say something else.

They used to think I talked too much, do yet; now they think I read too much. They give me authors and dominoes to keep me from reading so much. I get books from the library, which is open two afternoons a week. I was reading my *Arabian Nights* the Saturday before I joined the church. Mother came into the room and saw me and said she'd think I would be reading my Bible at such a time. I don't know why.

Linnie Baldwin is my best friend. We do everything together, so when Mother asks me if I would like to join the church I say I guess so and ask her if I can't see if Linnie will join too. Linnie'd just as soon. She says for me to ask her mother for her. We go to her house and stand near the door in their green sitting room, in front of Mrs. Baldwin in a sweet maroon dress. She is standing too; her face is sober and kind. I ask her if Linnie can join the church.

"Have you forgiven Mrs. Henderson for scolding you and calling you names for something you did not do that time?" she says to Linnie. I look at Linnie. She seems ashamed; she stares at her toes and shakes her head.

"Well, can you love that little Flaherty girl down at the corner?" says she.

Linnie jerks up her head disgustedly and bursts out, "Love her! A dirty little thing two years old and can't *tell* yet—does her bizness on the floor! How can I love her!"

She says Linnie cannot join the church; so I join by myself and partake of the communion for the first time. Our hired girl asks Mother, "Do you have to pay to partake of communion?" "Why, no, Mandy," says Mother; "salvation's free."

We are all walking along home from church in the quiet street, our best clothes on, our hymnbooks and Bibles in our hands, Father in his long black broadcloth coat and beaver hat. Suddenly Father leaps off from my side into the middle of the road, and there is a man driving a pig and beating him every step with a stick. Father grabs the stick out of his hand. He breaks it across his knee and slings the pieces so far they go over the fence into somebody's yard. He glares at the man and scolds him, and comes rapidly back to the sidewalk with his face as red as a beet, still muttering. How astonished I am to see him dart off like that—I hadn't noticed the man. I think he is mad at him. My mother says cruelty always makes him angry.

It is odd about faults. There are all kinds and if you do not have one kind, very likely you will have another. A minister exchanges with Father and preaches on Besetting Sins. He says we all have one. Paul did, even. And if we do not know what ours is, to ask a friend to tell us. I ask Linnie to tell me what is my besetting sin; but she won't do it. I guess Father's is acting before he thinks.

Aunt Anna visits us and it is hot. We sit in the hotel in her bedroom. She has on a camisole, thin, ruffled, because she can't stand the heat; and she has a large palm-leaf fan. They talk about chocolate.

"I never have any chocolate," I say.

"What, child?" says Aunty.

"Why, you are talking about chocolate as if there was any. I never see chocolate anywhere around."

"Never see any chocolate!" says Aunt Anna, "Mattie, don't you ever give chocolate to your children?"

"I don't think they keep it in the stores," says my mother.

"Nonsense!" says Auntie. "Of course they keep it in the stores."

She tells me to bring her purse from the bureau, and I do; and she gives me five cents out of it and says to run across the road to the drugstore and buy me some. I run across, kicking up the dust, and ask for chocolate. He says he hasn't got any. (Just as Mother thought.) I look around and wonder what to do now. There is the jar of black licorice. I like it so much better than stick-licorice, which many prefer. "I'll take a stick of black licorice," I say, and run back across the road sucking it and upstairs to her room. "Why, Nellie, I told you to get chocolate," says my aunt.

"Oh, they didn't have any; so I got licorice. I'll whack you off a piece from the other end, Aunt Anna. Wait a minute."

But she has turned very sober, and they both sit there; and suddenly I know something is wrong. What? I stand still and she explains it all to me. She says she gave me the five cents to buy chocolate, not anything else. When they didn't have any chocolate, I ought to have brought it back and given it to her, not spent it for something else. She says when you are trusted with money you must never spend it for anything but the one thing it is given you for. It does not belong to you to do what you like with; it is a trust. So now I know that money is a trust. I am sheepish at what I have done. I hate not to do things right.

Aunt Anna brought Father a fur-lined overcoat. He is going to send it to Grandpa. Grandpa will use it fifty times to his once, he says, and *he* doesn't need it. Grandpa will like it, on those Hector hills. But I think it would look handsome and stylish on my father going to church in the snow.

The Furniture has come. It belonged to Mother's uncles in New Orleans and was made in France. When they died, it was sent to their parents, Dr. and Mrs. Elisha North, at New Haven, who were Mother's grandparents. Dr. North was a very kind and good and learned man, wrote a book on spotted fever (a very old brown book; I've seen it), and used vaccination for smallpox almost the first of anyone. Now they are dead and gone. Aunt Julie is there at New Haven telling what to do with everything, and has sent The Furniture here to Mother to belong to us. There is an enormous wardrobe with a mirror for a door, the mirror lined behind with pleated red silk; and it has a large fancy brass key to the keyhole. There is a washstand with marble top and carved doors, and it is so big and square that Father has named it The Tomb of the Capulets. A little cunning carved commode, marble-topped, to stand by your bed at night, a rosewood bedroom sofa covered with lovely rosy brocade; and two other sofas, more for parlors, covered with maroon rep. Lots of chairs and armchairs, covered with maroon rep, and a grand mahogany bed with rolled-over headboard and footboard, big enough for the whole family if we ever wanted to do such a thing. There are a chess table that opens out and folds up, and a grand sideboard for dining room, carved and marble-topped. But as we do not use a sideboard, that can be for books, as it has shelves. There are gold mirrors and brass candelabra, and so forth. We take off the crystal pendants of the candelabra; they are *prisms*, and we use them to catch sunbeams and turn them into rainbows. And there are many very large pictures: "The Princes in the Tower," "Pierre le Grand Sauvé par sa Mère," "Upstream," "Downstream," and so forth. Mother

gives me the big down cover, chintz, with pictures on it of a
little boy and little girl sitting by a small lake watching swans,
all in dark brown and white.

Since The Furniture came I feel different. It lifts me. I
shall never feel the same again.

I sit in school at my desk. I see the word "perish" in my
book, and suddenly it seems strange to me. The meaning has
gone out of it. I notice its sound in a different way from ever
before, a curious way. Something has happened to this word.
The "per" and the "ish" are separate—don't belong together—
and neither one has any meaning to it.

There is excitement in school, a speechless thrill all over the
room. Something violent is happening. We stare at the teacher
talking in low tones to an unknown woman by the desk. We
look back and forth at each other. A strange girl appears.
Teacher takes her and brings her over to my side of the room,
which is the side farthest from the door, and hides her on the
floor under a desk near me. The school goes on as usual. After
a while she is gone. They say her father is after her.

We spell down. The whole room stands up on two sides, and
Miss Avery gives out the words quick and sharp. The poor
spellers go down first and don't mind it. Then the good ones,
and they are ashamed, or embarrassed, or they giggle. She
goes from easy to hard, and we get more and more stiff up and
down our backs and prickly all over us. She snaps out the words
and we snap back *right!* "Matutinal," "incomprehensibility,"
"phthisic" (but that's a trick word and all the good spellers
laugh when it comes; they know it, "ph-th-is-ic, phthisic").
"A-a-ah!" says everybody, sitting on the edge of their seats and
squirming, or standing up—the few that are left—and looking
braver and braver and more and more red in the face. I stand

stiff and still, waiting for the next word—*whatever it is*. My letters come out like soldiers; I order them, I don't let any letter go wrong.

Dave and I are left, the only ones in the big room standing, the whole room watching us, holding their breaths, teacher at the desk rapping out the words from the speller, hardly giving us time to answer. Back and forth, from Dave to me. We snap out the words and cast them away, and stand for the next. . . . . If this goes on much longer I shall *break!* . . . . Oh, Dave, how could you! To go down on "*sponge.*" No wonder you hide your face in your arms. I bet you're crying. *I have won.* I'd rather win with a harder word—but then, I went down myself on "queue" last time. Miss Avery shuts the book. I alone stand there. They all clap. I stand there; I have spelled the school down. A strange feeling. I seem like a soap bubble when we blow it up; I swell bigger and bigger; will I burst! But it is recess, and all rise and march out. My seat is so far away that I come out almost last on the platform at the top of the steps. They are all standing in a bunch on the ground around the steps. When I come they start shouting:

"Hurrah! Hurrah!"

"What's the matter? What's she done?" ask the big scholars from the room upstairs.

"She spelt the school down," they shout. I stand and don't know which way to look, but feel glory hallelujah.

Father is very proud of me. "She spelt the school down," he tells the callers, waving his hand toward me. Then he goes on and tells them I get a hundred most of the time. They look at me admiringly.

She is giving us long division. Miss Avery stands at the board and does us an example and the class sits on the bench and gawps at her. She runs her long limber pointer down as she figures, and explains. Dividend, divisor (just like short). Bring down the remainder . . . . Oh dear . . . . you go so

fast! What *is* a remainder? . . . . Oh dear, she keeps bringing them down so fast (perhaps this will stump me—nothing
else has). Divide and bring down the remainder . . . . I am not
getting it at all, there is no sense to it . . . . divide and bring
down another. And it ends with a remainder; doesn't come out
even. She seems to know just what to do about that, too. There
it is complete on the board, in a long flight of steps, and I'm
ready to cry (inside) because I don't understand it. She seems
to think she has told us. She gives out the next lesson and dis-
misses the class, and lets the room out for recess. We gather
around the steps and talk about long division. We feel very
sober. "Do *you* understand it, could you do it?" we say to
one another. "No, could you?" Nobody understands it; nobody could do it. We don't know that we ever shall.

Torchlight processions make me want to holler. So I do. We
are electing U. S. Grant to be the President. A girl in school
writes a sarcastic poem about Grant, sneering at his cigars and
so forth. She praises Horace Greeley. I write a much better
one in reply, sneering at Greeley.

> Grant stays at home and keeps his mouth shut,
> For Grant is a silent man.
> But he can do more than Greeley could
> Or than Greeley ever can.

That is one verse. Father wrote one too, but he says mine is
better. He says, "I have a daughter who can write a better poem
than I can."

The boys take a punkin and make a jack-lantern that looks
exactly like Greeley, put a fringe of white beard around under
its chin, and carry it in the procession. It is cheered. There is
a Democrat meeting to be at the hall and they sneak the jack-
lantern in and up to the front, and when the people come there
is their Greeley grinning at them on the floor at the edge of the
platform. Oh my, I wouldn't be a Democrat for anything.

"It reminds me of when I was a boy in Buffalo and ran down

the street shouting, 'Van, Van, Van, is a used-up man.' But I got into the wrong crowd and they *hustled* me," Father says.

"Hustled you? What did they do to you?"

"Hustled me," says he and looks solemn. He goes off singing, "Tippecanoe and Tyler too, with *them* we'll *beat* little *Van.*"

Perhaps you think our ancestral home is in Buffalo. It isn't; it's in Burdett. My father was born there. But Grandpa lived in Buffalo once and kept a drugstore and had a partner that *vamoosed* with the money and left my grandfather to pay the debts. Which it took him many years of rigid economy to do. It was an ill-advised venture. You wouldn't think *vamoose* would be doing wrong, would you? Sounds gay and lively.

I like the word "buffalo." It's like a nest of kittens. I never saw the animal, but I often ride under a buffalo robe in a sleigh in winter. Or even in a buggy when the fall weather is cold and the bright wind blows clouds of leaves off the whipping branches, ruffles them, and chases them along the paths and gutters. No frost, no wind can get me under that thick skin, curly outside, tucked tight around me up to my chin and a hot brick under my feet. It once kept a buffalo warm on the Western plains.

My father was a little boy in Buffalo, very fond of books (like me). One day a lady he went to see gave him a present of a large handsome book with gilt edges and a dark blue cover, and inside reading and many pictures. Father says there was *glamour* over that book. He went away from the lady's door down the street of Buffalo toward his home, with the great book open in his arms, turning the pages slowly and gazing at the pictures. He glanced up, and there was a beautiful little girl in a wide hat coming toward him, loitering along. They stopped, and he showed her the book. They turned the pages together and looked at the pictures. She thought it was lovely, but they did not talk much. Then she had to go on, and the little boy went in the opposite direction. He turned his head and looked back; she was standing, half going on and half wanting to see the book

some more. "Here, you take it," cried he, running back to her
and putting the book in her arms. In wonder she took it and
went along up the street away from him turning slowly the
pages. Father never saw her or the book again.

Mother teaches me the Sophie book at home, to learn French.
I have a primer, besides, with pronunciations and everything
else you need. Papa fume sa pipe; ma mère; mon père; le chien;
la plume; haricot (beans). Why do they call a pen a "plume"?
She explains. Almost up to now people made their pens of
feathers and a feather is a plume. Or rather a plume is a feather.
It is not a little soft feather we give the baby to blow, but a *quill*,
stiff, and with a strong hollow stem. They took their penknives
and cut off its end, clean and slanting, and then slit it a little
way to make it flexible and easier for the ink to flow down.
Pen-knife, you see; that is why that small knife is called a pen-
knife, although nowadays pens are made by machinery.

My father spoils his pens with great rapidity. For one thing
he writes a great deal; but he never stops to wipe his pen, just
drops it, and if you don't carefully wipe your pen, *every time*,
it rusts and gets sticky and dirty and clogged, yes, indeed, it
gets disreputable. And that's the way my father's pens are.
But he will not use a bad pen either; so he has to be always
buying a new one. He chooses them with great care, and it is
quite a burden. A kind friend of his sent him a box of pens
for a Christmas present, but Father did not like that a bit.
You'd think he would be delighted, but no.

"What does a man want with a hundred pens!" says he disgustedly.

Probably there are not as many as a hundred pens in a box;
but that is my father's way of speaking, in hyperbole. *Hyperbole!*

The more errands they give me to do at once the more fun
it is. I feel nicely loaded up and brace my shoulders and set

off. Run and not be weary, walk and not faint. I arrange my errands in packages in my head and take them out one by one when I get there. "Do the farthest one first," says Father; "then you won't have to carry it there and back again." Isn't that smart of him? I should not have thought of it.

I go with Mandy after supper to get some yeast in a pitcher. We get it at a grocery store and start home. It is growing dark. Some boys come along: "Hem-m, hem-m," they say. I don't know these boys, but they seem sociable. "Hem-m, hem-m," I say in return. Mandy catches hold of my arm and says "S-sh, s-sh!" and hurries me on; and when we get home she tells my mother what I have done. My mother looks very grave. She says I must never, never cough or clear my throat to attract attention on the street. She says if I ever do it again she will not let me go into the street. Imagine! Certainly I never will; but why, I should like to know? 'Tisn't one of the Ten Commandments, is it? Wrong, I suppose, but why—just coughing.

I don't see but I get along pretty well without rules anyway. But now that will be a rule, not to cough in the street to attract attention. Yet, after all, I rather like a few rules, to bolster me up. They are right there all the time, neat and useful. I can think of them suddenly when I don't know what to do. We have a few. Mother tells them to us. Some are proverbs, and some she made up: Don't contradict; speak when you're spoken to; come when you're called; don't slam the door; don't talk with your mouth full; don't chew with your mouth open; eat what's set before you; don't talk about your food at the table; don't make a noise when you drink (these seem to be all about eating); don't ask personal questions . . . . I did not realize we had so many. And there are others everybody has, like: you mustn't lie. But I never do lie; why should I? Not everything you do or don't do is a rule, of course. My mother says, "Don't do that, it isn't polite," or she says, "Don't do *that!*" and looks so disgusted you are ashamed of yourself without knowing why. And she tells us to "act according to your own judgment," which is what Rollo's tutor used to say to him when it didn't matter.

"How shall I fix it, Mother? Do tell me, this way or that way?" I am pasting a picture in my scrapbook. "Act according to your own judgment," says she.

"I can't, I haven't any; that's just the trouble. Would you put it crossways—or lengthways? I can't decide."

"Possibly it doesn't make any difference," says she.

"Oh. But yet . . . . ?"

"Well, count out," says Mother.

"Oh yes—aina, maina, dippery dick, delia, dolia, dominick, hytcha, pytcha, dominytcha, hon, pon, tusk—comes out to put it crossways. After all, I'd rather put it lengthways, I think."

Mother laughs. "Anyway it helped you to make up your mind," says she.

III

WOODWARD FARM

WE HAVE COME to live at Woodward Farm. It is the home of my ancestors; runs from the top of the Big Woods on the hill to the pebbly shores of Seneca Lake, in Hector Township and two miles from Burdett. The big white house Mary Woodward (Father's grandmother) built is on the Lake Road, and we live in it.

A long time ago I came here to visit. Uncle Horatio Woodward was alive, and Hannah Vosburg was his housekeeper. There were lace curtains at the parlor windows, held back in loops each side by silver disks as big as saucers. I looked into them and saw my face curiously pulled about. An iron mortar was on the pantry shelf with the pestle standing in it where they ground spice; on the veranda wall a tall barometer was hanging; in a dim corner behind the hall door a long leather-covered spyglass leaned. Uncle Horatio took the spyglass and went through the front door and stood at the top of the veranda steps; he pulled out an inside brass tube it had and looked through it to the hills across the Lake.

All is changed now. Uncle Horatio Woodward died one day alone in the front hall at the foot of the stairway. He sat down on the last stair step and shut his eyes and died, and there Hannah found him when she came through the hall. Our Great-uncle Richard, his elder brother, died just so, alone and quietly, but in his bed; and Hannah found him too, but many years before. The things have been taken away, Hannah has gone

home to her father's tiny house down on the Lake Road, and
we have come with our furniture and our things to live at the
farm. There are two tenant houses, Miner Bennett's and Lanterman's, to right and left of us along the road; and my father
will manage the estate.

The house is large and painted white. Across the front is a
long veranda, with two great rockers on it to sit in and watch
the gorgeous sunsets over the hills beyond the Lake. The gravel
walk up from the white fence is wide and clean, pear trees at
the side. A bush of flowering currant hangs full of fragrant
yellow blossoms. A lattice by the front steps holds up a rose
vine; the small yellow roses smell like violets and cloves.

We find at the back a great woodhouse ranked up with a
store of firewood to the roof. Across one end is an open loft
and a pile of dried bean vines there waiting to be threshed.
Under the loft are two small chambers, each with its window,
outside door, and lock. We have taken one for our museum,
and have already collected three lucky-stones, a sheep's skull,
and a very big, grey, paperish wasps' nest which we found
(deserted) hanging in a tree. In the back yard beyond the
quince bush and the morello cherry tree is a house the size of
a tall playhouse, roofed, shingled, painted brown like the woodhouse and wagonhouse, and a door that locks. It is to keep codfish in, out there because Uncle Horatio couldn't bear the smell.
The vegetable garden has a tall, brown-painted picket fence to
keep the chickens out.

In the wagonhouse yard we find a big black iron soap kettle
turned upside down in the grass. We put a board across it
and have it for a kind of see-saw, Bolton straddles one end and
I the other, and by kicking a little we sometimes whirl around.
Usually we fall off, the board slips from the round bottom.
Over the fence at the other side of the house is the ram's-yard,
with a tiny rill in it where Bolton makes dams and waterwheels.
Tall locusts stand by the house, at the sides there are old thick
lilac bushes growing.

Grandma's grandmother was pure French, Susannah de
Lucé; and this is the story of her father, the French Huguenot,
whose little old Bible in the French tongue they have at Burdett,
with its ragged leather cover nearly off and "Jno. de Lucé"
written in the front of it.

Persecuted for his faith, they put him in a dungeon with one
small grated window, his bed a heap of straw, and left him there
to starve. But every day a hen came and laid an egg outside the
window, and he was able to slip his fingers through the bars
and draw in the egg, and so was sustained. This went on for
two weeks. Then they came and found him alive and were
frightened, supposing a miracle had happened—some saint or
some angel had fed him. Not daring to kill him, they put him
in an open boat without oars and set him adrift on the sea, and
after two days a Yankee ship picked him up and brought him to
the coast of New England.

After a while his daughter, Susannah, was married to Richard Woodward, of Dedham, and that Richard is my grandmother's grandfather; and how John Lucé got his French daughter over from France and how she met with Richard Woodward
no one knows.

Parson Fowler, of Guilford, had two lovely daughters, Mary
and Sarah. I suppose he was not parson from his birth, but
Grandma always calls him that; and he preached in Guilford
forty years, until the time of his death—quite different from
my father. Mary married Peter Woodward, the son of Susannah de Lucé and Richard Woodward. Sarah married Peter's
brother Roswell, who sailed his sloop "Sally" (named after
her) to the South Seas and the Spice Islands. His sloop was
wrecked and he was drowned, and left her to marry again, a
Mr. Baldwin. And he died too. So Sarah came to live with
her sister Mary on this farm, both widows, and they were dear
friends and companions. "Aunt Baldwin" she was called. They
sat in two rocking chairs just alike, visiting together every day.

Peter Woodward was my ancestor (great-great-grandfather). Grandma was thirteen when he died, so she remembered him. She tells about him: "My father, Peter Woodward, was a lietuenant in the Revolution, a member of Washington's staff," says my grandmother, straightening in her chair. We have just had a short conversation in her shady sitting room. My Aunt Lidy has gone to the ravines. My grandfather is perhaps hoeing vegetables in the garden. I was announcing that I intended to do just as I liked—why not?—so long as I did not do wrong. My grandmother said, "Don't you care about the speech-of-people!" And what is that (though I am sure I know); I never heard of it before. Grandma straightens up and begins to tell about her ancestors. It sounds to me like history.

"With the rest of the staff he was dining with Washington the day the news came of Arnold's treason. The General was so moved he drank off three glasses of wine in succession, instead of one as his habit was . . . . He was a member of the Cincinnati." She has shown me from the garret a sheet of foolscap written in her father's hand, the minutes of their meeting, with the first plans for the Cincinnati Society all laid out. He was at Valley Forge; and four days they had a dog tied up thinking they might have to eat him, but did not. Peter Woodward said Washington sent for yarn at Valley Forge and set the soldiers to knitting stockings for themselves. "There was not a man in the Army who would not lie down and die for him," Peter Woodward said. He was there.

My grandmother tells these stories always in the same words. She gets on with it breathlessly and is interrupted now and then by the little fits of laughter she falls into. She repeats the speeches as though she were the very person talking; her face becomes that face, her voice that voice, and I can see it clearly in my mind.

"One day he was separated from the other soldiers, lost and wandering about half-famished. He saw through an open door a man sitting at a dinner table eating. He went up and knocked. The man looked at him: 'What is your name?' 'Peter Will-you-eat.' *'Peter Will-you-eat!'* (very much astonished), 'Yes, thank you,'—And he sat down to satisfy his hunger.

"He had to borrow for his college expenses—he left Yale to join the Army. After the war he found himself with no means to pay the college bills. He went to New York to seek employment, his entire fortune a dollar. He had this dollar in his hand crossing the ferry and accidentally dropped it overboard. He walked up Wall Street, very dejected, and met an old Quaker who stopped and said:

" 'Friend, thee looks sad, is thee in trouble?'

" 'I am a stranger in a strange city, and, what is worse, I am out of money and out of employment.'

" 'Thee come to my office at three o'clock this afternoon and I will see what I can do for thee.'

"He took him into his employ. This Quaker happened to be fitting out a privateer, and he sent Peter Woodward with them to keep the books. The ship took a prize and Peter's share was enough to pay all his debts." Grandma laughs, she thinks it so funny for a Quaker to be fitting out a privateer.

"What *is* a privateer, Grandma?"

"Ships sent to capture merchant vessels on the high seas— take them as prizes."

"Prizes? What to do with them?"

"They had the cargo for a prize—divided it up. Sometimes it was very valuable, thousands and thousands of dollars' worth."

"Stole it?"

She forgets to explain. She is telling how she used to run and meet her father when he came home from his office and "climb up on him" to search his pockets for the candy he would bring. "He was in the custom house of the Port of New York and had four dollars a day till the day of his death. He was sick for two years before he died, but a friend paid a substitute for him at the custom house office and he had his salary just the same." A great tall man, he was, fresh-colored with rosy cheeks, sandy hair and beard, "a fine-looking man well-dressed." In those days gentlemen were well-dressed—velvet, brocades, embroidered waistcoats, fancy buckles at foot and knee. Grandma likes it—and so do I.

"Uncle Russel was an aristocrat, his son Sam a perfect nabob. They were a younger branch of the Russels of the English nobility. Uncle Russel wore the finest of cloth breeches, long white silk stockings and low shoes, silver knee-buckles. His ships went to the Orient. He had his dishes made in China and marked with his initials, 'S.R.,' Samuel Russel. His handkerchiefs the finest linen cambric, his dressing-gown white broadcloth."

(I see them, those sailing ships crossing the billowing seas, to "the Orient!") "And *did* you see the silver buckles on Uncle Russel's fine breeches, and the lovely china?"

"Of course. The Russels and the Woodwards built next door to each other on Catherine Street, only the house wall between, and a big double garret over both where the children played."

I have to notice my grandmother's head when she lifts it up so. Small it is. Her hair has no grey in it, straight, black and shining, and done in a puff over the ears. If she has been lying down to read on the lounge and thinks her hair is mussed, she pulls out the very small side-combs, runs them through the locks that fall down, pats with her hand, rolls the hair round the combs with a smooth twinkling of her fingers and sets them smartly in place. She likes to have me brush her hair and I often do, standing behind her chair. I can twist the back knot for her when I am done; but she doesn't let me do the ears. "Here—let me—" and she snips the comb away from me, rolls them up like lightning, sticks them in exactly where they always go, and there she is!

"We lived well. Our furniture was mahogany, the best to be had, a sideboard, tall clock—we moved in the best society of New York City. My father was good to us. He was particular with our training, superintended our bearing and our walk and our lessons after supper around the table. Then he gave us a good romp before we went to bed and we saw no more of him until the next night."

"And, Grandma, what did you wear?"

"Elegant silks—for best—and satins. They were supposed to last fifteen or twenty years, so they were handsome. Mother had a white satin bonnet and dress for Sunday and a black satin bonnet and dress for everyday," says she.

"I wish I lived in those days," say I.

"Oh that was New York City," says she, "you couldn't dress that way in Burdett." She begins to laugh. She has remembered something else, and plunges in: "Mother wanted a new carpet and Father did not want her to have it. She went to town and bought it unbeknownst to him and got it home and upstairs into the garret. Father came home and found nobody about, came on upstairs, and there they all were in the garret, Mother and the girls and the Russel girls, sewing the breadths together. 'Mrs. Wood'ard, after this *I* will carry the purse.' He always called her 'Mrs. Wood'ard' when he was vexed with her."

The girls were "a lively set, lots of beaux." Fitzgreen Halleck and Rodman Drake beaued Charlotte and Jennet around. They'd make up a load of young folks and drive out to Westchester County where Rodman Drake lived with his two maiden aunts. "He was a gay fellow. Once he dressed up as a girl and went to a party and a young man fell in love with him." (Gusts of laughter.) "We had hosts of friends and a gay life."

Aunt Lidy comes sauntering in with ferns from the ravine and goes through to the kitchen. She will get a plate and cover it with a bed of moss and plant the ferns in it; they will grow there with water under the moss, and uncurl their green little young ones the same as in the woods. Grandma rises up suddenly and calls after her, "Lidy, we must have some Bermuda potatoes; Bermuda potatoes are in market."

"Grandma," I call after her, "haven't we any ancestors but the Wood'ards?"

She says over her shoulder that her grandmother Fowler was a Hart, very high-toned folks, "I visited them once in New Haven." I run after her into the kitchen. "Thomas Hooker, the founder of Connecticut, was my ancestor," she says, going through the back entry and into the garden to pick peas. I go out with her and pick and ask about Grandpa's folks. They are my ancestors too.

"The Browns came over in 1635, in the 'Susan and Ellen,' a good family. Your grandfather's mother was a Webster. Her grandfather came over in the 'Mayflower,' they say. Doctor's father, Benjamin Brown, was a giant of a man, famous, could outwork any four of his hired men in haying and harvesting. One Sunday he had a great field of hay down drying and a thunderstorm was coming up. He went out and got the hay raked and under shelter before it rained. The next day the minister rebuked him for working on the Sabbath. Benjamin never went near the church again."

I have two old uncles—my father's uncles—named Wesley and Alvin. They live in Homer, and Mother and I go to Homer in August to escape hay fever; we have it on the farm. Aunt Lucia, Uncle Wesley's wife, is very nice; born in South America where her father was consul, so she talks with a tiny accent and very crisp and witty. But Uncle Wesley is slow, and silent, and humorous-looking, and good, very like Grandpa (his brother). Uncle Alvin never married and used to teach school. He copies things out of books and papers—the population of Australia, the average rainfall in the British Isles, how many miles from here to Jupiter. He thinks they are interesting. He writes them very fine with black ink on small pieces of paper and sews the pieces to make little books, of which he now has many, and keeps them in a cherry-wood desk with many pigeonholes. His hair is long and bushy, and so is his beard, like a Prophet. But his eyes twinkle.

Uncle Alvin tells us often about his father (Benjamin Brown) coming out to Cortland County where Homer is, from their home in Connecticut, when he was only a young man, with a young wife, named Dorinda Webster before she was married, and two little boys. Afterward, Dorinda had many more boys, seven sons in all; and she only weighed a hundred pounds. One daughter there was, but she died. My grandfather, Edmund Brown, was one of the seven sons.

My Uncle Alvin says his father, Benjamin Brown, and two or three other young men came out from Connecticut to Truxton Township (which is in Cortland County) with ox teams, and horseback. It was early spring, the trees just beginning to leaf out. Each night when they made camp they cut down trees for the oxen to eat the young leaves, as there was nothing else to feed them. Their Negro slave boy, Mose, overate on maple sugar, took sick and died on the way. When they got to Truxton, after many, many days traveling in the wilderness, they located their future homes. Benjamin Brown chose a spot by the stream full-flowing with clear water, covered with great old trees, maples, walnuts, hickories, all the kinds we have now but older and larger. There he built a little bower among the trees beside the stream. He was proud of his choice. He went and brought Dorinda down, led her through the grass and bushes, brought her to the bower. "Here is the place; here is where our home is to be." Dorinda sat down on a log and looked at it. She threw her apron over her head and cried. She was young then. They built their house there; her children were born, she used to spin and weave. They made cheeses too. She lived to be ninety, they say, and she never got over being homesick for Connecticut, but she never went back home.

My grandmother is smart, for at the age of thirteen she made several very large water-color paintings after only taking a few lessons from her cousin. They are in a roll now in the garret chest. She brings out the roll and shows them to us. She says it was very hard to get the agonized look on the boy's face left alone to die on a peaked rock in the tempestuous ocean. The blue, the deep beautiful blue of his shirt and of the sea waves, that is *ultramarine*. She is proud of what she did at the age of thirteen. Another is a shipwreck, ship tipped over, many people drowning all around. Another is cows in a snowy wood. A milkmaid with a long red cape on and a hood is with them. The cows have bony flanks the way cows do, and wander along in the snow under the wintry trees. The best one is "Crossing the Brook," a lady holding her little boy's hand and guiding him over on stepping stones. The boy has curly hair. He is a little afraid, which you know by the way he holds his arms out and by the look on his face. His dress is thin and fluttery over his bare legs. It is pale yellow and his mother's is red. The trees by the brook stand up in dark green ranks.

Grandma jumps up and speaks a piece for us. "I will recite 'The Death of Marmion,'" she says. It begins, "O woman in our hours of ease," and ends, "Charge, Chester, charge, on Stanley on, were the last words of Marmion." She speaks like a dying soldier. Lifts her voice, yet not strong and clear, because he is dying. She waves her broken sword. She chants the words, she never misses one. With "were-the-last-words-of-Marmion," she comes down to earth, looks around at us with a little proud smile. She expects us to like it. She says she learned it when a girl. She reads all the time. She lies on the lounge and reads. She sits up suddenly and claps her two hands up to her head and cries out, "O-o-oh, how my head aches!"

Grandma tells one of her stories: "There was a servant whose master said to him, 'I must be undisturbed today. If anybody comes put him off with *irrelevant conversation*.' So when the servant heard a knock he opened the door and said to the man standing there, "Is your grandmother a monkey?'" Grandmother laughs in a funny gusty way, interrupting herself with it. Another one is this: An Indian was invited to dinner at a settler's home. He thought the changing the plates was very grand. He went back to his wigwam and told his squaw, "Put on succotash." She put it on. "Take off succotash." She took it off. "Put on succotash"—each time he ate a little bit. "Take off succotash." Grandma's catches of laughing stop her from telling any more of it.

My grandmother says the four dollars a day from the New York Custom House stopped when her father died. And there was nothing saved. Colonel Russel was in difficulties himself, so many of his ships were taken by the privateers on the high seas. His business declined, and he could give little financial assistance. They sold some of the mahogany pieces, some extra silver. Charlotte and Jennet were as proud as Lucifer, but they went to the stores and got sewing to do, and took the work back and forth after dark. Uncle Russel soon put a stop to that; he gave them his fine ruffled shirts to make at exorbitant prices. They moved to Spring Street, but Colonel Russel had them back again; he thought it too far out for safety. Peter Woodward's military services were paid for at the end of the war by grants of government land. There was a plan that Mary should sell one of these claims and with the proceeds buy a farm up where Fiftieth Street is now. "No, no," said Uncle Russel, "if you go to live in that wild place you will all be scalped by the Indians!"

Times were so bad for the Russels that they gave up the shipping business. They moved out to Hamburg, eighteen or so miles from Buffalo, and built a flour mill. For one year after he left New York Uncle Russel never smiled.

Then Mary Woodward sold her Cortland County claim and with the money took her family into the "Western Wilds." Charlotte and Jennet in their teens, Harriett twelve or thirteen, Horatio eight. They left Richard in business in New York, after a year or so at Yale. Up the Hudson they went by the Albany packet. "Sam Russel was our escort," says Grandma. "He was a lively young gentleman, and a regular nabob." Harriett's box was lost overboard on the way.

Parson Fowler owned a great handsome silver salver presented to him by his parishioners. When his daughters married he had this melted up and made into spoons and so on for their wedding dowry. Mary sold some of this wedding silver in New York. When they got to Albany Sam Russel helped her to dispose of the silver punch bowl for cash. But the great punch ladle they kept. I've seen it. They sold the mahogany case to the tall clock, "too heavy to take," and packed the brass works to carry along. Afterward they were put into a pine case; and that is the clock which stands in the garret now and does not go.

From Albany they went west across the state by carriage with fine swift horses. Horatio's box was stolen, and he had to have a new suit bought. The little pigskin trunks with curved tops and initials in brass nails came through and are in the garret now—hair still on the hide covering and the inside lined with pasted old newspapers.

They stayed with the Russels at Hamburg more than a year. The Russels lived in grand style, proper house and fine furniture, and servants standing behind chairs at meals. Still Uncle Russel "came down" in his elegant clothes and Sam was a regular nabob. The young folks did much riding about on saddle horses visiting friends. They rode into Buffalo to parties.

Mary Woodward's family left the Hamburg friends and went on to make their home in the frontier region of central New York. Their land, a mile square, lay on Seneca Lake, near the southern end. And Colonel Russel went with them to get them settled. Eighteen squatters had built their shanties on the land and "stole everything they could lay their hands on." Richard came on but was little help—cared only for reading and study. "Their cattle died and blighted was their corn," said Mary Woodward, and she said the initials on the bridal spoons—"P.M.W." for Peter and Mary Woodward—now stood for "Poor Mary Woodward." The girls (in their teens) and Mary, who "was not brought up to work," turned in and learned how. They built them a log house with a frame parlor to it. They cleared off the squatters; they had the fields planted, and saw to the stock.

"Girls, girls," called Mary in the morning, "how can you sleep when all nature is smiling!" And then drabbled off (says Grandma) through the wet grass to milk the cows. As she milked, she said her prayers, milking with one hand and holding up the other in an attitude of devotion.

"And why did she do that?" Grandma says in those days it was not thought proper to pray except in some formal position.

A good eater she was, and a good cook. She took care of her family and let them do as they pleased—"so that they did not break the Sabbath." Pious she was. "She read her Bible all the time, and whipped the children with the towel." She may have been "sanctified from her mother's womb," for when a tiny child, the daughter of Parson Fowler, there was an alarm in Guilford—*The British are coming! Take what you value most and run for your lives!* And in the terror and confusion little Mary was found lugging the family Bible—"most as big as she was."

Richard distressed her, she worried about his soul. He was a free-thinker, perhaps an infidel. He would not join the church. She wrestled with the Lord in prayer for his salvation. She prayed beside his bed at night, and Richard hated it and covered up his ears with the bedclothes; "but she kept on praying." She found him in the dark parlor one day reading an infidel book by a ray of light coming in at the corner of the window where he had the shade lifted a crack. She snatched it away from him and threw it in the kitchen fire.

"Oh, Mother, it was borrowed!"

"My son, I would rather pay for a thousand borrowed books than have you burn in hell."

The beaux of Charlotte and Jennet were not expected to come visiting on Sunday, but sometimes in the evening they did. Then she had them all into the parlor in a friendly way and set them down to read round in the Bible or in Flavel's *Fountain of Life*.

This great leather book, *The Fountain of Life*, as big as a table and weighs, I should think, ten pounds, I myself have seen. "Mary Woodward's Book" is written inside the cover. She has read it to rags, and the front pages are lost. There is plenty left: "The Righteous Man's Refuge," "A Treatise on the Soul of Man," "The Necessity of Christ's Humiliation in Order to the Execution of His Blessed Offices for Us, and Particularly of His Humiliation by Incarnation"—such things as that it talks about.

Their city clothes being unsuitable to farm life, the girls, before they left New York, had made themselves six cotton work-dresses apiece—*white*. They washed them in the Lake. And so in course of time the country folks joked and said "The Wood-'ard gals wear yaller" (because you can't get them white in lake water).

When their everyday things wore out they put on their silks and satins and protected them with aprons as well as they could, for there was no way of replenishing their wardrobes. The girls kept geese to get the down on them, and plucked it and sewed it on to their party dresses for trimming. They worked lace for trimming also, trimming they must have. They saved up their slippers and silk stockings. It was two miles uphill to church over a rough road, with ruts that cut the leather, or a stiff clay that made ruinous mud. So they carried their fine footwear in a bundle under their arm and wore their heavy shoes and stockings until they came to the bridge at Tug Hollow. There they sat down by the roadside and changed, putting on the silk stockings and the slippers, as was suitable for church, and hiding the others under the bridge. When they went home they changed again at the bridge. Unless they were accompanied by their beaux. In that case they walked right on over, chatting along, and came up the next morning (without beaux) and got their everyday shoes.

So big and buxom was Jennet that the first Sunday at church a country wench sidled up to her, after, and said: "I think I can get you a situation if you want it."

"Thank you," says Jennet, "I think I will not go out to service this year." She kept a straight face; but her sisters standing by giggled.

They swept the rooms and scoured the hearth, cleaned it first with sand to take off the dirt and then with brick to make it look like new. They scrubbed the parlor floor on their hands and knees. But, with all, no man ever saw them working. "They did it in the night after the beaux were gone." Then up in the morning early and off to some young folks's frolic, taking all day most likely. At least that is what Grandma says.

They went to parties on horseback to all the places near by and some far away—like Geneva, forty miles off, at the other end of the Lake; to Montour Falls beyond the marshes; to Ovid twenty miles the other way. And from all the little villages in the hills, and from Tadpole (as Burdett was then called), the gay young men who were in the Western Wilds seeking their fortune, came flocking to the farm to play with the Wood'ard girls. They came on horseback; and friends in New York thought it a fine jaunt to ride out through the countryside and spend a few days in a visit. Rodman Drake, the poet, came, and wrote a poem on Seneca Lake

> "On thy fair bosom, silver Lake,
>   The white swan spreads her snowy sail—"

This is one of the spots where my grandmother has to stop and laugh. "There never was a swan seen on the lake," says she, "or anywhere else that I know of."

Six cows they had, and that should furnish a plenty of butter; but Mary Woodward said she could not make butter with skim milk. The girls stole the cream to make waffles, and so they now and again went short. An admirer of Charlotte's, Mr. Wilkinson, who was a dyspeptic, came on from New York and stayed a week. Every day the same piece of butter appeared on the table, was passed to the guest for him to take his helping, and then to the family, who put out their knives to the plate and only pretended to cut off their bit. Finally, Mr. Wilkinson refused the butter. "Do have some butter, sir." He did not care for any. "Oh, Mr. Wilkinson, why will you not take some butter!" "Excuse me, I am loth to cut an old friend."

Charlotte (it is said) had twenty offers of marriage. My grandmother adds, "Charlotte was a case!" She married the Ovid minister and became that fat and comfortable Aunt Lounsbury I have visited when she was old, and well settled down I suppose.

Two brothers came to Hector Township in Schuyler County from Truxton Township in Cortland County. They were Edmund and Eleazur, young men, sons of Benjamin and Dorinda Brown; and the one, Edmund (my grandfather), was starting out as a doctor and the other, Eleazur, starting out as a lawyer. They came to live at Burdett. They courted the Woodward girls, Jennet and Harriett, and married them, brothers married sisters. My grandfather used to go to the Farm every evening to call on Harriett (Grandma), and when he bade her goodnight he put a letter into her hand which he had written her that day, a love letter. They are in the Burdett garret now, and I have sometimes seen the bundle of them. Eleazur and Jennet went to live in Buffalo, where they were prominent people but died young of the same fever the same month. Their two children were little, Horatio and Mary Jennet. Grandpa adopted Horatio and he was brought up as a brother to my father; and Grandma was so afraid she would show partiality to Horatio that she "whipped him with the soft end of the towel" and made night shirts for him, while Edmund, her own son, only slept in his shirt. Mary Jennet was adopted by the other "Woodward girl," my Aunt Lounsbury, and brought up as a sister to Aunt Lounsbury's daughter in Ovid where they lived.

IV

OUR DAYS

I AM POSSESSED to ride Old Katy. She was once a riding pony, milk white, now dirty yellowish, rather long-haired. She is safe for me to ride. I go up to Burdett and hunt up Aunt Lidy's sidesaddle in the garret and get them to bring it down to the farm for me.

Father cinches her up. There is a broad bellyband and he draws it so tight that she gives out a groan.

"Why, Father, you're hurting her!"

"Oh, pshaw," says he. He puts his foot against her dirty old side and jerks the band another hole up. "She swells out on purpose," he says. "She doesn't want this saddle on her. I'm not going to have it turn over and throw you."

I lead her to the wagon-yard fence and climb on to her back. I am sorry not to have a floating green velvet habit and a tall hat with a white (floating) plume. My short calico dress does not seem suitable; but (alas) these are all the riding habiliments I have.

Go along! Go along, Old Katy! I thrash her well with a lilac switch. She does not budge from a walk, but swings her tail around as though she felt a fly tickling her. *Go* along! She creeps sideways off the road; she sidles into the grass. Oh, the mean thing, she is trying to scrape me off on the fence! I will *not* be scraped off on the fence—even if I do have to mount from there. Get back into the road! I pull and jerk her; she only walks on.

My father and I and Flora, the dog, are off for a walk. We go up the grassy slope of the back yard, through the bars into the cherry orchard, past the trees we stripped weeks ago of their white oxhearts and black oxhearts, rosy blushing and ruby dark. We climb the fence into the great upper pasture. It is waving with green tall grass and daisies that bow and dance. There are hickory trees near the fence, two oaks standing alone by themselves, bushes and maples at the upper edge near the woods. The fresh summer air blows bright about us.

Flora is crazy with joy. She is spotted brown and white, with silky flopping ears and plumy tail waving. She digs at hummocks; she dashes far away and is gone for some time as we walk along, and comes picking her steps back slowly, saying nothing. She takes long chases; she leaps in glorious curves high above the tall grass, bounding and leaping, on and on. Oh, Flora, how lovely you are, nothing was ever more beautiful— spirit of delight!

Flora starts a woodchuck. "Go for him! Go for him!" my father cries, running after and clapping his hands. The woodchuck scuttles ahead; Flora bounds along, barks furiously; Father runs and swings his hat and shouts. I stand stiff and still; it is horrible. I cannot bear it. All is over in a minute. Flora has it and shakes it to death by the tree where its hole is, a good ways off from me. My father comes back panting. I am standing there crying. He turns sober and quiet. He says to me, "If I had known you felt that way . . . ." I am glad he is apologizing, but I wish he had not wanted Flora to catch the woodchuck. I feel terribly. Something that was alive is dead. It can never be the same again.

Next door to Grandpa's in Banker's orchard is a shed by a brook and a man makes gravestones. There is a rough table he lays the marble on in the middle, and uncarved stones or partly finished ones leaning against the wall all around. The shed is grey and cool, not very light because there is no window, only

the open door. It is pleasant and peaceful in there. I watch the
man cutting letters on a stone laid on the table; he cuts with a
chisel and a tapping mallet, and it is very easy. He has water
from the brook slopping around. He looks at me watching him.

"Would you like to try it?"

Me! Oh, delight! I can't begin quick enough. This kind
man hunts up for me a smooth piece of pure white marble that
he can spare, and puts it at the end, where I won't bother him.
He marks an N on it, shows me how to hold the chisel and the
mallet, and cuts a little himself to start it. Oh, let me! I cannot
wait to get hold. I work and work. This marble seems very
hard—a specially hard piece I suppose. I thought it would cut
like cheese. I persevere; I try to keep exactly on the line and
make it true. I am glad my initial is not S or G! I work on.
How long the afternoon is. I tap the chisel with the mallet and
try to keep it from waggling; it must be true. The man said it
must be, and I know it besides. I must finish this letter. I will
not stop until I finish it. My hand is tired. Pooh, that's nothing.
The man begins to put his things away to close up. The shed is
quite shadowy. I tap and tap, and just finish when Father comes
to the door to get me and go home.

"Father! See the letter I've made, carved in marble!"

Father is much pleased; he studies my letter in admiration.
"You may grow up to be a great artist, like Rosa Bonheur," he
says. This makes me feel calm and large. I look far forward;
perhaps I shall be a great artist. Yes, I shall be a sculptor when
I grow up. We take the square of marble with the N on it which
I have cut, home to show Mother.

I walk through the street at Burdett under the maples. Presently a faint, lovely sound begins to come in to me through the
summer air. At first it is so low I think I imagine it, but now it
grows. Oh, it grows like the moonrise, so secretly you cannot
know it, but soon—I look, I listen—it is here. Now it fills the
whole round of the world, the humming of a great golden bee.

I see no bee. I see nothing but the street under the trees, the quiet houses in their leafy yards. And still that melting, steady golden hum. It comes from nowhere, it fills the world.

I have heard of the music of the spheres—could I catch that music for a moment walking in a shady maple way? It is fainter now, but still round and full. I walk slowly on; it is less and less; the golden bee has winged away, gradually it is a dream, a thought—it is gone.

"What could it have been, Mother?" She asks me where I was walking. "It must have been old Mrs. Beasley's spinning wheel," says she. But, to fill the world!

My grandfather has come down from Burdett in a box-buggy to get firewood from the big woods; he stops and takes me in. We go up the pasture by a field road, and the wagon jolts along. When we come to the woods, a leafy green track winds up the steep under green trees. The horse's hoofs pad softly; it is still.

"Grandpa, I do love these woods. But I don't come here much, either."

"They are too lonesome for you," says he.

"Are they lonesome? Not when you are with me." My grandfather smiles.

"We hear wildcats at night in these woods sometimes."

"Are you afraid?" says he.

"No-o—at home in my bed! I can put the covers over my head."

My grandfather touches the horse's flank with the end of his whip and waggles the lines to get them out from under its tail. We come to the wood, cut in lengths and piled beside the way. Grandpa puts it into the back of the wagon, as much as it will hold. He lays an armful from the pile across one arm, turns to the buggy, slowly takes it off stick by stick and puts each stick just where it should go to make the load; then another armful; and so on. When it is finished we leave the horse and wagon standing and the horse crops grass, and go on to the spring to get a cold drink of water. It trickles out under a maple in a little mossy and stony basin; it is cold with a forgotten winter. We drink from our hands and from leaf cups I make. Up a few steps from the spring we go to see the view, for there we look down and far away at the Lake and the hills on the other side, and at the south the blue hills beyond Havana. "Seems to me," my grandfather says, "we can see from here forty counties." Nearer to us, yet far below, the country is in farms and checkered with fields and patches of woods.

Our wells at the farm are covered over with platforms and pumps and we cannot see into them. At my grandfather's the well has an open curb with a windlass and bucket and a spout at the side where the bucket tips and empties into the pail you bring. My grandfather dug the well and found far down the cold sparkling water in the earth. He laid up its deep shaft with stones from bottom to top in a smooth, true circle. He and my grandmother were beginning their first housekeeping, and the well is just by the kitchen door of the little house they built to begin with.

I look down it over the curb. There are cushions of moss on the stones, twinkling emerald; ferns hang down dripping. At the bottom I see myself in a round bright mirror leaning over to look, and behind my head the sky is blue, with a white cloud.

The garret at the farm has a beam on the length of its floor exactly beneath the ridgepole, so big we can hardly climb over it; we have to straddle up and reach down on the other side. In the roof is a trapdoor, at the top of a flight of open steps. The door unhooks, and we lift it and lay it out flat on the roof with a thud, poke ourselves halfway through the square opening, and stand there overlooking the world. We see over the Lake, beyond Watkins into the Havana hills, Lanterman's and Miner Bennett's houses, and Emmett's red barn up the road, the fields and bluffs that lie out from Terwilliger's, and the trees of the ancient graveyard. I get Ruth to go from her house in Burdett to the graveyard and wave a tablecloth (she consents after much coaxing; she does not appear interested) while I wave another from our roof. It works perfectly, far, far apart as we are. She won't do it again. As for me I find it thrilling—beacons on the hills, watchfires, and such things.

Under the garret eaves there is a black chest with two poke bonnets in it exactly like the pictures. We dress up in them. We have Sunday-school Exercises in the evening at Mullins Hall, and I wear one and recite "The New Church Organ." I borrow a black shawl from Grandma and wear it with my shoulders drooping forward, like an old woman, with a cracked, quavering voice:

> "They've got a bran new organ, Sue,
> Fer all their fuss an' search,
> They've done jest what they said they'd do
> And fetched it into church,"

and so on, a lot of verses—and many compliments I have afterward.

Father finds rolls of wallpaper in the chest, like the rooms downstairs, and he uses it to write his book on. Since the age of twelve he has had this book in mind, philosophy of history, I believe. He kneels on the floor and rolls out the paper. He weights one end with a book. He folds over the other end and presses and smooths it back and forth with the palm of his hand, working his mouth as he works his hand. He slits the fold with a case-knife, folds again, into small sheets, and slits them up. He carries the pile of rough grey sheets into his study and writes his book on them. They are quite ornamental on the back.

Gustav Stechert has sent him boxes of new books from New York. My father opens them and turns the pages of each one lovingly. They lie tumbled on the table and the box and wrappings all over the floor. We all help him look at them and arrange them on the shelves of the sideboard in the study: *Dawn of History, Freedom of Science, Outlines of History of Religion, On the Constitution of England, Education of the Human Race,* and so on. Louise and Eddie romp among the papers on the floor; they crumple them up and throw them at each other. "How do you pronounce this name, Mattie?" says my father. "De Toqueville," says my mother, pronouncing it right.

When we came, although the rooms were mostly empty, we found books in shelves and cases. Upstairs in a bedroom is a walnut case with doors. Out of this my father seizes a leather-bound book and gives it to me—*Pickwick Papers*. "Here," says he, "this will make you laugh." I read it twice over and expect to go on reading it the rest of my life. In the closet under the stairs we find some pamphlets by Dickens, parts of stories; but I go back to *Pickwick*. On shelves in what we have made into the study we find *Cobbett's Cottage Economy*, which says lard on your bread is good enough for poor folks, costing so much less than butter. I read *Jessica's First Prayer*, and *Mutineers of the Bounty*—never can get far in that one. *Queechy*, by the author of the *Wide, Wide World:* Fleda, in *Queechy*, keeps a list of the books she reads, what for I do not know. It seems to me an interesting habit and I intend to do the same. Fleda is always bursting into tears; my mother and I joke about it.

My mother says her father was strict about what they read; he did not believe in reading stories. He forbade her to read *Don Quixote;* so she took it and sat on the floor behind the bed in her room and finished it there. She says they could not write letters on Sunday. People are queer about Sunday. We go to church, and I like to go to church; and there is always plenty to do without being wicked on Sunday. Her father was strict, yes, but not harsh. In his portrait he is a very fine gentleman in a broadcloth cloak, handsome, red-cheeked, and plump. He was first a Presbyterian minister, then a banker; and he used to say he never asked but three women to marry him and they all did.

Terwilliger's, on a lonely bluff, overlooks the lake—a small low weathered house, empty, the yard rough with wild grass and bushes, a staggering old fence in front.

There is no reason for anybody's ever going to Terwilligers; but Ruth and I, on our way to the old burying-ground, turn toward it through a field where corn has been harvested. A few punkins lie on the littered ground among blackened, withered vines. Hickories stand between the field and the deserted place; they are russet from frost. We walk slowly, cross the ditch and the furrowed track that was the road, and stand by the gate. It hangs on one hinge and is propped aside against the fence. We meant to go in if we could. I look at her and she looks at me. Ruth's hair is in two long silky braids, brown-red; her eyes are a shining red-brown, her face is cream color.

"Shall we go in?" she says, in a low voice.

"But if we do—then we shall know what is there."

"Don't you want to know?" says she.

I am silent. Now that we are here, what did we come for? It is very still; insect sounds, the stirring and the dry whisper of the hickories in the light wind, do not make it less still. How forlorn it is, this deserted dwelling among its untended bushes. The tall pines behind deeply shadow it. We stand together by the broken gate looking across the yard at the huddled house. It stares from two blank windows, yet surely is asleep. Dead, it must be, not asleep; and nobody has closed its eyes. . . . We are uncertain what to do. . . . A shape crosses behind the empty window, we both see it. We turn and look at each other. Quietly we slip back across the road into the old cornfield, nip our way quickly through the ragged, blackish vines and the punkins; we climb the fence at the further edge. Here is a grassy slope with a round, clear, shallow pool lying in the swale at the bottom of it.

"Oh, oh!" cries Ruth, glad at the sight of it.

"That would be called a tarn if we were in England," say I.

"No, a tarn is a permanent pond up on a mountain," says she. "This is only some water left from the rain. Look at the grass in the bottom."

"Don't you like the word 'tarn' and the thought tarn?"

"Yes, I do. 'Tarn' has a wildness in it."

"Yes, there's no wildness in 'pond'—mill-pond. Pool is pretty good, it has a sort of wildness, too. Anything might happen at a pool. A nymph could use it for a looking-glass, or it might be to sail a fairy boat on, or if you drank from it you might suffer enchantment. A witch might have a pool of her own beneath her tower window and use its water in her bewitchments."

"This is a pool, anyway, if it isn't a tarn—a dear little, sweet little, tiny, grassy pool; and I love it," says Ruth. "I wish I were a sheep so that I could be washed in this pool."

We do not speak of what we saw at Terwilligers. I laugh at Ruth's idea about the sheep. It is not at all a sheep-washing place. There is a spot in Tug Hollow creek before it goes into the ravine. It runs through an open field; but there is one little fall, and there they wash the sheep in spring and shear them afterwards. Men stand in the creek at the fall, men on the bank catch a running, frightened sheep from the flock, hold her by both ends, and toss her into the brook. She is caught and they wash her good under the falls, squeezing and rubbing her mats of heavy wool. She is a poor, scared thing and struggles terribly. She thinks she is going to die; but it is good for her. They finish and boost her up the bank, and she gallops off blatting. Pretty soon she is caught again, and sheared, and the wool falls away in swathes from her thin white body under the great shears. Her small pointed face and head come up out of a collar of turned-back wool. "The sheep before her shearers is dumb" —she opens not her mouth.

We take hold of hands and leave the pool and go up out of the grassy swale on the other side. "Pretty little butterfly, I love to see you flutter by," says Ruth, suddenly. A butterfly, black and bright-brown, has flown across before us. There is a windy hill beyond. On its top a few trees grow and stand out against the sky. Under them are some old graves from long ago. No enclosure, no flowers, just thin small slate gravestones, slanting different ways, one broken and lying in pieces, with grass grown

over them. The graves are not even mounded any more; some
are sunken. The stones are rough from stormy weather and
frost and grimy with dust. We stoop and try to read them, but
they are all strange names to us. The letters are filled and
blurred with lichen. One man died of cancer and there is a
verse about his terrible affliction. One is a little child.

"They say all graves turn the same way. People are always
buried facing the east. Do you know why, Ruth?"

"No, I don't. I don't believe it's so," says she. We look
around at this old, poor handful; they are all placed one way,
east and west, headstones at the west.

"See, they are. And it is so they can rise at the Resurrection
Day facing the angel Gabriel."

Ruth turns her big eyes on me and has not a word to say.

As to keeping the Sabbath holy, you have to know what is
holy, and I ask my father about it. He says it is a matter I have
to settle for myself, as there are differences of opinion. He
gives me a book from his library to read named *The Sabbath*,
a nice-looking book with a brown cover. I read a little in it.

I myself like Sunday's being different. Some books I keep
just for that day. I do not go to school; nobody is fussing
around doing work; we dress up. Whether we go to church or
not, we had our baths last night and put on our clean clothes
this morning. And the beds have clean sheets.

Out in the side yard under the locust tree is a spot where I sit
by myself on Sunday, and think, and look at the clouds; I keep
it for that day. Or I sit in my little hickory rocker in my own
bedroom by the window alone. I have my books. I am in volume three of Daubigné's *History of the Reformation*—six volumes, but not so very thick, bound in black. I keep Daubigné
for Sunday; it is quite interesting, once a week. There are fine-
print notes at the bottom of the page. I always skip notes.
There is no sense in pulling you up that way in the middle of
something and telling you to look down below and you will find

something else. So they don't bother me, for I skip them and
am not interrupted.

I find a little fat book in the walnut case that tells about
Heaven, just the thing for Sunday. This book is wonderful and
beautiful to me, and I keep it through the week in my secret box
with Ruth's letters and the presents Jerry makes for me. I should
think Heaven would have been explained before. Everybody
ought to know about it, for some seem not to want to go there.
Not that it troubles me, even if I don't know about it; probably
I'll not be dying just yet.

This book talks about Heaven as a real place (like New York
or Burdett) with trees like ours you can walk under, and pretty
flowery fields, rivers and lakes, hills and vales; and walking
and talking together in it many people who like each other. The
Book of Revelation describes it as a real place, too; but you
cannot just believe it is going to be *that* way—gates of solid
jewels, pure gold pavements to the streets. That is the way of
story books. They don't expect you to believe it like dogs bark
and cats miaow, or twice two is four (for it *is* four and there is
no other way to look at it). The Book of Revelation and stories
are true; but it is in your mind they are true, not exactly in your
eyes and ears.

The Sunday-school teacher asked the class one day which
was our favorite of all the books of the Bible. I said Revelations. They were all surprised, most of them said The Psalms.

I like Mr. Trumbull's preaching; he is pleasant. We sit in
the fifth pew back on the right-hand side, with Grandpa's folks.
The Witherspoon family sit in front of us. In front of them
Deacon Heald and his family, Peter, John, and Mary who has
long golden curls, and Mrs. Heald when she comes. She is
something of an invalid.

Sunday school is before church, and Mr. Trumbull is the
superintendent. Ruth and I think Miss Ricker, our teacher, is
dull; and we talk it over and decide we ought to have someone
else—an important class of six girls like us. She is not very

bad either—sort of middling. But we are not learning a thing we didn't know before. A Sunday-school class of our age we think ought to be more alive—getting on to something new, the teacher should see to it. We sit in a row in the pew and she conducts the class over the back of the pew ahead, screwed around so she faces us. She reads out the questions on the lesson leaf and we answer them in a row; and that doesn't take long. She then tells us to be good and points out how the person in the lesson was good, Elijah and the Prophets of Baal, Abraham offering Isaac as a sacrifice. I ask her if it was really good for God to tell Abraham to do that. (The Bible says God is love.) She says God did not intend him to do it and provided a ram caught in a thicket instead. But think how Abraham felt before he knew about the ram! And a poor old man with his only son, the child of his old age.

Ruth and I talk it over. The class ought to have a better teacher. I say the thing to do is to go to Mr. Trumbull and tell him so. Ruth does not want to do it; she says, "Oh, no, *you*." I could, of course; I know Mr. Trumbull real well. But why don't we both go? Yes, we will both go, Ruth agrees to that. We will call upon him at the parsonage. This we do. We tell him—I mean I do, for Ruth will not open her head—that we are not satisfied with our Sunday-school teacher, and would like him to give us a new one. I speak politely. I do not want to hurt anybody's feelings. Mr. Trumbull is nice and polite; he does not say very much, and he doesn't tell us what he thinks of Miss Ricker. Soon we stop conversing; there seems nothing more to be done. "Good-bye." We go away.

Miss Ricker goes right on being our teacher. Probably he cannot secure anybody else.

My father has broken another lamp chimney, holding it crooked as he runs down the stairs in the night. They bounce off. Mother says we will have to buy them by the dozen. They talk at night; I hear them. He has "night fears," she says; and she has to wake up and be company for him so that he will not suffer. What are "night fears?" Afraid space will fall on him and crush him, and such things, she says. They talk and have long pleasant conversations about everything; and there is nothing she enjoys so much as talking with my father. About daylight he puts the pillow over his head and goes to sleep and gets up long after we have had breakfast. He can have his any time.

If he is busy writing when dinner is ready, he just sits there and writes away; and about two o'clock he comes out and says in a small, modest voice, "Mattie, could you get me a bite to eat?" She goes and gets it, and he has it on a corner of the table. She thinks it would be very foolish to interrupt his work just for the sake of eating with the rest of us. He has to write "when the spirit moves." Sometimes in the midst of his writing he calls, "Mattie, Nellie—could you make me a cup of coffee?" We do and take it to him at his desk; he sips it with his left hand, never stopping or looking up. "A-a-ah, that's good," says he.

An agent sells my father a patent bathtub. Very convenient, for we bathe in a washtub when we don't take a sponge. It is made of rubber, has a heavy hardwood rim at the top, which you put on a chair at each end to hold the rubber bag in a tub-shape. It is big enough to lie down in (a washtub isn't) and has to be set up in the dining-room, as the kitchen is too small. It takes a washboiler of hot water, carried in from the kitchen stove, and is emptied by pailsfull afterward. We use it some. It does a tricky thing, tips the chair over that holds it at one end, and collapses on the floor in a flood, with Father "like a stranded whale" in the midst. And now it has sprung a leak. Father is trying to mend it with some stuff the agent left, and glue, and paste, and solder. I see him there wrestling with it. "Goody! Goody!" says he, jerking and fumbling it around, and twisting his mouth. I don't believe he will succeed. He says himself he is not mechanical, that a stove damper is the only machine he can manipulate.

V

DAYS RUN TO YEARS

IT IS THE TIME of south wind and languid heat and flies in swarms. Mother and I take our fly-brushes, made of slit paper flour sacks tied in a bunch to old broom handles, and battle them out of the dining room after a meal. We shut the porch door, shut the blinds of the open windows, and arrange the slats slanting up outward. Softly we depart. Now the room is dark and the remaining flies who thought they were so cute to stay do not like it. They discover the streaks of light at the blinds and go and promenade up the slats and out. They fly away in the sunshine, congratulating themselves. It is her trap, her invention; she is so smart.

She takes the whole family to the ravine to spend the day. Gertrude, lunch, books, sewing, in the cart; and we take turns drawing it over the dusty hot road to the lower Tug Hollow bridge. We leave crazy Flo behind to mumble and grumble and get on with the ironing. She is a fat unpleasant old darky we have to keep because we've got her—and that is something. She "sets around." When Mother tells her to do something extra, she growls, "Got 'nuff to do without."

In the ravine it is wet and cool, dripping rocks, ferns and green moss, airy trees and bushes rising up the banks to lightly shadow us, the stream like a live companion laughing and leaping down the falls, babbling over the flats, dancing around the corners—sparkle and spray, and lovely long riffles quivering with light and colors. We put on some old thing we have brought

along and bathe in the pools. We run up under a fall and let
the white water pound our bent backs. We smother in laughter
and foam, and rush out again to save our lives. One or two of
the children fall in again after they are all dried and dressed.
It doesn't matter. We spread their clothes on a sunny rock and
they are soon dry.

She sews, my mother, sitting in a cool nook of the bank, or
reads, or dangles her bare feet in the brook, and picks up pretty
stones and turns them over in her hands, studying them and admiring them. Her feet are the round shape of a baby's, small
and soft and white; I love my mother's feet. She looks at the
small plants just starting up from the ground. She touches their
young tender leaves with her fingertips: "I never get over the
wonder of a growing thing," says she.

Sometimes my father is with us in the glens. He wades and
frolics with us in the water. Everybody splashes everybody else
with handfuls we scoop up; everybody is streaming and dripping and laughing. We forget the flies and heat and old crazy
Flo. He wanders among the rocks; he finds a scarlet flower of
the mountain balm; he snatches it off its stalk and snuffs up the
smell as though he were eating it.

The fire roars in the big stove, we are burning hickory butts.
At night Father puts the chunk in, and another in the morning,
and keeps the fire all the time. It is evening; we read by the
table. A knock. My father takes up the lamp and goes through
the hall to open the front door. Mother and I hear a murmur of
voices.... "Death telegram...." The outside door shuts; my
father holds up the light, pulls a paper from an envelope....
"It's bogus!" he cries and dashes it to the floor. He looks as
though he were going to burst into a flame. He rushes out on
the stoop. He shouts to the men; they are getting into the buggy
at the gate. Everything is dark because of the lamp in his hand;
he pitches it down into the snow and it goes out. He runs to the
gate; but they have started the horse and got away up the road.

He chases after them, but they are gone. He has to stop and come back home, very angry. They said it was a death telegram and there was five dollars to pay; and he paid it, and *it was bogus!* They are gone. . . . What a delightful word, *bogus.* A new one to me.

Evening. The Updykes are here talking business with my father, all quarreling badly. They are men hired to work in the big woods cutting dead trees, cleaning up brush, getting out hickory butts, and so on. My father is very careful about the trees, and the Updykes have not obeyed orders. What's more, they are "crooked" about money; they don't live up to their bargain. They are scoundrels. More and more talk, getting loud—"Eyktie, eyktie, eyktie!" as Gertrude says to herself (playing with her toys on the floor) when she hears a dispute going on.

The two men rise up, clap on their hats, go out through the hall, still talking. As soon as they are off my father thinks of something else and starts in a rush after them. "Don't go, Edmund!" says my mother. But we run along out and down the steps and down the walk to the gate. Very dark it is. They have got off. We run along the road after them, their wagon is on ahead of us . . . . We cannot catch up. My father stops and hurls after them, "So *that's* an Updyke!" He turns around, growling, and we race back home. We need not race; but my father seems to have to. He is puffing and red when we burst into the light sitting room, Mother waiting there in her chair. He comes to himself and notices me; I did not suppose he knew I was along. He looks at me. He turns to my mother and says, "She went with me." Then, *"She went with me*—why, they might have shot me!" Of course I went with him, why shouldn't I?

My father preaches at Peach Orchard Sundays, seven miles away. He rides Old Katy. But why does he not get home? We wait here in the bright, warm sitting room. It is very cold and snowy out, and long past his time. We put in some more wood and look at the clock—again.

"I don't see what can have happened," I say. My mother and I always wait for him together Sunday evenings; I sit up past my bedtime to keep her company.

"I don't suppose anything has," says Mother. "When he comes he will have it all explained, easily. There are so many ways of being delayed."

"But he isn't usually . . . . You haint no worrier, are you?" This is what Mrs. Flagg says—*she* "haint," when she sits and rocks in her dirty dress and reads a story with the dishes all over the kitchen and the flies swarming. Mother shows her dimple. All the same she looks at the clock and does not seem to settle to her reading.

We hear a sound at the back and a call in my father's voice. We pick up the lamp and hurry through the hall to the back porch. We open and there is Old Katy standing with her head almost in the doorway.

"I've hurt myself," says Father, quietly. "The horse stumbled and threw me and my arm is hurt. You'll have to get a chair for me to get down with."

We get a chair and set it close to Katy's side, I hold up the lamp, and Mother supports him as he climbs off. She puts her shoulder up and he rests on it so hard that she almost staggers. He drops into the chair. "Does it pain you, Edmund?" "I should think it does!" he says, still quietly. He is pale and wan as the light shines on him. "I mustn't stay here in this terrific cold—" He gets up; we all huddle him into the house and up to the fire. Very gently Mother and he together get his muffler and overcoat off; but he says, "There—no more."

They send me for Miner Bennett to go to Burdett for the doctor. Father sits by the stove; its sides are rosy hot—oh, he is so cold! It happened two miles up the road; he supposes he threw out his arm to catch himself and that was how it got the weight of the fall. He lay there in the snow and thought he was dead with the pain; he thought he could not possibly move. Oh, pshaw, he thought, that won't do; if you stay like this you soon will be dead—frozen. So he crawled up to the fence, pulling the horse by the bridle, and got himself onto her back from the fence. "Goody, how it hurt me!" says he. He could not stand the jar of trotting, and he just poked along to ease himself, though he guessed this policy might result in freezing him and Katy together in their tracks before they got here.

The doctor comes. They uncover my father's shoulder and chest, peeling down the clothes as he sits there in the chair. How white his flesh is, and smooth. Yes, the arm is broken at the shoulder. The doctor sets it. We get him to bed.

Miss Beam is letting down my summer dresses and making me some new longer ones for school next fall. I don't suppose I shall ever have the free use of my legs again. I go down in the lake woods and run about and climb trees in my calico. I stop and sit down on a log and think about it. Next time you come to these woods probably your skirts will flop around your ankles and hamper your footsteps so that you cannot run or climb trees never any more, say I to me. Besides, with long dresses you feel statelier and don't want to run; at least I suppose I shall; there will be a change. Or else why put on long dresses? Oh, but you have to put them on when the time comes; there isn't any reason for it that I know of.

Miss Beam has kindly come for a while to help with the housework, besides sewing, as Mother has been sick a long time and no girl can be found. The big bed is in the study and Mother in it, to make it easier, and the desk moved into the front room. 'Tis but a step across the porch corner from dining room to study, now my mother's bedroom. It is hard to see her clouded over. She lies there and looks unhappy and cannot seem to get well. Every other day Dr. Witherspoon drives down from Burdett and sits by her and feels her pulse and leaves quinine powders for her to take. He's a nice old man.

"Nellie, I fear you will not have your mother with you much longer." Miss Beam says it in a meek, put-on voice to me when I am sweeping the sitting room. Oh what blackness falls upon me! The bright day turns into night. I never thought of such a thing; I cannot answer. How I hate you, Miss Beam, it can't possibly be so! I run away by myself . . . . Suddenly I forget all about it because I *know* it is not so.

We have all kinds of a time with the work, and I learn how to do plenty of new things. My mother tells me from her bed. Father brings home a lot of small fish and tells me to cook them for dinner.

"Why, I don't know how."

"You better learn how," says he. "Just cook 'em," and off he goes.

I get the bread-board and lay it on the porch floor and start to slit their bellies and clean them as I have watched people do. I begin to cut off their heads, then discover their heads are already off—I am cutting off the meaty part of the body. I scrape their scales up backwards, and fry them in lard, and they are first-rate. Everybody laughs about my not knowing whether a fish has its head off or on.

"Fish have awful eyes," says Bolton. "I should think you would know by their eyes."

"I should think she would know by her own eyes," says Father.

"There isn't one single brown eye in our family," Louise says, thoughtfully. "Ruth's eyes are brown."

"We have a brown name," says Eddie.

"Aye, aye!" says Father, meaning *eye*. He is a great joker. We laugh and laugh and somebody says you wouldn't want a single brown eye anyway —one brown and one blue, like a deaf cat, and mother calls from her room to know what we are laughing at. Miss Beam is the only serious one; she is naturally so and cannot help it.

We do not have fish often. Ezra Spiller, who lives down the

Lake Road toward Watkins, brings Father a fine big fish he
caught in the Lake, wrapped in a newspaper—Father was good
to him and went to see him when his wife was sick. But Father
will not take it; he is sorry not to (and so are we), and thanks
him; but it is against the law to fish in the Lake at this season of
the year. So he goes home again and the Spillers eat it.

My dear Aunt Anna comes and cures my mother right away
and takes her back to New York with her to make a visit. Father
wrote her to come. He got desperate with Mother sick so long,
lying there, and quinine powders no good. So here she is
coming up the walk from the gate and Father carrying her
satchels and shawls. I run and clasp her and hang on her neck;
and we come on to the house and bring her in to my mother in
the big bed in the study. The next day Mother is sitting up on
the front veranda in a handsome green cashmere wrapper Auntie
brought her, trimmed with striped green and black silk down
the front, open over her nightgown. Aunt Anna sits in the other
rocker; I sit on the top step, and Gertrude on the gravel walk
making a pen for her Noah's Ark animals out of stones. Louise
and Eddie caper and shout all over the front yard, playing
horse, until Aunt Anna calls to them to go around back with
their romping. But they stop and come and sit on the steps with
me. They do not care to play in the back yard where she cannot see them. Two days later Mother is up and dressed and
Father ready to drive them to Watkins to the train. She does
not seem tired. Miss Beam and I did her packing.

"Oh, Mother, hadn't you better lie down on the bed until it
is time to go?" She is sitting in Aunt Baldwin's chair, dressed
and ready, and I am afraid she will overdo before she even
gets started.

"*No!* I never want to see that bed again," says she, snap-
pishly. Then she laughs. She is like herself again. In a few
moments they are gone.

Miss Beam and I pull off the sheets and make up the bed

fresh, standing on each side. "It is the south wind makes her sick. She can't stand the heat. The south wind takes all the tucker out of her, and it does me, too."

"Your mother is going into a decline," says Miss Beam.

"She isn't. There is nothing the matter with her, Auntie says so. She's not in a decline now, dressed up and gone to New York."

Miss Beam shakes her head mournfully. She gets a pair of pillow shams and spreads them on the pillows, ruffled, "Goodnight" and "Good Morning" embroidered on them in red.

"I hate those shams," I exclaim. She looks at me surprised, and at the shams. I suppose she is trying to find out what I hate. Really they are rather stylish, but I always do seem to have to spat with her.

"Your Cousin Kate worked them and sent them to your mother for a Christmas present," she says, reprovingly.

"I don't care if she did. I don't see why clean cases aren't nice enough without shams over them."

Miss Beam smooths them with her hand. "Oh, no," she says, "these are much more recherky."

I flounce upstairs, I throw myself on my little bed with the door shut and have a good cry, because I love my mother so, and my auntie so, and she is sick, and now she is better, and gone away from me for I don't know how long, and the big bed where we took care of her is all made up with clean sheets and shams over the pillows.

She is all right in New York, Father gets letters. I write her almost every day. I send her visiting cards. I am sure she will need them in the city so, and she has some nice ones in a Scotchplaid box: "Mrs. E. Woodward Brown." Only two or three I send at once, on account of the postage.

Father has us all out in the back yard to see the northern lights. It is evening. Faintly they stream up in great pale fan rays from behind the darkness of the hill. I look and look. I see color coming and going, yet secretly—perhaps I only thought it. The Aurora Borealis. But it is cold; I think it has to be cold for the Aurora Borealis. It is lent us from the lonely north. We are lucky to see it; we were warm in the house, and it makes no signal, not even a silver trumpet sounds before it. Still, Father would know, even if it came at midnight and he were sound asleep in his bed, he would somehow know, and spring awake and rush out to look and call us all from our beds to come and see the northern lights.

But it is cold. My father hangs comforters over windows and builds up the good fires in the different rooms. He sits by the stove and looks over his manuscript. He is always writing his book. He is in his socks, and holds up one foot and then the other to the warmth as he turns the pages. He says, "I am like an ant with this book, staggering along; sometimes I am on top of it and sometimes it is on top of me!"

The children undress by the sitting-room stove. They frolic and hate to get off to the cold beds. Mother and I help them. We have hot soapstones ready, and blankets hanging over chairs by the fire, and canton-flannel nightgowns warming. "Pooh," says Bolton, "I don't need a blanket. I'll run fast enough to keep me warm." But he condescends to undress behind Father's big chair. He and Eddie tear ahead up the stairs and leap on the bed like goats. Then they sit huddled with their knees up to their chins, dreading to get in between the stone-cold sheets. We race the younger ones upstairs and cuddle them down, two to a bed.

When Father goes to bed he comes into all the rooms, even mine, and tucks us up. I rouse a little with the light and the feeling of his hand. It is sweetly comfortable to have his strong hand pull the covers closer around me and push them in at my back. He will not have us cold, he hates to be cold himself.

Grandfather is sick with pneumonia. I stand at the door of the little bedroom off their sitting room in my cloak and hood;

I have come up to see him. He is propped up dreadfully on
the pillows. His face is ashen; his eyes are closed; he is breathing roughly and loud—so different from his gentleness, he always does everything gently. Oh, dear Grandfather, you do not
know me . . . . it is tearing you . . . .

Aunt Lida is in Florida with Aunt Louise, so Mother goes
up every day to be with Grandma. My father and mother talk
of what comes after death; no one understands it. "Whatever
happens to us at death you may be sure it will be *natural*," he
says. He sits and reads the Bible. Whenever special trouble
comes he gets the Bible and sits quiet in his chair and reads.

Mother comes home one day toward evening. Father is up
there. She stands at the hall door in her bonnet and cloak with
her cloud wrapped round her head and shoulders. We look
up quickly at her and wait. "He is gone." Her face quivers into
tears.

I stand with my father in Grandma's parlor, it is dim and
peaceful. We are alone there beside the coffin and look down
at my dear grandfather's still, closed face. How beautiful he
is. He has no age—younger than I ever saw him, yet old like
himself. Around his mouth is his smiling look; he is quiet and
serene—he is always so. Ah, not like the day I saw him breathing terribly and loud with pain-shut eyes—not knowing me, his
smile and strong gentleness overcome. Now he is himself, for
always.

We stand around the grave in the snow in the churchyard.
They lower the coffin; they spread evergreen boughs down over
it. I am between my father and mother there in the wintry
graveyard behind the church, in the snow.

Dinner is ready at Grandma's, and we are sitting down. My
father comes and pulls back his chair; then he turns away
quickly and goes out into the woodshed; he is shaking with
grief and tears. "It is because of sitting in his father's place,"
my mother says in a low tone to the one who is next her. For
they have put him at the head of the table.

It is summertime. I wake in the night in my small, dim room. I hear a crunching, a stealthy scraping and crunching. I slip out of bed and go softly to the window and look down the locust-tree trunk to see what makes that quiet sound. Dear me! only Pedro crouching on the grass in the moonlight gnawing the old ram's-horn. He is a very ordinary dog, white with purple-brown spots, probably a coach-dog the way he trots under the back of the buggy. We never taught him to do that, and we had him as a puppy and named him Dom Pedro after the Emperor of Brazil.

Once I got out of my window and climbed down the smooth, straight trunk of this locust, clutching it and clinging round it and sliding to the ground. When we first came I could not be satisfied until I had done that. I do not need to do it again.

Another time, when I slept in a downstairs bedroom, I climbed out of the window and went to the upper pasture to see the sunrise. The window opens into the lilac bushes; but I scrabbled through. I went up the yard in a wonder, everything looking different, and the light dim, yet not as it is in the night. The grass was wet with dew, the tall field grass, drenching wet, so that my shoes and stockings were soaked. It was astonishingly cold and still. All things removed themselves from me, and I walked in a sort of apology: "I don't *mean* to intrude," said I in my mind to the world. It is not a time when humans are supposed to be about, the pale solemn hour of dawn. I got to the pasture and sat on the rail fence and looked toward the hill woods, waiting for the sun. I shivered to my bones with chill. The sky grew lighter, grew milky, grew pink; and the pink caught the little cherub clouds over the hill. It takes the sun a long time; he will not hurry for me. The cheeping birds began to keep me company. At last he burst up clear and golden; he beamed, and the strange world was, suddenly, just as usual. It had put on its mask.

I ran down the fields to get warm, bedrabbled but full of joy. I got in as they were finishing breakfast.

"Where *have* you been?" says my mother. "The pancakes are cold."

"I went to the upper pasture to see the sunrise." My voice was small, I know, and I felt I must go take off my wet things.

"Oh," said she, and looked at me.

I walk alone in the Lake woods; softly I go on cushions of moss and padded mats of packed dry leaves in the hollows. The slate rock crops up, but moss and squawberry and ground-pine grow over it and will not let it be rough and hard. Moss-pink, in spring, covers a great rock table I know of with a lovely bloom. Columbine with honeyed horns, liverworts at the roots of trees, spring-beauties, anemones that some call the wind-flower, a few wild sprays of honeysuckle, blossoming in coral, these in spring. The anemone has a divided leaf that silvers under water. I pick a branched leaf and stoop and hold it in the lake. It cups itself and turns up a bright silver under surface with little bubbles of quicksilver for trim. On the ragged rocks of the shore the delicate harebell blows, always one alone, hanging its cool blue flower over the water.

Down here I have for my pleasure a cove, a miniature bay, under the cliff. The shore curves an arm around it, sheltering it in from the spread of the lake. A dwarfish, twisting juniper, the Son of the Rock, digs his roots into the crevices and stands up on top of my rampart against the sky. Here I sit solitary and play with the lipping water that curves gently in. The chamber is no larger than my own room at home . . . . Perhaps this is the very spot where the Wood'ard girls washed their white dresses and dried them, maybe, on the rocks above while they sat and skipped stones, and hunted lucky-stones with holes in them, and talked about their beaux. This little pebbly beach has lucky-stones in it. I myself have found them.

The rocks of the shore lie out in shelves over the water, and the shadowy, shallow caves beneath have always in them a low chuckling from the motion of the waves. Up the bank I wander, where it is silent even from the secret sounds of the water. I sit on a floor of fallen pine needles and make a chain with green needles I pull from an overhanging bough. The ground is softly billowed with a plushy, deep-green moss; and a little thin grass grows in spots; and there is a pattern of grey lichen on the rock.

All around me on this floor of the woods are scattered thin shreds of a kind of bark, some strange tree casting them down carelessly. They are satiny and brown, all sorts of shapes, none very large; some are roundish, some long with scalloped edges; some have holes through them; some are comical like gnomes. I can see that they are material, that they are suitable for diminutive architecture, cut and beveled and smoothed. I collect the dry, faintly perfumed flakes in my lap and drop them from my fingers and pick them up and study them one by one. I set up a house, a village, a colony, at exactly the foot of a straight young pine tree . . . . Their lawns of green velvet spread away; parks and gardens lie enclosed in the sweet red-brown carvings I have been given; a beautiful tiny civilization, different from anything we know. The woods are still and mysterious.

I kneel long at my work; it blooms out under my hand; it grows—strangely—no one knows it but me . . . . Now it is done; there is nothing more. And now it is a sacred thing; it will endure always, for I have made it. There is a meaning; I do not know what it is.

I rise up to go home, I turn away quietly, never touching it to spoil it. I walk under the trees back to the sunny fields, up through their mullein and thistles, across the pleasant orchard of old gnarled apple trees, and come to the bars. There, across the road, stands our house—just as I left it.

Eddie's goat is so ramptious today he is climbing the slat ladder up the pear tree! When he gets there and butts his head into the bush of branches he is not very happy after all, he corkscrews round and leaps to the ground and bounds to the house and jumps to the porch and then *through the window*. I suppose he scrambles on upstairs, which is one of his favorite precipices, for I am in the hammock in the front yard and he soon comes galloping out the hall door with Mother after him flopping her apron—*"Shoo! shoo!"*

It is a sticky, south-wind day. Everybody is trying to cool off after chasing the mocking bird. It took the whole family and came to nothing; for, alas, he is gone.—Aunt Louise brought him to us from Florida last spring. Bolton and I built him a large cage out of candle rods we found in the woodhouse chamber, and there he was happy I am sure. But he would not sing. He would not mock our robins and other birds. Father sang "Yankee Doodle" to him, but he wouldn't even mock that, putting his head on one side and looking down at us, flirting his tail, going for a drink of water, anything but singing. They said he had to get wonted; they said he was moulting; they said it was not his singing season—it was not.

Then, today, right after dinner, Mary Burns called out, *"The bird's got away—the bird's gone!"* Everybody ran to the back porch and stared at the cage with the door swinging open. *"Oh, there he is!"* Sitting on a lilac bush he was. Off he flew as we came near. And off he flew every other time we came near; and we chased him up the yard to the quince bush, to the codfish house (and he waited on the roof until we had crept close up under), to the morello cherry tree, to the orchard bars, all over the orchard, flitting about among the cherry trees .... Finally he was gone; we could not find him anywhere. We trailed back home; Bolton shut the cage door. Louise wept quietly, seated on the kitchen step; and Eddie sat beside her, saying nothing, very sober. Mother and Father went into the house, and Mary Burns began to wash her dishes. I took the hammock; and then the goat burst in. His ramping around makes me think of Mother's trick to settle our nerves. When we get cross and fidgety being in the house too long Mother says, "Go out doors

and run around the house three times as hard as you can go."
We do that and come back all freshened up—like the goat.

Zaidee is our baby now. She sits in her clothesbasket on the
back porch. She is crying. The puppy jumps round her to amuse
her, but she keeps on wailing. The puppy goes off and finds a
bone; he wags up to the basket and drops it in—surely that will
comfort her. Good little puppy! But she does not care about the
bone and keeps on wailing. Mother comes out the study door.

"You poor hot child, no wonder you fret." She sees the
bone and the anxious puppy wriggling around. She laughs at
him and takes Zaidee in and undresses her in the study. She
brings a firkin half full of water and sets it on the porch floor.
"There," says she, plumping the baby into it, "now you'll be
more comfortable." Zaidee gasps at the cool water, then lifts
her two hands and splashes, and shrieks with delight at the
shower she makes. Better than bones, doggy. The rings of her
light hair sparkle with the water drops, her eyes shine with their
blueness. The puppy dances and yelps with joy.

The south wind blows up a shower at last. Thunder, but not
very loud or long; the lightning is far away. But we will get
the skirts of the storm. Already the dull hot air is fresher—
oh, the cool, sweet puffs, we breathe them in, they smooth our
hair back from our hot faces. We go into the yard to see the
great clouds over the far hills and the grey slants of the showers
coming down from them like straight gauze curtains across the
distant fields and woods .... Here come the first big tempestuous drops. "Run in! run in! you will be drenched!" We
gather in the porch beside the baby's tub. Bolton and Eddie
race round the corner from the front.

"Mother, Mother, can we go naked in the rain? Can we?"

"Yes, do!" says she. They strip in the kitchen and dash out
into the warm soft beating rain. It comes now in sheets.

"It's raining bucketsful!" Eddie shouts. "Raining cats-and-
dogs!" shouts Bolton.

They caper over the grass; they run up under the flooding gutter spout at the kitchen corner; it splashes down on them. The puppy yelps; he jumps around them. The goat shut into the wagonhouse yard bounds and blats. The hens huddle against the woodhouse wall and oil their feathers with careful bills. "It is going to be a long rain; see, the hens are oiling their feathers," says Mother. Mary Burns comes to the dining-room door and stands looking out. Her face is mild and quiet; her hair is a pale brown and wound around her head in two braids. She has on the blue-and-white checked gingham that I like her in. She came when Zaidee was born and helped take care of Mother then, and we hope she will stay with us forever. She is the best hired girl we ever had.

My father preaches at Dresden. He takes me with him occasionally. People come crowding around me after church—"Is *this* little Nellie Brown!" Naturally I am not so small as when I was born there. My mother and I sit on the front stoop in the two big chairs and wait for him Sunday evenings. He takes the train at Pen Yan. The headlight comes in sight far away northward at the top of the hill across the lake. "There it is," we say. We watch it as it glides slanting down the black hill toward Watkins. It seems to move slowly, we hear no sound; it is like a still, traveling star in the distance. We know Father is with it. The air is softly warm; we rock quietly, speak sometimes a little, say how fragrant is the night. We get sleepy. Some nights there are fireflies in the gloom by the gate, sometimes there is a meteor.

Aunt Anna wants us to move near New York where we can see her oftener. So my father goes candidating to Breakwater. It does not amount to anything. They have been without a minister sixteen months and trying candidates. He preaches twice for them and they say they guess they will have to leave their decision until they have heard a few others they know about. There is nothing there at the depot *but* the depot; it is hard to find any village anywhere except a huddle near the church; the missionary society is quite ossified; all the elders are old men. The society is rich enough, but tight. He thinks the church building old-fashioned, but neat, with a table turned upside down for a steeple. The people are kind. They ask him how many children he has. He says he has six but he will kill off a few if they wish. Louisa's eyes get very big.

"Would he do that, Mother?" says she.

"Probably not," says Mother.

I am a peddler—of flowers. My wagon is filled at the back with house-plants in pots. Geraniums; a fuchsia; an artillery plant that has red, small, fire-crackery, hanging blossoms; a lovely pink begonia; a cactus like a green fleshy ear of some creature, spines in bunches all over it—just one ear, sticking up. Father and I choose them out of a hothouse in Watkins and he pays five dollars for them. It seems so much; but Father says I can easily sell enough to repay him and have a profit left over for myself. We talk about prices as we drive home and decide about that. The artillery plant is so rare that it ought to cost more; we put it at fifty cents. The maidenhair fern anyone can get for themselves by going to the ravines, but Father says many a busy farmer's wife never has time for ravines and would rather pay fifteen cents than go there anyway.

Now I have been out four days. If I have some left we can keep them ourselves; we'd like some house-plants in the windows in the winter. I start after breakfast and get home for supper and drive my buggy-load of plants many miles over the country roads. The people say such funny things to me. They are always astonished, for nobody ever heard of a plant peddler. I never did myself before. They seem to think I am a child. Because I am small, I suppose, and my hair in a braid. I am going to do it up next year. Everybody speaks about its being so thick; it's a yard long. I like it myself.

One woman will not even come out to the wagon to look.

"I've got some already," she says. I take peach pits in exchange if they have them saved up. There is a place in Watkins where they buy peach pits, I don't know what for. One woman is sick abed and calls me to come in; the door is open. She is tickled to see me, and we have quite a visit. Her husband is not good to her, so she is glad not to have him around; she doesn't mind being alone, even if she is sick, only it is nice to have someone (like me) drop in to talk to, as they are off there on a by-road where there ain't no passin'. I go out and bring two different geraniums and the artillery plant for her to see, all I can hold in my arms. She admires the double red geranium; she will buy it if I will let her pay in peach pits. They're in a firkin in the shed. If I will just go get as many as I think is right for the pay. I take two quarts in an old box I find there that she says I can have.

Bolton thinks he will peddle, too—chromos. He has some that Father let him get in Watkins one day and he is crazy about them. They are beautiful; "Fruit," a couple of big blue-purple plums and a red-and-yellow peach together on a plate—a spray of wild rose, "The Barefoot Boy," standing, barefoot, on a mossy stone in the middle of a brook, "Wide Awake" and "Fast Asleep," a pair every one likes, and I should think Bolton could easily sell dozens up and down the Lake Road. It is the same little girl in both, golden curls, pink cheeks, a blue dress, and around her neck a daisy chain. She lies on a pillow. In the first she is wide awake, laughing, in the second sound asleep with hands still mixed up with the daisies.

It is the thing to speak pieces for your friends in case you cannot sing solos or play the piano. So I do. Here is "The Dutchman's Baby." It is considered very amusing:

> Zo help me gracious effry tay
> I laffs me vild to zee der vay
> My schmall yung paby dry do blay!
> Dot cunnin' leedle paby.

> He bulls my nose und gicks my hair
> Und grawls me ofer ervere,
> Und schlobbers me—but vat I care?
>   He iss my own schmall paby.
>
> Und ven der vindy vind vill grawl
> Righd in his leedle schtomach schmall
> I am so sad to hear him schquall,
>   Dot's too bad for der paby.
>
> Around my neck dot leedle arm
> Vas schqueezen me so nice und varm—
> Oh may der neffer gome some harm
>   To mine own leedle paby.

Another is named "My Mother"—

> *Who* dressed me in my Sunday clothes
> And taught me how to wipe my nose,
> And told me to turn out my toes?
>   *My mother.*

The funny ones take better, though I have others: "Stand, the Ground's Your Own, My Braves," "Divided"—

> An empty sky, a world of heather,
> Purple of foxglove, yellow of broom,
> We two among them wading together
> Shaking out honey, treading perfume.

Then they come to a rill "green like a ribbon to prank the town," go along its banks taking hold of hands across the stream, one on each side. Of course it gets bigger—"the beck grows wider, the hands must sever,"

> He prays, "Come over"—I may not follow,
> I cry, "Return"—but he cannot come:
> We speak, we laugh, but with voices hollow;
> Our hands are hanging, our hearts are numb.

And so on, there is a lot of it. I like the pictures the words make.

When we get into a real gale they pounce on me and make me say the *"Oh,* Doctor." I can say it faster than anybody else; in fact I don't know anybody else that can say it at all. The point is to run it together so fast that they can't understand it possibly. It is a boy who has been sent to the drugstore to get some medicine "quicker'n blazes." "*Oh*-doctor-mother-sent-me-to-the-shopecarypop-quicker'n-blazes-bub's-sicksidickens-with-the-pickenchocks-t'get-a-thimbleful-of-ballygollick-in-this-din-tip-per-cause-we-hain't-bot-a-gottle-and-the-kint-pup's-got-bine-wit-ters-init-*gottany?*"

We make Mother say her "Betth's Settin'Out." She always says "Oh, I do*want*uh"; but she will after a while. She sits up in a chair as though she was making a call. She draws in her mouth as though she had no teeth and talks with a sort of a lispth. She tells how Betth was goin' to git married and they all turned in and gin her a settin' out:

"Sal, she gin her a pair of flatirons—they was old 'n' rusty, one on 'em was broke where they had cracked butt'nuts, but they was good 'nuff fer Betth. Mame, she gin her an armchair —hadn't only three legs, but you could prop it up on a box and 'twas a real comf't'ble armchair. Good 'nuff fer Betth," and so on with every ricketty old thing you can imagine—"good 'nuff fer Betth." And Mother can think up the funniest old things and have the most ridiculous accidents happen to them. Then Betth gets married and goes to live in Podunk and they don't hear of her for a long time. At last she goes to make a call on Betth, and this is the wind-up:

"Betth," says I, "be you well married?" and she said she was.

"Is your husband good to yuh?" and she said he was.

"Betth, do yuh own yer own home?" and she said they did.

"Have yuh got any chillun, Betth?" and she said she had.

"Betth," says I, "be they boys or gals?" and she said *they was* . . . . Here Mother suddenly turns back into herself, and it is done, we never do know which they was.

Father does a trick with a knife and three little pieces of paper. He sticks them on the blade in a row, says, "Now I will cause them to disappear." He rolls his eyes, says off a line of

Greek—it begins with "A bomini" and ends up with "sedusus" —does something quick with his hands and holds out the knife blade toward us, the papers are gone. "Now I will bring them back." He rolls his eyes, stares at the ceiling (and so do we to see what he is looking at), exclaims "abracadabra" or "Open, Sesame," holds out the knife, and there in a row are the three little bits of paper again.

His best time is Christmas, and Blindman's Buff is his favorite. We open the stockings first; we cram ourselves with candy and look at our presents and play the new games in boxes we get, and scare each other with the new jack-in-the-box, and say how nice it is to have a fresh Noah's Ark with *all* the family and not just Noah's wife, the rest being lost. We read the books we get; we try the puzzles; we play checkers with the new set. Then we begin to play the lively games, and Blindman's Buff is our favorite. After dinner—turkey, or at least chicken pie, and probably the Burdett folks down—we begin to just sit, reading or visiting together. Father then gets the book and reads us the "Ode to the Nativity." Every Christmas he reads it. The beautiful words and his beautiful voice speaking them are a music I many times remember to myself afterwards:

> It was the winter wild,
>   While the heaven-born child
> All meanly wrapt in the rude manger lies,
> Nature in awe of him,
>   Had doffed her gaudy trim,
>   With her great master so to sympathize.
> . . . . Peaceful was the night
> Wherein the prince of light
> His reign of peace upon the earth began.
>   The winds, with wonder whist,
>   Smoothly the waters kissed
> Whispering new joys to the mild oceàn
>   Who now hath quite forgot to rave,
>   While birds of calm sit brooding on the charmèd wave.

The road we travel afoot to school each morning we call The Hill of Difficulty. Sometimes we have the Slough of

Despond spread before the gate, clay mud from fence to fence. Sometimes, beyond Lanterman's, we have to walk the lower rail of the fence around the mire. If it is too stormy we are taken, by somebody. Bolton and I argue as we go, which passes the time, and we play Pilgrim's Progress all the way. Louise trudges along. We carry our lunch in a tin pail, usually gingerbread. At Tug Hollow bridge we stop and rest before the steep pitch, and halfway up we loiter at the little thorn-apple tree by the fence, and, if it is the season, pick and nibble the sour fruit. It is red and no larger than a cherry.

A wild apple has a charm. We know our tame apples so well, large and satisfying, punctually ripening in the orchard and afterward to be had from barrels in the cellar. Like our house, Mother and Father, the well, and the woodshed—ordinary apples. But that such a thing could grow wild of its own accord, untended, in the fields and woods, it is amazing. Our tame apples have no thorns either, and their leaves are different from these; still, this is an apple, for that is its name and it has core and seeds, and we eat it. Tiny and bitter it is, but a lovely red, the thorn-apple.

The hill gets to its top after a while, and there come grassy sidewalks, a few boards along, in front of yards and houses at the edge of the village. We arrive at the Brick Schoolhouse and are late. We are always late, because we live so far away (out of the district, but Father arranged it). Mr. Smith is used to it; he only sometimes makes us stand up in front of the school ten minutes for tardiness.

Mr. Smith is big and jolly; his hair is red, his face is red. He sits in front of the school in a wooden armchair tipped back against the wall; and the legs of the chair have worn the floor to splinters, with his being so heavy. Ruth and I have chairs at a long table at one side of the front because the desks are full and we, being big girls, can use the table. We are quite special friends of Mr. Smith. We have good times with him. But we learn a lesson not out of books the day we draw a funny picture of him on the slate and *show it to him*. He does not seem to find it funny, no laugh out of him, he gives us a sharp word— he disapproves! Suddenly we are ashamed of ourselves and understand we ought not to make fun of our teacher. Everybody likes him. Even when he takes the ruler to the big boys and makes them behave.

It is forbidden to fight at recess, the boys will do it. One day Mr. Smith jerks a big boy in out of the snow by his collar and stands him up in front just after school is called. He must hold out his hand for the ruler. The boy's hair is all mussed up, his clothes are tumbled and snowy, his face flaming. He looks awful. He flinches from the strokes. He is crying out loud, sobbing and blubbering; and he calls out in a rough, mad way, between his blubbers:

"I don't care! My father told me to fight for my rights. He *told* me I wouldn't get anywhere if I didn't fight for my rights!"

The schoolroom is very still. Everybody sits immovable, staring at him. It is appalling. The boy clumps up the aisle to his seat and drops his head in his arms on his desk. We can hardly get to work again. It was so different.

The oldest girl in school sits back against the wall. She has long dresses, brown alpaca or merino. Her dark brown hair is in long, smooth, careful curls to her waist. I admire her more than I can tell. She has a long upper lip; her face is calm and elevated, and she is always quiet. One day we are telling our favorite flowers; someone asks her what is her favorite flower. She says, in her low, sweet voice, "I like the violet— because it is so modest." I think I have never heard so choice a sentiment.

Ruth is my best friend. Her brother Jerry is older, the best scholar in school and respected by all. He cuts me finger-rings out of buttons. He makes me the most exquisite basket from a walnut shell, beautifully smoothed and shaped and the handle firm and dainty. It is a work of art. So is the tiny cup with a handle he whittled out, about the size of a thimble, painted with a spray of flowers and "Nellie and Ruth" cut on the bottom in a circle. How can he make such a perfect, such a delicate thing!

We have a play we are in all the time and a secret language we invent, and write letters to each other. It's a lot of bother to use the language. I forget and have to look out the words in the key—a nuisance, I can't keep up with myself. There's a locust tree by the fence in Ruth's front yard with a good hole in it. The hole is our secret post office, and she is Pocahontas and I am Aurora Borealis.

Ruth says that Jerry thinks I am beautiful. He told her he loved me and when I get to be seventeen he is going to ask me to marry him . . . . I go along the street by Mr. Howe's yard where the walk is paved with irregular flat stones and grass grows up between, and think about having beauty. No one ever told me that before. I have never thought a thing about it. What a delight to be beautiful! It lifts me.

Noon spell, the girls are finding out their future husbands. Emeline Weaver has the Bible from Mr. Smith's table and the door key. We all gather round her in the back of the schoolroom where her desk is, and she hunts up the part where it says, "Turn, my beloved, and be thou like a roe or young hart on the mountains of Bether." They tie the key in there between the leaves, wrapping string around the shut Bible to hold it, with the handle out. A girl lifts the Bible up by the tips of her two forefingers held under the loop of the key. She says "A—turn my beloved and be thou like a roe or young hart on the mountains of Bether." If her beau begins with an A the key will turn in her fingers and then she knows. If it happens to be Peter or Zeb, she has to begin at A and go on through the alphabet without skipping or else it won't work. They jabber it off, some get so impatient they just say after the letter, "Turn my beloved—" and go on to the next. This isn't fair. I don't try it, don't care to. Who wants all the girls standing round watch-

ing and teasing and joggling your elbow when you say the
initial of some boy that happens to sharpen your pencil once
or twice. I'd rather go outdoors and play pom-pom-pullaway.
Of course we know there's nothing in it, Estelle tried it twice;
first for F (Frank Jerrold) and then for H (Hal Evans), and it
turned for both!

Eddie has begun school. There is a low bench against the
wall up front and Eddie is so little Mr. Smith has put him at
the end of this bench right next me at the long table where Ruth
and I sit. I can lean over and help him with his primer lesson
without getting out of my chair.

Mental arithmetic is my delight. We stand up for it with
toes on the crack, and leave off head, like spelling. Some just
can't do it; but Mr. Smith makes them, somehow. He backs
them up, and untangles their tangles, and starts them over and
puts in a word if he has to, and leaps them into the *therefore*
before they know it. They think they have done it themselves.
But some like it and gallop it off smooth and perfect like the
multiplication table. I do. You can't do that unless you see
through it from beginning to end—and that's the fun of it. Mr.
Smith likes that; his smile gets broader and broader. His face
flushes—more, for it is pretty red anyway.

How big you are, Mr. Smith! He fills the whole room, the
whole world, marching back and forth in front of the blackboard with his pointer like a javelin in his hand. Jab goes the
javelin, straight at Marshall's tiny mistake (Marshall always
makes mistakes, but just little ones), and whack-whack-whack
it beats on the board. Don't you *see?* That's such a foolish mistake—what did you do that for? Oh, Marshall didn't know it
made any difference. Difference—*difference!* All the difference between right and wrong. Oh, Marshall didn't understand
the example. Understand? Well, see *here.* Mr. Smith cools
down his breath, pushes down his hair, straightens up (he looms
so big), and sets off in a quiet, even tone, and fairly skins that

example from beginning to end. So clear it is when he gets
through everybody sees it. Even Marshall. That mistake
nobody will ever make again. (We hadn't better.) He loves it,
Mr. Smith does, I guess he is rather glad of a mistake to give
him a chance to explain. He makes arithmetic seem—beautiful
(I can't think of any other word for it). Though he would
jump over the moon before he would think of saying a thing
was beautiful. Mathematics is my favorite. For real study, I
mean, not amusement like reading and writing. I get my teeth
into the problem and worry it and worry it and flounce the life
out of it and *make* it come right. Ruth and I resolve we will do
the miscellaneous examples in the higher arithmetic without
looking at the answers in the back of the book. We can prove
the answers and find out that way if they are right. Mr. Smith
is tickled that we like our arithmetic and algebra, for they are
his favorite studies too.

In the summer he is a farmer and lives over toward Bennets-
burg on the hills. One Friday when we speak pieces he brings
his little boy and has him speak a piece:

> "I'll never chew tobacco, no;
> It is a filthy weed;
> I'll never put it in *my* mouth,"
> Said little Robert Reed.

After that the big boys go around chanting (to themselves,
so Mr. Smith won't hear) "I'll never put it in *my-y* mouth,"
and then chewing hard with great big twists of their jaws—on
nothing, of course. We girls have to laugh—all of them doing
it in concert and as sober as owls. When Mr. Smith suddenly
looks up in his sharp way not a single jaw is wagging, everybody studying their lessons innocently.

In the back of the geography there are different types of
people, pictures and descriptions of them. Mr. Smith is "san-
guine." "Phlegmatic" means heavy and stupid and slow; and
Pete Stowell is phlegmatic. He is filling up the door at recess;
I can't get out:

"Oh, do get along, Pete, let me get past you . . . ."

"What's your hurry? Rome wa'n't built in a day."

"You'll never build Rome."

"Oh, I dunno," says Pete, dropping himself down the steps like a bag of sand. He's the one that always answers "lead" when you ask which is the heaviest, a pound of feathers or a pound of lead.

My Uncle Horatio is of the "melancholy" type; his face looks rather dignified, but he breaks into his hearty laugh just like all the ministers, and I like him first-rate.

Bennie Nickerson has begun to make elegant covers for our bookkeeping books. We have foolscap sheets for the accounts, fastened together at the back into a book, and Bennie has discovered he can decorate handsome covers for them. He takes a pencil and makes a broad band across, or some other shape, of wreaths and sprays and curling, whirling tendrils like grapevines. Sometimes it is in a circle, sometimes the whole cover has it, sometimes he just makes a border all around. It is not the picture of anything, just a flowing prettiness. He puts our name in the middle in fancy letters and perhaps the word "Bookkeeping," all trimmed up. "Oh, Bennie, will you do me one tomorrow"—"Bennie, do *me* one next, won't you"—"No, Bennie promised *me* next, didn't you, Bennie!" He is awfully goodnatured; he promises everybody and sits in his seat working over them at recess and nooning and after school and forgets every other thing in the world.

Jerry goes to school at Havana Academy now. Ruth says he wants me to forgive him for kissing me; he told her to ask me. He is home for summer vacation, and he came a piece with me the other day after I had been up to their house, as far as Tug Hollow bridge. So when he stopped and said good-bye and started to go back, he just kissed me for good-bye. I didn't like it—or, no, I mean I don't think it is right. I don't believe in it. I told him I was offended. Why, I don't even kiss Ruth.

He wants me to correspond with him, but I don't think I'd better. It doesn't seem quite the thing. He writes to Ruth.

Jerry wants to be an architect. When we go to Homer for hay fever I write Ruth a description of the streets and buildings of the town, and tell her about the beautiful little room with oil paintings in it and a large globe and shelves of books to the ceiling on all the walls, which is their town library. I wish Jerry could see it all if he is going to be an architect. The library has a sort of an incense smell to it. I am all alone in there. I am perfectly, perfectly happy; if only I could be there forever, just that way.

Books are different from anything else to me. I like to look at their backs standing on a shelf; lots of them I couldn't understand, and don't want to read anyway; but that does not make any difference. I put my arms around them all and hug them; they are mine, all, even never mind if I don't open their dusty old covers—Father's big Commentaries, I mean, on the bottom shelves—and I don't believe he opens them very often either. He thinks the world of them. Dr. Bolton, my dear Aunt Anna's husband who died, gave them to him when he was beginning his ministry, preaching at Alexandria, Virginia. He studied them seriously, he says. I don't think commentaries help him to write his history of civilization, or whatever it is. But yet he likes to preach. I guess he preaches out of his head now instead of out of books. Anyway there is always the Bible; he must be full of that.

Father and I drive over to Ithaca where he has to see a man about getting out timber. It is a pretty, rolling drive through the green country and we talk along, about twenty miles. We come to the edge of the town where we can see it spread below. Father points across with his whip.

"Cornell University," says he, and I look and see the buildings on a hill.

"Umph-humph," say I.

"How would you like to go there to college?" says he.

College! I never thought of such a thing. Doesn't just school go on forever? What is a college? I only know about Yale where Father went. . . . . I don't know whether this is a question Father expects me to answer or not. I steal a look at him; really I cannot think of anything to say. So I say,

"Yes, I guess so."

VI

WILLIAMSPORT

Uncle Horatio, Aunt Mary, and I are on the train going through pretty hills in Pennsylvania. I have left my home, left Woodward Farm, and shall go to school this winter at a select girls' school kept by the two Miss Wilsons in Williamsport. Uncle is minister there and I will live with him. How will it be, I wonder. Shall I love my cousins Alice, Bertha, Clara, and Lester like my own brothers and sisters? I suppose so.

This morning at prayers before we started, Father prayed for *me*—for "her who goes out from her home for the first time." It was beautiful, but I was surprised to be mentioned specially. I looked at Mother as we got up from our knees; she had tears in her eyes. Dear Mother! Can it be you are sorry to have me go? I never thought of such a thing. Why, they *love* me, they will *miss* me, even! Leaving has not been in my mind, only getting there. I think of them as we go rattling along in the train; this is parting. I never understood before what it is to be parted.

We come to Williamsport and I see the fine big house they live in. Aunt Mary is lovely to me, gives me a little bed by the window in a large bedroom next hers, with a door between. The room has also a double bed in it, and Alice and Bertha sleep there; it is their room. My work is to dust the parlor, a pretty parlor with a piano and pictures. The kitchen is down cellar and nobody goes near it (except Aunt Mary to poison cockroaches in the evening before going to bed), as there is a hired girl. We all do our own beds of course. I never heard brushing teeth, and so forth, called "duties" before. Aunt Mary says, "Alice, Bertha, have you done your duties this morning?" It means brushing teeth, making bed, putting bureau in order, and "redding up" the bedroom. The house is always in order—everywhere. I never heard of such orderliness. At our house Father drops his things all over, and so do we all of us. The first morning I sat down to read a book right after breakfast. Aunt Mary said to me so sweetly and gently (she thought I had just forgotten): "Hadn't you better make your bed before you sit down to read, Nellie?" The idea surprised me; I always read when I want to. But I rather liked it, too—not to come in the middle of the day and see that dreadful mess of a bed there just as you left it when you got up hours ago.

School has not yet begun. It is hot. I have nothing much to do, though I tell the children stories out of the *Arabian Nights* and they like it. But every day, though I love them all here, my heart gets heavier. I feel doleful. My own family that I've always had is far away. Not one of them is here. I write to them every day, and I get letters and postal cards all the time. But that's not it. I'm so homesick; and I did not think it would be like this. I feel dreadfully, for it exactly seems as if they were *all dead!* So then I write a mournful postal card again asking if I may not come home, and afterward go into the shady parlor and sit alone in the green stuffed rocking-chair and think about the heaviness of my heart.

I have a little bit of hay fever. I know Mother is in Homer avoiding it, and Zaidee with her. If I had a lot of hay fever I should have to go to Homer, too. I could see my Mother and Zaidee. I have written that I have it and begged to go to Homer.

I am out in the yard under the plum tree. Plums give me hay fever very much. The world is very black today; I must go home. I take the plums and squash them all over my face; I rub the plum leaves over my face, and snuff them up my nose;

I eat plums and they make my throat itch like fire. My face burns, my eyes run; so does my nose. I sneeze and cry. I never was so miserable in my life. I *must* go to Homer. I *will* go, to get rid of this awful hay fever.

So they said I might; and I have to spend the night at Ithaca, because it is a long journey from Williamsport to Homer and you change cars much. My Great-Aunt Athalie, a French lady my Great-Uncle Harvey North married in New Orleans, happens to be in Ithaca staying at a grand hotel and they wrote her about me and would she take care of me the night I had to stay there? I have never seen her before.

I come into the hotel alone in the evening, not knowing who to look for; but she comes to me at once with her hands stretched out and is sweet and loving to me. I belong to her before hardly a word is said: Straight, black, shining hair, parted and smoothed down on each side, and a small knot at the back (no frizzes). Her head small and neat, her eyes brown and clear. Her dress astonishes me, though she does not seem to be thinking about it. She looks so very different. Our dresses have ruffles and puffs and pleats all over them; it makes them stylish; and everybody wears overskirts. Now the dress I am wearing is my garnet cashmere Miss Beam made me to go to Williamsport with. The basque is short, pointed in front and behind, with fancy buttons. The skirt is tight, gored of course, with a row of box-pleating on the bottom and above it another row of knife-pleating, narrower. On one side of the overskirt is a deep narrow pocket which Miss Beam copied from a fashion-plate. She calls it a "parasol pocket," because it looks like a parasol, closed. It is trimmed with rows of knife and box pleating to match the skirt. The basque has one of the new choker collars, the first I've had; and I wear a ribbon bow in front, under my chin. I think a bow under a person's chin is so pretty.

But Aunt Athalie has on a dress that is per-fect-ly plain. The skirt is gathered and sewed right to the waist at the belt— instead of a basque, and no overskirt, nor ruffles, nor pleats.

Jet buttons, a narrow lace collar, and a lovely cameo pin at the neck. Why, she takes my breath away! The dress is black silk. She is a very great lady I suppose.

Yes, yes, Aunt Athalie, I had a lunch with me, I ate it at supper time. No, I didn't mind traveling alone, nor coming from the depot in the hotel bus. Oh, no, dear Auntie, I'm not afraid of the dark! We laugh merrily together. She has a cunning accent. She asks me about my people in Williamsport and about my family in Burdett. She talks to me kindly and beautifully. We go to my bedroom, and she looks about to see if I have everything, and tells me not to blow out the gas (I knew it before). She kisses me goodnight on both cheeks and leaves me. How dear and fine she is. She has a daughter of her own, a young lady, named 'Thalie. Tomorrow I shall be with my mother and Zaidee.

It was lovely to be with Mother and Zaidee in Homer. I discovered *Paradise Lost*. That is, Mother gave it to me when I asked her for something to read, a little green leather book she used to parse in school, with "Mattie Coit" written in the front. There were pictures, Adam and Eve lying around in the Garden of Eden, and others. It took right hold of me. I devoured it. I sat cross-legged on the bed in the hall bedroom and read it and read it straight through, and it took two days. I never had anything make me feel the way that did.

The frost came; the leaves rattled down from the trees; the air was like wine; we went beech-nutting in the edge of the woods. Hay-fever time was over. But I did not want to go back to Williamsport—homesickness is so dreadful. How could I bear it to begin again! No, I could not go back. Mother needs me at home. "Mother, how can you get along without me to help with the children? *Need* I go back?"

"If you really cannot bear it to be away from home," said my mother, "why, then you will have to give up getting an education."

Appalling!

So I get into the train and go on back to Williamsport. School starts up; Alice and I both go; I get acquainted with everybody; I never have one bit of homesickness any more.

My seat-mate is Jenny Mudge, a tall girl, rather quiet. One day she passes me a note (no whispering in school) and begins to do her studying very hard, not looking at me. It says "Are you a Christian?" My heart bounds. I write on it "Yes" and shove it back along the desk. We look at each other and smile, and now we are the dearest friends. Not that we talk about *that*.

May Partridge sits in front of us, small and fidgety, dark hair tied in a bunch of curls behind at her neck—she's a chatterbox. Mr. Partridge is a pillar in Uncle's church. May has six new dresses—six, all at once! I never heard of such a thing. She shows them to me hanging up in the closet. My Cousin Alice has two school dresses, a brown camel's-hair and a navy-blue merino. She wears them a week about, and Aunt Mary cleans and mends the one she takes off on Saturday and hangs it up to put on a week from Monday. I have my garnet for best. For school a green *drap-d'été*, made over from Mother's, faded some, but it has a nice overskirt puckered up behind. I never had two new dresses at once in my life, and why should I, there is always an old dress to be wearing out that serves as a change.

It is closing time in the schoolroom, and we are sitting waiting. Miss Jenny Wilson goes up and down the aisles and lays an envelope on each desk. It is a bill, Jenny Mudge gets one, but I do not. Miss Jenny is younger than Miss Wilson and wears her hair in a pretty way, a coil behind, and the front caught back with combs on each side of her face in a cascade of brown curls. So long they are, and springy; they touch her shoulders, and the curly ends fall this way and that. She wears a trailing princess dress, dove-colored, or sometimes brown or plum. Miss Wilson wears the same sort of princess cashmeres, I like her best in her wine-colored one. They have little trains, and generally narrow pleating around the bottom—one row.

Miss Wilson—Miss *Sophia* Wilson, has grey hair, not curly, but done in a puff at the sides with combs, and a coil behind. After dismissal I go to the desk and say to Miss Wilson that I have not been given any bill. She likes me and I like her. She smiles and says:

"I should never present a bill to a member of my pastor's family." Alice has none either. I am glad to write that to Father.

In the morning when we are all there and it is time, Miss Wilson opens the door from her own hall. She stands a moment; we see her; she says, "Good morning, young ladies," and glides to her table on a low platform. She takes the Bible and reads the chapter. When we are dismissed at one o'clock, we take down our things from the rows of hooks at one side and put them on, quietly, and go out by a door on that side. She stands on her platform looking over at us. As we go out, each girl turns at the door and says, "Good afternoon, Miss Wilson," and to each one she returns a little bow and "Good afternoon." She loves to teach. Jenny says she told some one that if it were not for frightening the girls she would like to die in the schoolroom, teaching right up to the end. She will stand no nonsense, either. She says: "You may not think it matters how you act now, but you will be grown up some day. When you are grown up and have your own children, think of your behavior being such that they will *criticize you!*" She rolls her eyes at us, and purses up her lips in a way she has, and we realize the dreadful prospect.

Uncle Horatio is deaf. It is a great trial to him; he often mentions it. He carries a large black ear trumpet the size and shape of a quart dipper; but he hates the ear trumpet. The shiny, japanned finish of the dipper part is so offensive to him that Cousin Mary Jennet, who humors him to death, has made a neat black broadcloth slip to put over it. But you must not cover the top where the sound goes in, and that is bright brass, perforated, like a skimmer. It is very humiliating. He is tall and dark, with dark hair thrown back from his dignified face. His hearty laugh shows his big white teeth. His voice is rich like my father's and flows in waves when he preaches and reads the Bible and hymns.

Cousin Mary Jennet makes Uncle Horatio long dressing-gowns of flowered cashmere or delaine, which he always wears in the house. Usually he is writing sermons in his study, or pacing back and forth across it thinking up sermons. He has worn a bare track in the Brussels carpet cater-cornering across the room doing that. He hates to write his sermons, he preaches the new one Sunday morning and an old one Sunday evening. He groans when he sits at his desk writing, sometimes.

The study is the best room in the house, the one intended for the parlor, at the right of the front door. There are tall windows looking into maple trees, tall bookcases to the ceiling, and the desk in the middle with the new-style student lamp on it. When he is in the sitting room he is in his reclining chair, reading. He spreads out the fingers of his free hand like a cat its claws, back and forth. As he reads he says to himself through his nose without opening his lips, "Umph, imph," because he is deaf, I suppose. He is splendid when he and Aunt Mary go out to make pastoral calls, which they do twice a week. He is in his fine black broadcloth and beaver hat. Oh, how proud I am of him!

Aunt Mary is tall, too, not a dumpling like Mother. She has a long, nice, cream-colored face, brown eyes, and a great shining coil of auburn hair. Her best dress is a grey-and-white pin-stripe silk, and she looks very handsome beside Uncle in his black. And pearl-grey kid gloves.

Aunt Mary is my greatest admiration. I love her, too. She does everything. At night after poisoning the cockroaches she goes to the pantry and gets the silver basket with all the forks and spoons in it and takes them upstairs with her to her bedroom. She puts the basket on a shelf in her closet and shuts the door till morning; and in the morning she brings them down again. One day I open the door of her room suddenly and she is kneeling by the bed praying. She rises up when I come in. I am confused and sorry, but I ask her what I came for, whether it is true that every time you catch a cold it uses up some of your vitality, so that you will not live quite so long as if you did not have that cold. She says she thinks it cannot be true. Uncle talks over his sermons with her, as do all ministers—or else why do they have wives? Lester cannot stand it to have his broken jumping-jack fixed by anybody else. She makes clothes for everybody all the time, and attends to pastoral duties. Only Alice goes to school, she teaches the others at home, and though Alice is ten, this is her first year at school. Uncle Horatio considers home training the best for young children.

I'm beginning to do things regularly. At home we flourish around and do the work as it happens. We are so busy doing the things we like we don't get around to the others until after a while. It does make a clutteration sometimes. But we don't mind it. Here it is different. I think we would mind it here.

I wish I was quiet and dignified. People who are reserved and quiet are so much more respected and have so much more to them. Now, I tell everything, and so sorry for it afterward. Aunt Mary is quiet, never anything else, and good without remark by anybody. She never raises her voice—yet she does not appear to be holding in either, like a cork to a fizzing bottle. I love her. She is perfect. She is going to begin with Alice's music lessons. "Nellie," she says, "I am going to give you lessons, too." Oh, isn't she dear to do that? How I shall like it! She plays beautifully and—when she has time—sits down and plays for me certain pieces that are my favorites.

Aunt Mary is going to a party—she looks beautiful in her silvery grey dress with its trail. She has a real-lace collar and jabot at the neck. Her thick, soft, rich hair is in its large loose coil, and softly curving back from her face. In front of the glass she sits and lets me put the flowers in her hair, lilies-of-the-valley and violets. I thrill to do it, but I cannot get them right. I fuss and fuss; they will not suit me. I keep pinning them on and taking them off.

"You are not arranging them in a ring around the coil, are you?" she asks, in her sweet voice.

"Oh, no!" (I had intended to do just that) . . . . "There, it is done. Take the hand glass and see if you like it, Auntie." She likes it. At last I have just bunched them in a hurry at one side and they droop almost to her shoulder.

The instant dinner is over in this house every member of the family goes and takes a nap, all in their bedrooms, shades pulled down. Uncle Horatio says it is the thing to do, everybody does it. Everybody but me; no one obliges me, because I am already brought up and may do as I like, at least about anything not religious. So on Saturday afternoon after our busy marketing and bathing morning, I retire into the shaded parlor, all in order, and I dusted it before breakfast. The house is perfectly still. I curl up in a big green-rep rocker, very soft and cuddly, and think. I go over in my mind what I might write about for my composition. We have one every week, and it is this way I write it. I choose a subject: "Small Boys," "Crooked Sticks," "Our First Camping Out," or whatever. I think it all through, all about it and how I will say it. I love this; my body never stirs, but my mind goes like a silent little mill, round and round go the thoughts; I marshal them. They study out the whole thing for me. When I raise the window curtain and fly to writing, it comes too fast to put down, almost. They don't have to be long, a page or two, nothing hard.

Miss Wilson goes over our compositions with us each alone, so she can say anything and we can ask anything, no matter how silly.

"You might use 'foliage' here instead of 'leaves.' You said 'leaves' in the previous sentence."

"I like 'leaves' better than 'foliage.' Why should I use a different word, Miss Wilson?"

"To enlarge your vocabulary," says she. I am so pleased with vocabulary (rolling around in the mouth like smooth pebbles!) that I forget my objections.

Once on my composition she wrote on the margin, "This is very beautiful." What she said was beautiful was this, "like the touch of a soft hand felt in a dream." I dreamed a touch like that once.

Miss Wilson says she "never can think of a person as truly educated who has not studied Latin and Greek." But I do not study the dead languages; my father says it is all poppycock, and he wants me to have French and German instead. So I do. I translated his remarks to Miss Wilson, as he would wish me to do. He had to learn Hebrew, Greek, and Latin in college (seven years wasted, he says) because he was going to be a minister and had to read the Bible in the original.

Miss Wilson is my *beau ideal.* Her elegance is a revelation to me. She glides about the schoolroom with small invisible silent steps, the little train of her princess dress never acting up. When she leaves the room she turns quickly as she opens the door (whether anybody is looking or not) and slips through it backward. Why, of course, what a polite thought, your face then is turned to the people in the room when you go out, instead of your back. I shall always do it. Her movements are swift but ever softly noiseless.

I need a new calico dress, and I want a net, the girls are wearing them, and they are wearing Alsatian bows, too, but that takes too much wide ribbon, and I need a lead-pencil, and my purse contains ten cents, and my debts count up to one cent. Anyhow, I've lived within my income. I trim over my hat and make it into a little bonnet with blue ribbons tied under the chin. I buy a shawl, a soft lovely summer blue shawl, reduced in price because it is autumn; many times I go and look at it in the store before I can decide. I want it so much, I long for it. I don't long for it just because I need it, I'm afraid—I do need it, but so pretty, basket weave, blue like the sky—it pulls at me. I buy it with the five dollars Grandma gave me. Perhaps I should have saved it for stockings or shoes, some things you *can't* go without. Shawls you can—wear your cloak.

We choose mottoes, some of the girls together. Jenny Mudge takes "To thine own self be true and it must follow as the night the day thou canst not then be false to any man." May flaxes around in the book and finally settles on: "My purpose is to sail beyond the sunset." We laugh at her, because everybody knows May is a flutterbudget and never sticks to anything more than a minute. But tears are in her eyes—she really means it, so we stop right off. She is a great favorite.

Mine is not out of the book. I found it before and copied it out because I thought it was beautiful: *"Le meilleur, c'est assez bon pour moi."* That is mine and always will be. It shall be on my banner, like "Excelsior" (only I always feel that "Excelsior" is rather showy). It is my gonfalon! I presume a gonfalon is silken, fringed with gold. All in color it must be, some golden color full of rainbows: *"Le meilleur, c'est assez bon pour moi."*

Jenny and I want to be real helpers to the poor and anyone else that needs us. Jenny wants to be a missionary. Aunt Mary has two sisters in the mission field—India. She would probably be there herself, only she married Uncle. We start a girls' mission circle, and they elect me secretary. I propose its name, "Ministering Children." Jenny and I take a walk quite far off on the edge of town, and the street is about empty. There comes along a poor old washerwoman carrying a big heavy bundle of washing. Jenny and I look at each other; here is a chance for us to help. We go kindly to the old woman and ask her to let us carry her bundle for her. She stares at us. She is surprised, and does not seem to like us. Then she rather snorts, or something of the kind, without even answering. She pushes by us and walks off as fast as ever she can go.

"Well, if she doesn't want to accept our help she needn't, horrid old creature!"

"Oh, Nellie, don't say that. She's a soul—I suppose."

"I don't like her snort," say I.

"People can't help their snorts," says she, "any more than they can their color. Look at the Negroes."

"I don't mind them a bit. I like their color, and they are so nice and shiny. Don't you?"

"Like it! No. A colored person makes me shudder—I hate to say so."

"The idea! Why?"

"Well, I don't know why, and that makes it all the worse. It just is, inside of me. I hate to own it."

"Yet you are going as a missionary to India—they're black."

"That's why I'm going," says she.

"Oh chickie, chickie!" says my Uncle Horatio. He drums on the table and looks gloomily across at Aunt Mary, and says that to her in a tender despondency. She gives a sort of quiet chuckle and looks affectionately back at him.

My uncle disapproves of many things. Thanksgiving he preaches a sermon on all the things we as a nation have to fear: communism, Mormonism, naturalized foreigners, ignorant Southern Negroes, poor whites, the labor and capital question. He ends up with a big thunder against the papists, tells startling things they've done (gives his authority) and what the Catholics themselves declare they will do if they can get the power. Two common laboring men in front of us nod to each other with knowing glances. They nudge each other at the emphatic points. "That's so!" "True, every word of it!" they whisper. Three other ministers are in the pulpit with Uncle and they too seem pleased, smile at each other. It is grand. We are very thankful, certainly. We go home and eat the best turkey I ever tasted, seventeen pounds, roasted crisp and brown, cranberries, hot biscuit, and all.

His children must not bang their hair, nor think of such a thing—no, no. He inveighs against the abominable fashion. Bertha was toying with the idea. She is an independent little piece, she speaks up at the dinner table: "Why, Father, you talk as though bangs were *wicked!*" Uncle laughs, has to, and shows his teeth. For all his fierceness and gloom he often has to laugh. Nobody is in the least afraid of him. He is so large and handsome, and quite a great man, I think.

Cousin Mary Jennet idolizes him. He has lately taken a notion to skull caps, on account of his catarrh, and she makes them for him out of black silk. His parishioners think the world of him, though he is always intending to hand in his resignation at the next session meeting—because he hates to write sermons and does it so poorly (he thinks), and because he is deaf, and because, I suppose, of the state of the country. "I am of a melancholy temperament," he says.

Three times a week Cousin Mary Jennet brings out the battery and gives Uncle the electricity for ten minutes. I don't know what for. I take it, too; I think it is good for me. I hear they are going to make lamps for our houses with electricity. I hope so, I'm sure; I hate kerosene lamps, greasy old things. Father keeps ours smutty tipping them around, and to clean the chimneys is a mean job. Mother uses a crumpled newspaper and gets off the worst of it dry instead of putting them into suds with all their black upon them, which is the stupid method. My mother never used a stupid method in her life. My hand will go into a lamp chimney and into a fruit jar, too; most people's won't.

The gas goes out at Sunday evening church while Uncle is preaching. He sits down; the choir sings a hymn; the gas goes on escaping; we begin to sniffle and cough, and get out our handkerchiefs. A tall, very old Negro gentleman (apparently) in a long black coat begins to walk ver-ry slowly up the aisle from the back, mounts the pulpit, opens a door behind and brings forth a long pole. With this, still deliberately and reverently as befits the sacred place, he—lights—the—gas. Uncle resumes his sermon; the gas stops escaping; the floating fumes fade away; the congregation cease to cough; and the long black Negro in time reaches again his station in the vestibule.

Down at the corner they have the new telephone contraption. I go with Auntie and talk into it to someone in another building, successfully. Bolton and I did that with two baking-powder tins connected by a long piece of wire. We talked into the cans and heard each other perfectly.

She says there is a surprise for me in the parlor—Aunt Mary comes into my bedroom where I am studying and says that. "What is it, what is it?" She will not tell me. "Go on down and see." I fly out into the hall, down the stairs, Aunt Mary follows me, I run through the lower hall, open the parlor door. There on the sofa, with her things on, and her dimple, sits my mother! How my heart surges—I can hardly breathe. I never thought of such a thing—I choke. I throw myself into her arms and burst out crying. "Why Nellie, Nellie!" says Aunt Mary with her soft laugh. My mother has come to see me! My heart is full, I never knew such happiness as this before.

VII

COLLEGE LOOMS

THERE IS a great snowstorm and I home for Christmas. It is almost time to go back. See the drifts; see the new snow fly; see the lonesome empty road, a smooth sheet of white no horse or cutter has gone through today. Every morning we look out to see, and the day when I must go draws nearer. The farmers drive through, breaking the drifts, their teams bravely flounder in the snow.

The "old woman in the sky" has stopped picking her geese. The morning comes, Father will drive me to Watkins, the stage went through yesterday and reports the road broken. Even across the Head of the Lake where the wind sweeps and the flying snow drifts.

Extra warm we wrap up, for it has turned very cold. Hot bricks on the cutter floor, the buffalo robe and all the blankets, and my father stands me up by the stove for ten minutes before we start. "You have to get *toasty* warm," says Louise in a motherly way. But, after all, I cannot go; we take the long cold ride to Watkins and find no trains are running; railroad blocked with the snow, and they don't know how long. We leave my trunk in the baggage room and turn homeward. I'm not so toasty warm as when I left the sitting room some time ago. The north wind is blowing up—icy. It whirls the top snow in the air and sends it scurrying about in a silvery spray. Along the white surfaces of the fields these little fairy clouds and wreaths skim and curl. My thick bérège veil, wet and frozen from my breath,

135

makes me shiver. I open it a little; the flying snow stings my face. The road comes into the woods and it is more sheltered; yet the cold seems terrific. I ache all over. Father urges the horse, whose breath comes in white puffs as he trots knee-deep in snow. He shakes his head impatiently. I am stone cold inside of all my clothes, I suffer, it seems to me I cannot stand it. My father keeps chatting and urges the horse — "*Go* along, old church steeple!" he says, and makes me laugh. I grow sleepy; I do not notice the cold so much. Father talks and pokes me up with his elbow . . . . Here we are, he jumps out and bundles me to the house; he makes me run up the snowy path.

He lays me down right on the floor in front of the stove with my things on. The windows have comforters hung over them; the stove has red spots on its cheeks. The family gather round. I soon get warm. I sit up in Mother's chair and drink hot milk and recount my adventures. We always recount our adventures when we come in.

My dear Aunt Anna ought to be careful about the style of the clothes she sends. Not but that her own are always handsome and fashionable, though black because of Uncle Bolton and her being a widow. But she has taken to sending us things her cousins, the Chappels, give her to dispose of after their girls are through with them. I guess they don't part with them until a long time after. They are lovely material and can—sometimes—be made over. Two linen lawns I had last summer, white ground with a small black sprig, and pretty. They were just waist-and-skirt, which is always in style for wash dresses.

But Cinderella's godmother herself could not make over this highly durable, perfectly good, black broadcloth coat with which I am at present afflicted. Because it is cut up with a hundred seams, fitted with darts front and back, trimmed with rows of silk braid firmly stitched on, and has a cape! Of all things! Nobody wears capes. This is a flappy, ripply, full cape around the shoulders and (horrors!) it is matched by the short skirt of the coat, which flares and undulates all over the hips at a time when we wear our hips skin-tight. It is lined and warm (oh, me!); it is not the least bit shabby (alas, alas!); it fits me, I haven't any other winter cloak, I wear it. Cousin Mary Jennet admires it; she thinks it must be an imported garment. No doubt. One day, taking my walk, two street boys jeer, *jeer*, they call after me, "Oh, what a coat!" It is horrible. I feel like an insect on a pin and nearly die of mortification. Partly because I know it is true. A plain, inconspicuous black coat might pass even if old-fashioned; but this is too dreadfully jaunty! I have a homely pair of shoes Aunt Mary recommended me to buy, being such good quality and for sale at a bargain, only a dollar. I wrote home and they said I'd better get them if they fitted (they do), and sent me the dollar. So I did. We are wearing buttoned shoes; but these are laced. Instead of coming up high on the ankle with a curving top, they cut the ankle bone right in two, as much as to say "there, that's enough shoe leather; cut her off square, no sense in curves." They are warm in cold weather. They are not pebble-goat, or morocco, or the thin French kid best shoes are made of. Kid they are, yes, but a regular old-lady's kid, thick, and dull, and wear off blue. I think about it when I stand at the blackboard in front of the class. However, as they are not the kind that ever wear out, I am lucky to get them for a dollar. Father hasn't much of any money. I have bought me two pairs of red woolen stockings, though; those are nice.

The black ostrich tip Grandma gave me I left at home for Mother's bonnet; but she is not using it, and I send for it for my hat. The white wing is worn out. I fix it over and change its shape, and it will do another season. I send my old hair-ribbons home to Louise. I am ashamed to do it, but she can wear them around home after I cannot at school. When I can I tuck in a new one. I ought to be earning money instead of spending it so fast. But what could I do to earn? District school, perhaps? I've only spent sixteen cents this month and it is now the twenty-ninth, excluding what Cousin Henry has sent me to get my picture taken. I shall need two new white petticoats, I'm afraid, as mine have been let down twice, and being scant at the top and gored cannot be lengthened again, and are now too short.

Mother writes that she has had to make a rule that Bolton shall sit at the table fifteen minutes whether he eats or not. He runs his legs off, never walks anywhere—a waste of time. So he will not waste time eating, either, and snatches up any little things he can bolt in one or two minutes and darts off again. He is thin and lanky, and now she has made him this rule. When he is obliged to stay in the house from weather or anything, he crochets mittens and scarfs and wristlets. He does something every minute. He was crazy to learn the sewing machine, possessed to make himself a pair of pants; but when he sewed up the legs all wrong and they did not turn out legs at all, he threw it away and never touched the machine again.

He touched it again, yes, but for a different kind of experiment. This happened when I was home in the summer. He wrapped a very long rope tightly around the rod which hitches to the wheel and turns it. When the rope was all wound on he took the end of it and set off full tilt through the door up the back yard as far as it would reach. Of course the unwinding rope whirled the wheel around as he ran, and faster and faster. This set up a motion in the machine itself and it began to bounce—I don't know why. Bolton came racing back, dragging the rope, to see what was happening, and when he got to the door there was the machine *jumping gaily across the floor,* and at the other side by the hall door Cousin Mary Jennet with her eyes popping out of her head. She, seeing no cause for such behavior, thought it was bewitched!

Mother says Bolton is as good as a nurse for the younger children. He builds water-wheels and sawmills, and pens for wild animals, and traps to trap them, and hunts curiosities—

we find Indian arrowheads in our fields sometimes—and sets up museums, and many other things. The children help him, and he bosses them and everybody happy. They tag him all over. Mother keeps school for them at home a good deal; it is so hard for them to traipse up to Burdett. Bolton has found a bed of smooth, light-grey clay such as they make fine china of, he says. We have clay in plenty in the road right in front of the house, and a great nuisance, too, but not the fine china kind, I guess. He shapes it into flat forms, rubs the smooth surfaces with lampblack until it is like a clean slate, and then with a sharp stick and some other little tools he draws a lovely picture on it, white on the black ground. We think they are beautiful and put them up in the parlor to keep and to look at. He is always drawing, but had no good rubber. He uses bread crumbs a good deal, which Mother taught him; she did that when she learned. When I come back to school I buy him one and send it to him. I look for a good one and pay ten cents for it.

I am president of Ministering Children this year. It would be great to get the ladies to give us their plain sewing to do, we have to earn money for the heathen. I go around and see them and gather in some towels and pillow cases. . . . . The girls ought to sew at home besides at the meetings; the ladies cannot wait forever for their things. I tell them that. But they don't do it. They forget, or hadn't time, or went for a ride last Saturday. They come back to the meeting with plenty excuses, little accomplished, and very poor indeed what they do sew. Lena Dart does a terrible hem, knots sticking out, and big and dirty at that. Oh, I am so disappointed, and ashamed. I scold them well. Of course, Lena must do hers over; we cannot take money for such work as that, even for the heathen.

They put me on a committee with Miss Porter to go around and drum up new scholars for the mission Sunday school. It is in the Negro district; but the Negroes have a school of their own, so we only go to their houses by mistake. But I wouldn't mind seeing more of them. One mother opens the door to us, and there she is banked up with about "ten small children and one at the breast," all staring with their bright, buttony eyes. When we finish and come to the end of the street, there is the Bunting mill right in front of us. Ed Bunting keeps books for his father and does business in the mill. Very convenient, I am sure; for as he is the superintendent of the mission school, we should go in and report. We do so; we report in a proper manner. We warm our feet, which are very cold, we are very gay over nothing.

It is not the thing in this house to take a walk on Sunday. The nursegirl did, once, and there was a great to-do. At home Father goes to walk with us Sunday like any other day, if he is not away preaching. Perhaps it is different in a city. Perhaps "wickedness stalks the streets" in Williamsport. I get my exercise, plenty enough, on Sunday without "going to walk"—walk to morning church and Sunday school; home again; to mission school after dinner, way over the other part of town (I teach a class), and back, to the church again at night for young people's meeting and the preaching service—and back.

Sundays at five o'clock, after I get home from mission school, comes the catechism. The children learn it just like any lesson and recite it Sunday to Aunt Mary; and I have taken to doing it, too, because I like to. Father and Mother learned it in childhood, but they never regularly set us at it. I started it over and over because I liked it; but Mother forgot to hear me say it, and I forgot to study it, and so never did get beyond about ten questions, there are one hundred and seven in all: "What are the Decrees of God?" Answer: "The Decrees of God are His eternal purpose, according to the counsel of His will, whereby, for His own glory, He hath foreordained whatsoever cometh to pass." That is question seven. I love the roll of the language. When you have learned that you have *got* something. Of course I know the Creed.

Our set does not dance, of course; I don't know whether any of Uncle's parishioners do. But some of Miss Wilson's girls do, and some people think it is wicked and some do not, and I'd like to find out about it. I don't know why pretty exercising to music should be wicked. I look up the references in *Cruden's Concordance*. There are only a few, and they do not shed much light—David dancing before the Ark, and such. I cannot find a word about whether we ought or ought not to do it.

Aunt Mary is sick—would be sick abed if she were anybody else, a bad cold and really suffering. Lester is sick. The doctor gives him a hot pack, which he hates, so it takes all the doctor's strength to put him in the blankets. Lester can't bear water, especially warm. He comes out of it seeming at peace, looks around on us, smiles sweetly, and goes off to sleep. Alice has just got over being sick, which she was last week. Annie Roan, the nurse, has a cold on her lungs, and coughs. Uncle is in the Slough of Despond. It is a good thing I like to nurse the sick. I take clear comfort doctoring Aunt Mary, I bathe her feet, I smooth her head, and give her aconite pellets, until I know she is tired to death of me. I mustard-plaster Annie's chest, much against her will, and dose her for her cough with stewed quaker.

"You don't think you can mesmerize away a headache that comes from the stomach, do you?" That is Uncle Horatio, and rather a contemptuous tone of voice. Of course I can. I smooth away their headaches whenever they have them wherever they come from. Said to be mesmerism. Dear Uncle, how very yellow you look, stretched out on the lounge. Aren't you doleful, though! And not so handsome as usual with that curl of the lips. Come, let me smooth you.

"I can—let me try it."

So I stand behind him and stroke his forehead softly, and close his eyes softly, and stroke, and stroke. "It's getting better . . . ." (drowsily). More smoothings, more, more, gently. "I guess you have real mesmerism in your hands . . . . who taught you to do it . . . ." (drowsily). "Nobody," say I, and go on stroking. "Thank you . . . ." and he drops off.

It is Gertrude's birthday. Seven years ago I stood in front of the calendar and said "Sixteenth, sixteenth; I shall never forget this baby's birthday." Another dress for Zaidee is finished. I make them so neatly, just as Aunt Mary does; stroke all the gathers, fasten all the ends. I have finished the underclothes, waists and drawers, petticoats, all made just as Aunt Mary makes them for the children. She shows me, and I use her machine. I have been at it all winter, and it must be completely done when I go home in June.

Auntie comes up the stairs; I am crying, coming down. "Why, Nellie, have you had bad news?" for I have a letter in my hand.

"Oh, Aunt Mary, Mother has a baby!"

"Why . . . . why . . . . but are they all right?"

"Yes, oh, yes—it's a girl." More tears bursting out, which I cannot help.

"What makes you cry? Aren't you glad?"

"Yes, oh, yes—but I ought to be there. They need me. I ought to be at home to help . . . ." (tears).

We go down into the sitting room and talk it over. I did so much when Zaidee was born; they needed me so, it seems to me I *must* go right home. How can they get along without me—I do not see . . . . I want to go so much. But my school, says Aunt Mary. Oh, I know Miss Wilson will understand—*it's a baby!* Hadn't I better go, Aunt Mary? At last she says perhaps I had better if I feel so strongly about it. She advises me not to start right off by the next train but to write home and say I will come if I am needed and wait for the answer. Oh, how can I wait! . . . .

Father writes they do not need me; they can get along very well without me until vacation; I'd better stay and finish my year's work. Louise writes a separate letter in a tiny blue envelope: "I think the baby is as nice as Zaidee was, she has very thick hair. I wear my bunnit when the sun shines. Zaidee likes the baby and wants to give it everything she has got, even to her teeth. Mary bathes the baby. We have not any other girl, but Mary and Father and I take good care of Mother and the baby, so you will not have to leave your school to take care of her."

Of course I understand, there is no nurse, Mary Burns does the work and bathes the baby and tends to Mother, and Father helps. If I must stay here, I must. Mary Burns is a treasure. But I want to go.

Home again, home again! Father brings the baby to show me before even I get my things off. He always carries a baby like a king's crown on a pillow, and a mysterious look on his face—as much as to say there's more in this than meets the eye. She is so slimpsy—I wonder if something is the matter with her.

"She can't hold her head up yet," says Father, laying her in my arms. How long and black her hair is.

"Her hair is her distinguishing characteristic," says he. "When Pedro saw her he thought she was a woodchuck. He said *woof!* and had to be restrained from chasing her."

She is named Harriett Henrietta, after Grandma. Grandma is pleased, promises five hundred dollars for her education. Also after Mother's dear sister, Henrietta, who is dead.

Zaidee is tickled with her new clothes. I can hardly wait to get them out of the trunk and try them on. She looks like a fairy in the dresses, blue-and-white pin stripe is one, another pink, another a dainty vine on a white ground. The blue one has ruffled elbow sleeves—oh, Zaidee's dear elbows, with the dimples in them! She is the only one who has a dimple—in spite of Mother's big one. Hers is very little, not in her cheek but at the corner of her mouth, coming and going, faintly—mostly going.

It is my third winter at Miss Wilson's. I am going to Cornell next year and I shall enter up, for I am taking the first-year work here. Miss Wilson says it will be hard work, I shall have to *study*. Goody! I like to study.

How odd geometry is! They prove that three angles and three lines equal a triangle. Then that three lines and three angles equal a triangle. Then (not satisfied) that a triangle equals three angles and three lines, and also that a triangle is equal to three lines and three angles. *Therefore*, a triangle is equal to a triangle. Hence a triangle *is a triangle*. Corollary: If a triangle is a triangle and is equal to a triangle, then a triangle is not any other kind of an angle, hence the theorem. Prayer-meeting bells are ringing. I go. But the fun of it is that you know all that about the poor old triangle the minute you lay eyes on it. So why all this dragging around?

In Higher Arithmetic we have got to "Miscellaneous Examples" on the last page, Jenny and I alone in the class and vowing to do all of them, every one, by ourselves without help from anybody. There are eleven. Miss Wilson glories in us and sics us on, Uncle shakes his head; we cannot do it, he says. Right after dinner I go back to the schoolroom; Jenny is there waiting for me. All alone in the great sunshiny place where it is perfectly quiet we work from half-past two until six. We accomplish two and a half problems. I work at home after supper till ten at night and do two and a half more. Each day we dig. We have got our dander up and don't accept assistance even from each other.

"Jenny, have you done the fourth yet?"

"No, I spent an hour on it and got worse and worse all the time. I am going back to it. I got the eighth last night at ten. You got it yet?"

"Yes, I did the eighth this morning before breakfast. I've worked on it off and on for three days . . . ."

We take our time—being all the class there is—and one by one we conquer them. All the eleven are finally done—com-

pleted—wrestled with and downed—understood from A to
Izzard. Hurray! I'm several inches taller than I was before—
though the Bible does say you cannot by taking thought add to
your stature. Miss Wilson continues to glory in us. Says Uncle,
"You have done wonders."

Mother writes about a sermon Father preached on Woman.
I'd like to have heard it; I can imagine what he thinks. Everybody ought to be free anyhow, man or woman, that is what he
would say. Liberty, says my father, is our most precious possession. Everyone thinks that, I presume; but Father is different. He never tries to make us have our liberty the way *he*
wants it. The sermon was a chapter of his book, doubtless. I
shall get my book out before his, I do believe; but then mine
will not have to roam all over creation first. He has named it,
at last, "The Life of Society." Mine will be Sunday-School
books at the beginning of my career; they are easy, and there
must be a great sale for them. Cousin Mary Jennet reads them
all the time. Then I shall write a novel or two, then a book of
poems, and finally a great treatise on "The Science of Mathematics."

At Dickenson Seminary, where I might have gone instead
of to Miss Wilson's, the young lady boarders are not allowed
to go outside the grounds, and the young gentlemen boarders
are allowed to go out "at the discretion of the faculty," which
means whenever they want to. If I went to a school like that I
should go out instantly whenever I got a chance. The idea!
Are not girls as much to be trusted as boys? Woman's Rights
comes into that, I guess.

My first trained dress! Ecru camel's-hair, trimmed with
plum silk ruffles, and a bonnet to match, with plum silk ties.
How very elegant I am switching around at the church social,
helping with the ice cream. I recite "The New Church Organ,"
too. Mrs. Everett looks very funny when she hops up on a chair
and turns down the gas that has been squealing for five minutes

excruciatingly and not a man noticed it. Her cloth gaiter shoes
and white stockings are decidedly conspicuous; she has conscientious, or other, scruples against wearing her skirts below
the ankle. You'd think her scruples would be the other way,
she seems a modest person. But one of the kind that are "sot
and the meetin' house couldn't be sotter." I suppose she got
sot in her clothes a long time ago. She dresses to suit herself,
and fashion be hanged. Naturally Mrs. Everett does not express
herself that way—but she thinks it! Her waists (not basques)
are sewed to her skirts at the waistline; plain they are, and her
skirts, likewise, absolutely. Not a ruffle, not a tuck, not a pleat
(box, side, or knife), no overskirt, no polonaise, or redingote,
or princess, no puckers behind, no drapery in front (caught up
with ribbon bows), no puffs, no passementerie, no lace or braid
or sequins, bangles, or buckles, no panels, no fringes or ribbons, no pipings or reveres, no scallops or points. Just one
concession—a row of plain black buttons down the front of
her waist, and she has to have 'em to keep herself shut. She
wears no waterfall, or chignon, or a braided switch around her
head, nor even one of those long false curls over one shoulder
I admire so much when I sit behind it in church. How bare and
undecorated she must feel. Crazy old lady!

There has come a new *Our Talk* with some of Father's
funny poetry:

> Like a ship
>   I'm bound for Williamsport,
> Like a beau
>   I'm round its girls to court.
>
> Daughters of
>   Horatio and Mary,
> Corner of
>   Bennett and Mulberry
>
> Tell Nellie
>   To read and rest her,
> Greet Mary J.
>   And smile on Lester.

A MOOD

Nature is in despair this afternoon,
A lowering heavy cloud rests on the lake
The gusty winds their strangest wailings make
And swaying branches sing their strangest tune.

The storm-wind wildly flies above our heads,
High in the air we hear it crying loud,
It catches at the grey skirts of the cloud
And madly tears them into silver shreds.

The merry sun peeps down between the shreds,
And suddenly in answer smile the waves,
But still the wild wind storming moans and raves
And flies in terror high above our heads.

The sun retreats, the shadows fall again,
And damper grows the gloomy chilling air,
A hopeless sadness settles everywhere,
The brooding cloud bursts weeping into rain.

The startled wind has wearied out its strength
And moaning low is sobbing out its fear,
The shivering twilight leaves the landscape drear
And black night covers all its breadth and length.

My contribution to *Our Talk*, the best I could do. Many's
the storm I've seen coming over the hills and over the Lake.
Father has written a sweet piece called "Glamour." He says:
"Glamour is not real but a kind of idea. The mind, the fancy,
the imagination, makes glamour, makes it on anything. He
who sees glamour is very happy . . . ." He remembers always
the moments when he saw it. It comes when it pleases, to some
and not to others. "When I was a boy I saw it once on a new
Latin dictionary, once on some library books with colored pictures. Sometimes glamour comes over a new place, a new
acquaintance, a face, if you are a young man."

How beautiful! I have scarcely heard of glamour before.
But I have known it. Father says "it is apt to deceive"—oh,
no, Father, never. But he says "in itself it is always the cause
of very deep and unalloyed pleasure. Few things can recuper-

ate, reinvigorate, and inspire as one sight of glamour does."
Oh, glamour, you loveliness; come along and let me have you
whenever I will! No, no, says Glamour; only when I please.

The girl lets me in and seats me in the silent, shaded parlor.
Miss Wilson doesn't come and doesn't come; maybe the girl
forgot to tell her. Here I sit in my best dress wondering what
I shall be. Miss Wilson is so wise, she knows us so well, I trust
her so, that at last I thought I'd better lay it before her ere I
leave her forever.

Nobody seems to be about. Saturday forenoon, perhaps they
have gone to market . . . . It's late for market, though; must
be eleven . . . . I wait and wait. There is a cuckoo clock somewhere; it tells the quarters . . . . Ah, here she comes, just like
herself, slipping in with that silent quickness from the hall. She
goes and pulls up a shade, a spray of sunshine falls into the
room, her lavender princess sweeps the roses of the carpet. She
was taking her bath, she says, and apologizes for keeping me
waiting.

We talk. I do not have to go all the way round the barberry
bush and waste a year or two in preliminary explanations. Miss
Wilson leaps right into the matter from the first, just from her
own gumption. Not that you can possibly imagine my dear Miss
Sophia leaping—but, yes, there is a leap. It is her mind that
does it, not her legs. She knows I am to earn my living after
college. I am going to put Bolton through. That is the way
Father has planned it. They will put me through college, as
I am the oldest, and after that each one will put the next younger
through, and so all can get their education easily.

The point is what shall I *do*. Teach? Most girls do that.
I could; perhaps I shall have to, but don't want to. I don't
know why. Linnie Baldwin's aunt, Miss Fidele Hamilton, is a
woman doctor. But I have no desire to be one . . . . Behind
everything, hiding in a dark closet, is my small hanker to write.
I cannot get the courage to drag it into the conversation . . . .

There! Her leaping thought has discovered that glimmering wish deep down inside me, and she asks me in a matter-of-fact way if I have ever thought of writing as a career. I confess to my aspiration. She says I have a good start, I write very well, as my compositions show.

"Do you intend to marry?" says she.

I am astounded. *Marry*, how do I know? Am I going on a trip to the moon some day? I can hardly reply; it puts my mind in such a whirl. What has marrying to do with it!

"Yes, it does have a great deal to do with it," says she. "I think you would have to choose."

My bewilderment is such that I am quite unfit to carry on the discussion. We leave the point undecided and talk about something else.

"Good morning, Miss Wilson."

All the girls who are finishing this spring have been invited to a dinner at Miss Wilson's, eight of us. We file meekly into her handsome dining room. I was in it once before, when she dissected the sheep's eye, it was not dressed up for company then. Here are beautiful glossy white linen, sparkling goblets, shining silver, a small nosegay at each place, with pin, and a grand bouquet in the middle. Dear Miss Sophia at the head of the table, Miss Jenny in her curls at the foot. At one side, opposite me, sits Miss Annie, pale and withdrawn, in a pearl-grey silk, princess like her sisters. Miss Wilson introduces each of us to her; she bows and says not a word. She eats her dinner silently and afterward vanishes away alone and we see her no more. We go into the parlor and talk.

Miss Sophia presently begins to ask us one after another what we intend to be. Half in fun she is but yet three-quarters in earnest. The girls answer as they feel like it. Jenny says, in her grave way, she will be a missionary, if the way opens. Effie says "a teacher." Sally says "a lady of leisure" (rather pertly, I think). I have been thinking about being a kinder-

garten teacher, because I love children and have had plenty
experience, and can take care of them and amuse them, and
kindergartens are something rather new, and it would be rather
interesting. Mother thinks I could. Besides, writing isn't a
thing I want to blurt out before a roomful of people anyway.
So when my turn comes I say,

"I think I will start a kindergarten."

Miss Wilson is in a kind of little gale of her own, for some
reason. "Yes," says she, "I believe you will, and begin with
one infant."

Mean of her, wasn't it!

VIII

CERTAINLY YOU MUST CRAM

I AM AT MY grandmother's, supposed to be "cramming" for the Cornell examinations. We had reviews at Miss Wilson's, but no examinations. At the brick schoolhouse we finished the book and were through, and began another. I was scorning the very idea; I can imagine Miss Wilson's contempt at stuffing your head one day for the sake of emptying it next day on paper. But Father says: "You'll have to cram. We crammed at Yale. We had biennials! Goody, I guess we did cram!"

I will have to pass in every little old study I ever had and left behind me, even geography. Weak I am in geography, and certainly never expected to have it thrown at me again. It is because I have no certificates of any kind, save Miss Wilson's monthly report cards, which won't do.

Father and I prance down to Watkins expecting me to capture a state scholarship. But, unfortunately, the examiner requires to know what school I have been attending; and, when informed, he comes out with the objection that the Cornell scholarships are only for the pupils of the New York public schools. We argue the point, feeling that four generations in the state give us rights (and Father is counting on the scholarship). But no. The only other applicant is a farmer girl from Kittridge, and she gets it and we come home. Maybe she needs it more than I, for Father will send me anyway. Though how he is going to compass it nobody knows. He is out of a place, and has a nervous breakdown, and can only write his book. The

151

Woodward estate is to be divided among the heirs at last and we are moving to Ithaca in the fall. Mother managed it.

"Mattie, I cannot bear to leave my ancestral home," says Father, snuffing at a sprig of pennyroyal he brought from the woods.

"Pshaw, Edmund, I guess if you saw a good parish in the offing you would leave it quick enough."

"You bet I would," says he. "Do you spy one in the direction of Ithaca?

"We've got to put the children in school," says she.

Mother has taught the children at home a good deal. Bolton needs a real school; Louise, too. So Father goes off and reads the Bible. He intends to educate us; Mother thinks this is the first step. I argue for me to teach district school a year or two and save up my money, especially since I get no scholarship; but they will not have it. Father says to stick to my studies three years longer and I can earn a good salary; now I could command only a pittance. I hush up after that; the "pittance" crushes me. Aunt Anna urges the move and offers to pay our rent—"Then you will at least have a roof over your heads." She says the farm is bad for Mattie, zero in winter and broiling in summer, and no social life whatever.

They send me to stay at Grandma's and do my studying; there is so much going on at home just now. I protest, for they need me, but am told my duty is to *enter Cornell*. I intend to do that, of course; but why this fuss about study? I have learned all these things thoroughly as I went along. Mother says I will get rusty and that I haven't looked at my German in a year. Aunt Lida says, "Nellie, I expect they'll examine you in the primer. Are you sure you know your primer: 'the-sun-is-up-the-sun-has-left-his-bed'?"

Father declares I must bone right down and *cram*.

"You'd better study up your German," says Mother.

"Oh, well, yes; I will go over the verbs. I suppose I'd better."

"French irregular verbs, too," says she.

"Oh, Mother, I know my French verbs. Miss Wilson hammered them into us day after day, and week after week, and month after month, and year after year, and century after century. I *know* 'em!"

Mother laughs. "Maybe you do," says she.

The Burtons are in the little-house. Ernest and I have a tournament of checkers on; we play every day after I get my cramming done. I have to pass entrance and first-year examinations both, as I am entering sophomore.

I ask Jim MacNeal if I will be obliged in the examination to remember the numbers of the geometry theorems. Miss Wilson had us learn the theorems by number and asked us for them that way in recitation. It is easy to learn them, but they slip away afterward. Jim is very superior and informing, because he has graduated at Cornell. "When you once get to Cornell," he says, impressively, "you will know that they do not stand for *that* sort of thing." Oh, my!

Mr. Trumbull detains me after church to talk about my going to Cornell. He seems uncommon solemn, and he is usually so pleasant.

Says he, "When you get to college the professors will tell you one thing and the Bible will tell you another. Remember that what the Bible says is the truth."

Miss Beam hopes she can make my college "gowns" for me. But I'm making one or two for myself.

We are settled on Tioga Street, with a peach tree in the side yard and a pump and a vegetable garden in the back, and a grassplot as big as a door mat in front. The furniture, disposed in the parlor and sitting room, makes us feel at home, mirror in the sitting room as usual. The stoves are up, and a pipe through the floor to a drum in my room to keep me warm in winter—although at present it is terrifically hot. Hannah comes with us; and lucky she does, for no girl looms in sight. Mother is in Homer.

Father looks for a girl, does not find any, comes back and tacks down carpets, takes care of children, goes singing around the house. He carols old Yale songs with Latin to them and anon drops into "Yankee Doodle." The first Sunday he marches us all to church. We file in conspicuously, me at the head—Nellie, Bolton, Louise, Eddie, Gertrude. Even Gertrude; he would have it. I believe he would have suggested Zaidee and Hattie if he had dared. He shows us into the pew looking as proud as Cuffy. A lady behind us leans over and whispers to me, "Are all these *your* children?" Idiot!

Mrs. Estey and the minister's wife call to see us. Our next-door neighbor, Mrs. Thompson, will mend and sew for us if we want her to, a white-haired woman, awfully kind, always running over. She talks temperance every minute day and night because her husband died of drink.

I go with Bolton to buy him a school suit, and get a good one, brown check, that ought to last him two years. I stand the boys up in the parlor and give them a lesson in deportment:

"Mr. Smith, may I introduce Mr. Jones? . . . . Go ahead, Eddie. Bow. Say something, 'Mr. Jones' will do . . . . Oh don't be so goggle-eyed! You needn't be embarrassed, it's nothing to be introduced."

" 'Tis, too, embarrassing to be introduced to your own brother," says Eddie.

"I'm not your brother, sir. I don't know you, sir. My name is Jones, not Brown."

"Stop fooling. Do you know how to enter and exit a room?"

"Just come in, don't you, and go out?"

"Well, do you *burst* in or *enter?*"

"Oh, I always en-ter," says Bolton, elegantly.

"Do it," say I. I turn them into the hall and shut the door. "Don't ever come into a room without rapping," I call to them. "Why not?" shouts Bolton. He knocks on the door so low I can hardly hear.

"Come in."

They come in slowly and gravely, measuring their steps, and advance to the middle of the parlor.

"Very good. Now go out."

They wheel around and pace solemnly to the door.

"Hold on."

"What's the matter? We're not bursting."

"No, but you are presenting your back to the company. You have to turn around and go through the door backward, with your face to me."

"Oh, pshaw!" says Bolton. "I never heard of such a thing."

"Miss Wilson does. It's polite. You don't know anything about society manners. Brought up on a farm, how should you?"

"I shan't do it. Don't you do it, Eddie. If you want to exit a room hind foremost, you can do it for all of me. I've got a perfect right to go with my face in front of me."

"I guess that's a lady's rule," says Eddie, pleasantly.

The school begins. Everybody starts in, all different grades, of course. I do hope Bolton will get a good arithmetic teacher; he hates it and cannot learn it, and Mother has had quite a time, even Mother, who teaches better than anybody else.

Father takes us to Cascadilla and Fall Creek gorges, and to the flume, and to the paper mill. There is a glass works we are going to see. The walk through the marsh at the corner of the Lake is lovely; we take it Sunday afternoon. And there is a Buttermilk Falls somewhere we haven't been to yet.

At last a girl! And Hannah has gone back to the Lake Road. She was glad to be relieved, poor thing. I caught her crying once from sheer weariness, hidden in a bedroom; but she would stick by until we got somebody, once she set her hand to it.

Lizzie Mulvahill, if you please, is as big as a barrel but not nearly so neat, strong as a horse, good-natured enough: "I'll bake pancakes for the childers, su-u-r-re," says she. She gets mad at me because I give her some particular directions about making the bread. "I'll not be bossed by a little chit of a gur-rl like you!" says she. But she has to, as Mother is in Homer.

If I had a few more inches on top of me and did not look so like a twelve-year-old it would help—and my hair tied behind in a bunch. I did not realize it would be at this awkward length just at the time I entered college and wanted to look particularly grown-up or I would not have had it shingled in Williamsport. The barber did not want to cut it, when it was down and spread out. He asked if my folks were willing I should have it cut. I wrote them. Uncle thinks all children should wear short hair, and his do. I wanted to have mine cut so it would grow out curly, which it did not, only a wave like Mother's. They did not answer about the hair. Silence gives consent, thought I, and went and did it. Then when I came home for vacation they were sorry. "The glory of a woman is her long hair," said Father. But they were nice about it.

I grab my father in the upstairs hall and pull him into my room.

"See here, Father, the examinations begin tomorrow— *tomorrow!* Here it is in the catalogue . . . ."

"I guess you can take them whenever you want to," he says. "I don't see how you can take them now. You are needed at home."

"But here it is in the catalogue." (I show him.) "September 11, Monday, Entrance examinations, September 12, Tuesday, Entrance examinations continued . . . ."

He takes the catalogue and reads it earnestly. It is unmistakable. We look at each other, startled. We don't know what to do. We cannot go against plain print, down in a book—the rule. But how *can* I attend college just now. Mother away, the children to be seen to, the older ones have begun school, but Zaidee and Hattie must be taken care of. Lizzie is not capable of running the house without looking after; she would leave the broom on the front steps and wash the dishes with the dust rag, likely, if I were not here. "Why, Father, how can I take them tomorrow!" He gives another swift look at the catalogue. Something flows into him suddenly like wine in the veins; he straightens up.

"I guess you'll have to, Pussy," he says. "I'll go with you. Let's see what you have to pass." We droop over the fateful page.

"All students unless provided with certificates and diplomas [that's me] must pass entrance examinations in Geography, political and physical; English Grammar, including Orthography and Syntax; Arithmetic, including the Metric System [I never had it. "It's easy," says Father, "all tens."]; Physiology, Plane Geometry, Algebra through Quadratic Equations."

"Six," says Father, "and several of them elementary."

"There is more below." I run my finger down.

"For the course in Science, Science and Letters, Mathematics and Chemistry and Physics [I shall take either Science and Letters or], Mathematics; French Grammar and translation *or* German ditto [I shall take both of these because I have had a year of German so that I may enter sophomore]; Algebra *entire* ('any of the larger ones'); Solid Geometry; Trigonometry, plane and spherical." That makes six more. Well, a dozen examinations. We'd better get at it.

Next morning early Father and I trail cross-lots up the hill through the cemetery and the sumach patch and the fields below the University buildings and present ourselves according to directions at the office of the Registrar. What a dear, kind old gentleman is Dr. Wilson, his tie rather crooked, his white hair rather long and untended. I like him. He talks in a swallowed, chopped manner and says all kinds of things, rapidly; but his eyes are gentle, he tries to tell you what you want to know. We inform him that I am to enter for the second year, as I am prepared for it. He waves it away and clips and rumbles on about such a thing not being possible because of this and that, to our bewilderment. We have understood for a

year that I am to enter sophomore. Anyway, the first thing is
to take the first examination, and the hour, eight o'clock, is
about to strike.

Father has found out what room it is and hustles me to it.
Physiology. He puts me in at the door, wishes me luck, and
goes off to read in the library. I have had Steele's *Fourteen
Weeks* in preparation for just this. I spread out my paper con-
fidently. Question 1, "What first happens to milk when taken
into the stomach?" My goodness! We did not have a thing
about what happens to milk in stomachs—only How many
bones in the human body? Answer: Two hundred and six
besides thirty-two teeth, and Miss Wilson dissected a sheep's
eye for us in her dining room. Well, well . . . . Oh, I know.
I haven't seen nursing babies puke all over themselves for
nothing. It curdles. That's one right anyway.

Father is in the hall waiting for me when I come out. "How
did you do?" says he. "Oh, it wasn't hard. Now what next?"
He knows, and conducts me to English Grammar, including
Orthography. We laugh at that, for me who always spelt the
school down. Grammar I've had, of every description, since
I was knee-high to a grasshopper, including diagramming (something like tit, tat, toe) and False Syntax—"Circumstances alters
cases—what rule is violated."

When Grammar including Orthography is over, it is noon.
Father comes and gets me. There is a Quaker girl taking the
examinations, too; and her mother in plain gray silk and a
white lawn bonnet comes for her at the door. By this time we
all nod and smile; I presume tomorrow, if she keeps on, we
shall tell each other our life histories.

We leave the buildings by the back and scramble down the
hill and into the sumachs, already turning scarlet. Suddenly—
"Why, I have to be back for the next examination at *one*. There
won't be time to go clear home and eat my dinner . . . . I'll go
without dinner. I *have* to be there at one."

Father grabs out his watch. He looks at me in astonishment.

"You won't have time," says he. Then that wine flows into him; he stiffens:

"Here, you sit down under the bushes and rest you," says he, "I'll go get you something to eat." He is off, running down the path, before I can wink.

I sink down gratefully; I lie down flat, and the sumach branches stir idly around me. Oh me, I am tired. How hot it is! I had not realized . . . . Oh me, how this boil on my chin hurts. We poulticed it at home with bread-and-milk. But you can't go to examinations with a poultice on your chin—the idea! How *hot* it is! *Ah-tchoo-oo*, plenty of hay fever I have . . . . *ah-tchoo-oo*, I must get up out of this grass . . . .

"Why, Father, how quick you've been!" He comes bounding up with bundles in his hands.

"I only went to the corner grocery. I've brought you crackers, and cheese, and raisins, and" (rapidly undoing them) "sardines . . . ." I cannot bear sardines, but I do not tell Father that. He opens the tin with his jackknife and eats them with relish. We have to scurry, our eye on the watch, McGraw tower informs us of the quarters. Finished, we jump up and race the hill.

"Father, are you puffing!"

"*Puffing*—you go to grass. I am a mountain climber. I'll beat you."

I love to run, if necessary. "You haven't much to carry," they always say. Oh, plenty, ninety-six pounds.

Two more examinations this afternoon, Father escorting me and doing the library between. We finish and saunter away down the path—hot, hot, how hot it is! Father swoops into the meat market and buys a grand beefsteak, and we have it for supper. "You must be *fed*," says he.

Next day the same, except we carry a lunch and eat it outside in the lee of McGraw where we find a shade. Same heat as ever. Same hurting boil. "Oh, by doze, I sdeeze ad bloze"— which is our hay-fever anthem. I'll tell you the rest of it when

I have time. When night comes we have another elegant steak for supper. Lizzie springs to and broils it to perfection, seeming to realize the situation—I must be fed. That is a charming Quaker lady. Today we spoke.

The sun has blazed all day; the heat is terrific. I can't stand heat, especially late-summer heat; I am nearly dead. Examinations keep coming like a spring freshet. The German I cannot take, for it is set at the same time as the French. We talk with Dr. Wilson about it. He says it is either *or*, and I should not take German *if* I take French; it is not required. But I am going to enter second year. I am prepared in the German; I want to take the examination and "pass it up." Now. "She wants to enter second year," says Father. Dr. Wilson starts off again. He says, as near as we can understand his rapid mumble, that I cannot enter second year; it is not allowed; I cannot take the German examination—it comes at the same time as the French. And more. Do I wish to substitute it for French? I can do that—either *or*, I am not required to pass both.

No! (But I cannot possibly *shout* it to him.) "No, sir, I wish to pass my French *anyway*; but I want to pass German, *too*, as I am entering sophomore." He gives me a long sort of a look. Father's face seems quizzical; he stands one side and glances first at the Registrar then at me. I feel he will support me to the bitter end.

"How *can* you take the German when it comes at the same hour as the French?" Dr. Wilson leans kindly toward me over the table, his deep-set eyes mild behind his glasses.

"Yes, how can I? That's just it. Couldn't I take a special examination in German, somehow? I'll have to, won't I, in order to enter sophomore?"

He leans back; he seats himself again in his armchair. He starts rumbling rapidly, and we listen close. He seems to say it could (or it couldn't) be arranged. He seems to intimate that I'd better go along and take the French anyhow. We hear something about it's not being required and—just as we go out the door—that it is not possible for me to enter sophomore.

"I understood him to say the distinctions between classes, freshman and sophomore, etc., are not recognized at Cornell," says Father.

"Yes, I read that in the catalogue," say I.

"Then why did you use the term sophomore," says he. "I presume that is all that is the matter. Better say 'second year' next time."

"Oh, Father, we've said 'second year' over and over; it means the same!" I am so sticky-hot and tired. Dr. Wilson's obstinacy is too provoking. Here I have been planning all the past year, and having all the required first-year work with Miss Wilson; and she has known all about it, and Father has, and I have. And I am fully prepared to begin at the second year. Now to have Dr. Wilson act this way—it is too bad! Of course he will have to give in, because I *am* prepared; he can't get around that. And Father says I'd better not attend classes until he has agreed to it, for he is not going to have me start in as a freshman. Three years I am to do it in, as arranged, not four.

I slip into the library and find Father, in an alcove, placidly reading. He looks up quickly, "How early you finished. I hadn't thought of coming for you yet. How did you do?"

"Failed," I whisper, pursing up my lips to keep them steady.

"What!" says he, nearly bounding out of his chair.

So then I draw him into the deeper part of the alcove where we can talk better, and tell him. The heat got the better of me. It seemed to me I could think of nothing but how my boil hurt, and how itchy were my nose and eyes with hay fever, how my throat was burning. It was trigonometry with those logarithms to remember, the last examination on the last afternoon. I looked at the paper and read down the list of questions. They meant no more to me than if they were Greek. I pounded myself, stuck pins into myself (mentally), and said "Come, come,

Nellie, this will not do." No use. I had a gleam of sense and did the first problem quick while it lasted. After that no more. I was simply imbecile. I could not have repeated the multiplication table, or added two and two, and me with mathematics my forte! Suddenly the heat surged over me, an intolerable wave in that cramped, glaring, ugly, upstairs classroom like a torture chamber. I rose and handed in my paper and went to find my father.

"It is the eleventh examination in three days . . . . ; and if he'd let me take the German 'twould be twelve . . . ."

"Here," says my father in a low quick voice, "you sit and read awhile and rest you before we go home. It's cool here." He goes and brings me Carlyle's *French Revolution* from the shelves and begins to read again himself.

So I sit here, spent, in the library. It is still, nearly empty. Whoever is here is reading; the books have it all to themselves. So many books, so quiet in their places. Up and down the long high room—so many books. A middle space runs like a broad hall, with shelved alcoves giving into it on each side. Each alcove, lined with its books, has a tall window, a table and a chair, and a tiny iron gallery above, got to by a toy iron stairway; and the shelves go on up. The hall is beautiful. It comes into my being, a possession, I shall never lose it. Banners reach out from the sides, high up, and hang glowingly in the central space. They catch me up, one after the other, bright their floating color, yet soft in the shaded air. They catch me up and carry my heart in a secret dance, up and down, up and down.

After awhile we must go home. "Do you suppose failing in trigonometry will prevent me entering sophomore?" I whisper.

"*Second year*," says Father, correctingly; "we'll have to see the Registrar about that."

How big the French bed is in this little (but cozy) room.

College women of the 'eighties

Its glossy chestnut-colored mahogany rises up at head and foot and rolls over and makes a handsome frame for Mother and the baby. Mother's hair waves against the pillow; her eyes are blue, large; her dimple shows. Dear Mother! How I will take care of you. The baby sleeps, smelling of warm flannel and sweetness.

The bedroom is off the sitting room and easily kept warm. We've fitted it up for Mother with the big bed and the Tomb of the Capulets and the marble-topped commode, and the carpet is like the sitting room. A leafy bush looks in at the window, next Mrs. Thompson's.

We are gathered around, discussing what we shall name the baby. We do this every evening after supper regularly. I have decided on Elizabeth—and call her Bessie. I have a great deal to say about it and go on talking, saying it. The rest interrupt with their ideas; and Mother lies there with her dimple, and listens. I do get to the end finally. I run down and stop. There is silence in heaven, as the Bible says. Then Mother, quietly:

"I thought I would call her 'Agnes'," says she. "It means a little lamb, you know."

There is a good nurse, praise be, Mrs. Wiley from just around the corner. Mrs. Thompson buzzes in and out by the back door, everlastingly kind and obliging. We don't let her into Mother's room if we can help it; she talks so much . . . . Poor old barrelly Mulvahill comes up to the scratch nobly. Occasional tempers; but she's got over not being bossed by me. "The childers" get what is coming to them as far as her lights go.

Father and I go up the hill frequently to see Dr. Wilson about my entering second year. He says I can be "conditioned" in the trigonometry—something I never heard of before—and pass it up in December.

"And so I can enter second year, now, just the same as though I had not failed?"

He says no. I cannot enter second year, it is not according to the regulations. Especially if I have a condition.

"But what am I going to do? I am fully prepared for the soph . . . . second-year work. I can't enter freshman?"

"She is *prepared* for second-year work. She did her first-year work last year, at her preparatory school," says Father, politely.

I don't think Dr. Wilson knows I am not attending classes. I suppose he thinks I am just pegging along as a freshman, hoping for the best. We cannot make him see it right. I can't begin college anyway till Mother's up. Meantime we lay siege to the Registrar and expect after a while to get the matter straightened out. He says so many things—and we understand so few of them.

Today is my special examination in German. I go up the hill and hunt out Professor Elgar's house on the campus. The girl lets me in. She takes me to the study. Professor Elgar is seated at his desk, tightly buttoned up in his clothes. He remains seated, looking glum. I feel like a lost child, for I read no welcome or genial consideration in that cold round face, in those pop-eyes. There is an explanation between us that I am to have a special examination in German. I tell him as patiently as I can that I am entering as a second-year student and that is the reason I am taking examinations in two modern languages — only one being required. (I remain standing.)

"Why are you entering late—what have you been doing all these weeks since term began?" very brusque.

Now I've had about enough of this. Bother this examination! I am distinctly nettled.

"Taking care of children," I reply, with hauteur.

Professor Elgar is flabbergasted. He looks helpless, he looks different. Without a word he hands me paper and questions from the desk, motions me to sit down, and buries himself behind a book. I never saw a person so completely buried behind a book in my life.

I am alone upstairs in the study sitting on the floor. Getting my German lesson in *Die Piccolomini*. I am backed against Father's big black *Commentaries* in a row behind me, my feet out before me; the carpet, red-and-black in a small pattern, stretches smooth and flat off to the door. It is my first day's study, I began classes this morning, six weeks late, and all in the middle of things. I had astronomy; they are calculating eclipses, but that is only geometry. I took my first notes, Dr. Wilder's lecture in zoölogy, I never took notes before, didn't know how, felt at a loss—but I shall soon learn it.

But this German—so hard. We never had such long lessons at Miss Wilson's. This is my first book translating, too. And I had my German over a year ago, Mother *said* I would be rusty.

I labor and labor. Nearly every word I have to look up, tedious, and it slows me up so. I cannot haul these stubborn lines around into English sense. I work and work. *Die Piccolomini* is the hardest reading I ever struck. The page before me gives me the shivers; it is a hieroglyph; I shall never understand it, never! I plod on, more looking up, more ingenuity about outlandish phrases. Ingenuity wasted, there is too much of this . . . . why, I cannot possibly get over the whole assignment this afternoon at the rate I am going! And what about the other lessons I have to get? I struggle, and time goes by.

Suddenly a dark wing shuts down upon me; a new and somber knowledge comes to me. I shall never have time in any afternoon to learn such lessons as this, college work is different from school work. *I have not the brains for it.* I have bit off more than I can chew. A keen discerning despair possesses me. I know it now; here is a thing I cannot do . . . . *I never thought there was such a thing.* But now I know . . . . How still the house is. I sink into myself against the books and drop *Piccolomini* on the floor.

Thus far I have seen myself, in the Mirror of Time, a child, and have spoken with frank garrulity, lived again with you the trifling days that were the whole round of existence.

Now the child first encounters the Insurmountable Obstacle. Her saucy banner—"The best is good enough for her!"—and she with it, are prone in the dust of first defeat. On the floor of her father's study, supported by his tall, black-covered, gold-lettered Commentaries, *she is suddenly a child no more . . . .*

Now I cannot let you in so guilelessly; for I am become grown-up, self-conscious. If there is to be more—and indeed this moment of fathomless despair was not the end, for she rose, flaunted again her gonfalon, and graduated in three years—*if there is to be more it must be in the mode of maturity. You shall find me as accurate as ever, and I trust as sincere, although the completely adult tongue treacherously seeks the cheek while I say it; but the mode is different. This Book is closed and over the page is a new one.*

Part Two

TRANSPLANTED TO CALIFORNIA

O. L. E.

IN GRATITUDE

IX

WE GO

* * * * * * * * * * * This row of
stars—I have asked the printer to count them and put in just
twelve—represents now a lapse of twelve years. You can imagine
me at the third star graduating from Cornell. By this time the
family was really flowering out and we were terrifically poor.
Not that we minded, but it had to be dealt with. So, when I
was chosen to be one of six student speakers to give Orations
in Library Hall at my Commencement, I had to flax around to
get the proper costume for the platform. Father was found to
be impossibly idealistic; said he had no money to buy me a
new dress, and advised me earnestly to "graduate in calico"
and thus (he averred) "go down in history" as a heroine. But
Mother came quietly forward and gave me her beautiful glistening grey silk which had been her one really dress-up dress for
many years, and it was made over for me by a dressmaker.
Father was regretful at this; he tenderly fingered the silk.
"After you have 'spoken your piece' and graduated in it, I want
you to have it put back," he said, "just as it was before, to fit
your mother again. I always liked her to have this dress for
nice."

Be that as it may, when the time came, I stood up in the
demure grey silk (but with that glisten to it), secure and self-
possessed. I was five feet tall and weighed ninety pounds; a
jacqueminot rose, deep red, was under my chin; my buttoned
shoes were French kid and new, size two and a half; my hair

was done up on the top of my head in a heavy coil; and I
delivered to an astonished audience a message right from
the shoulder on "Hand-Workers and Head-Workers: A Social
Study." Instancing the triumphs of the machine age, I told them
that we had "a glorious inheritance." But "look again at the
page," and, when they had looked and "read between the lines,"
they found that for all our "Corliss engines and Great Easterns"
we had been turning *men* into machines to tend our inventions.
And this, said I (at some length, passionately), would never do.
College people ("head-workers") must not go on "rounding out
and perfecting themselves" in scholarly leisure and seclusion
while "hand-workers" wore out their days "feeding buttons into
a cylinder or sharpening the points of pins." (I knew so much
about it because I had worked for six weeks the previous summer in the Ithaca button factory, Father delightedly egging me
on, sewing white pearl buttons on to cards for so much a gross,
and had earned thus my first money, besides getting the labor
problem early under my skin.) It was a good long oration. The
dignitaries of the University and the five other student speakers
sat on the platform behind me. The audience in front of me
crowded the hall, my family there too, and even Aunt Anna,
who had come from Hartford to see me graduate.

In conclusion the speech declared that hand-workers were
"not *masses* but *men,* not *factors* but *souls*" and each one had a
birthright, "a birthright which is not the right to have or the
right to get, but a nobler privilege still, *the right to be!*" Tumultuous applause! I was ahead of my time, and the audience
couldn't get over it. I daresay I looked very juvenile, a sort of
a child wonder, I suppose. It is said that for some time afterward I was known to the local public as "that girl that graduated!" And wasn't Father proud? "Why, Nellie," he cried,
with admiring looks, "I didn't know you had it in you!"

Along somewhere in those twelve stars I was married and
set up housekeeping with Leslie, a teacher of English at Cornell.
He did not aim to teach English; he had trained for economics,

but the English instructorship offered and he took it because then we could be married instead of dangling along engaged indefinitely. After a while, in another star, we had a baby; named him Louis for Robert Louis Stevenson, who was at the time our literary love and had just put out *A Child's Garden of Verses*. My husband studied for his Doctorate and I corrected the English themes of his classes to give him more time. He wrote his thesis, on the "Tariff Controversy in the United States," and in due course was awarded his Ph.D. Now, being ready, he naturally desired to begin teaching his own subject; and in the eleventh and twelfth stars we were putting out feelers for positions in economics and building air castles about our next move. Our special joke was, "If nothing else turns up, let's go to California," as that was the most unlikely spot we could think of short of the moon.

On a day in the month of March 1891, I was broiling a thick juicy porterhouse steak (such as we used to have) over the glowing hard-coal fire in the kitchen range. I turned and turned the long-handled wire cage which held the fragrant, browning slab. I was supposed to have a hired girl, but the ninth one for that year had gone (she tippled from the brandy bottle), and her successor had not yet been achieved; so, flushed but not unhappy, I stood cooking our dinner. Leslie appeared. He said, "How would you like to go to California?" The joke, of course. I attended to my broiling, turned out the steak on a hot platter, peppered it, salted it, buttered it. He waved a paper at me which looked like a telegram. Before I tasted my steak the whole of my life was changed, and the lives of my children and of theirs, and of all the persons we were to touch in the half-century to come. The telegram was from David Starr Jordan, President of Indiana University, whose message said: he had been named president of the new university in California founded and endowed by Leland Stanford; he would require a secretary; would Leslie care to come on to Bloomington at once and take the post and accompany him in June to California?

You could have knocked me over with a feather, though I cannot see what good it would have done. Would he! But we had to find out about salary, sum not mentioned in telegram; the answer to our inquiring dispatch seemed reasonable (we should have gone anyway, if merely gratis); we accepted and Leslie became thus the first man on Stanford's payroll. Dr. Jordan was in active service at Indiana University until the end of the college year; it seems not to have occurred to him to claim two salaries in the meantime.

Leslie departed as soon as he could disentangle himself from his engagements and collect his shirts and collars. He left me to sell the no-account furniture and box and ship the rest, to visit my relations and his, and to meet him in June and proceed with the party to Palo Alto—the name of Senator Stanford's horse ranch and estate, not of the town celebrated as the home of our ex-President, for there was no such town then in existence. Our California destination would be Menlo Park, and there our letters would be addressed.

Arriving at Bloomington, Leslie found a prodigious mail, dating from the moment the public knew of Dr. Jordan's appointment as president of the new university. Mr. Stanford had suggested fifteen as about the size of the prospective faculty, enough for the modest number of students he was expecting; but hundreds of teachers wrote in, desiring a place on the faculty list. Students from everywhere sent inquiries and applications, hoping to be found worthy—either as prepared or unprepared, for this university was rumored to teach everything, especially things you could make your living at, and its scope would be "from the kindergarten up." Besides, it was in *California*. The lure was not diminished by any word of the new president. Dr. Jordan had caught fire instantly, like a pitch-pine kindling—he appointed a professor the very day he accepted his own position—and nothing could put him out. He had a great body and a warm rich nature; the size, the novelty, the human implications of the work inspired and challenged

him; he never rested, but carried his enthusiasm and his buoyant plans and forecasts about, lighting up the population from
his torch.

I remained in Ithaca for some weeks and Louise was there
to help me. We price-tagged the belongings and the neighbors
came in and bought them. We got Bool's men to box and freight
what we were taking. We wrapped and boxed the books; we
made traveling clothes for Louis and for me, and sent for the
doctor to come and vaccinate us. We sold the canned fruit put
up in new Mason jars which I hated to part with, and a ten-
gallon crock of washing fluid, crock and all. We sold the dipper
for five cents, though worth ten I am sure, and the stove shovel
for a two-cent copper. I was glad to be rid of the ugly bedroom
set, the bed with that high towering headboard which I always
thought was going to fall over on me in the night. I expected
some enchanting sort of article to take its place when we got to
California. And, finally, after paying the landlord sixty dollars
more than we had received the worth of—our lease running to
August—we abandoned the house and Ithaca, and went to
Burdett.

Father was preaching there, and the three younger girls were
at home going to school. Bolton had graduated from Syracuse
University, in the art department, and was teaching. Louise
also had just finished her art course there. Edmund had lived
with us in Ithaca, gone through Cornell and graduated, and was
teaching. Gertrude was being trained in Philadelphia as a kin-
dergartner, Aunt Anna paying her expenses. She was the only
one of Father's eight children who did not go through college.
She begged off: arithmetic stumped her, languages bored her;
people, not books, interested her; she wished to teach a kindergarten. She had a singing voice of a pure contralto quality and
she played the piano.

Our amazing prospects, our astounding luck, the romance
of the adventure before us, threw my appreciative family into
a whirl of excitement. Mother, it seems, knew all about the

Leland Stanford Junior University from reading the papers. She told us of the quadrangle and the arcades. She said the sandstone columns supporting the arches were carved, each one with a different design; the pavement of the cloisters was to be of marble set in squares of alternate colors. The architecture was Spanish, suitable to a country full of Spanish Missions. Cousin Henry had traveled in California; he wrote extensive directions about the journey, and said we must on no account "go tourist." Los Angeles was in the public eye, "City of the Angels"; *Scribners Magazine* ran an illustrated article about it. Father recited bits of San Francisco history—the gold seekers particularly intrigued him—and his impulsive bursts made history and myth and the past and the future come alive.

Chunks of information and feathers of fancy came in the Bloomington letters: Dr. Jordan says this, Dr. Jordan says that. We learned that the rose vines grew forty feet high and reached the housetops. We heard of the white-fenced paddocks of the racing horses which were bred and trained on the Senator's ranch; and that one great horse hero, now dead, was honored there by a formal grave with monument and inscription. "Paddock" and "ranch" were delightfully exotic in our ears; we imagined—thinking of Lanier—the live oak drooping over this strange tomb. There were great estates, Dr. Jordan said, close by the University property, belonging to millionaires. The mansions were grand and aristocratically secluded among gardens and groves—something like the Vale of Cashmere or the Gardens of Damascus, we inferred. A good neighborhood to settle in; we foresaw these gentle millionaires coming through the turnstiles which (probably) separated their grounds from ours to welcome us and get acquainted. The endowment was twenty million, wealth that would have gone to the idolized son. There would be a series of great quadrangles, besides the one already up, with stone buildings, tile-roofed, to house the departments; the courts were to be gardened, the campus landscaped. Stone cottages with tile roofs would be erected on the

campus for faculty people, *the rent nominal*. The Founders
overflowed with generous plans.

Fed thus day by day—it was spring, and Burdett and the
glens and the Lake were lovely—the household developed a
sort of whipped-cream mentality. We went around mooning.
We lisped in numbers, for the numbers came. Glamour en-
thralled us. Louis and I, soon to depart for this land of dream,
were enshrined in wonder and walked among our kin as gods.
But when in June the time came to go, kisses were kissed and
good-byes were said, and we climbed into the democrat at last
with the trunk in behind; when Father gathered the reins and
said "giddap" and the horse began to step off toward Watkins
and the railroad, that was parting. Then my mother—so Aunt
Lida told me afterward—went back into her house, soberly,
and said, "I don't suppose I shall ever see Nellie again."

Late in June the Stanford party left Bloomington. Dr. and
Mrs. Jordan, with Mrs. Jordan's three-year-old boy and her
twelve-year-old stepdaughter Edith, were accompanied by Professor Richardson (chemistry) with his wife and mother, and by
a young man going along to enter the University, Albert Fletcher.
They proceeded to St. Louis. Leslie went to Indianapolis to
collect Louis and me, whom he found awaiting him on the station platform. We also went to St. Louis, and from there all
journeyed on together.

The train was hot; there were cinders and old-fashioned
smells. Young Elliott and young Jordan got heartily bored with
each other in the irritating confines of the aisle. As we came to
Kansas I began to think about Burdett; I thought about Burdett
all across the state of Kansas, which took us eighteen hours. We
kept stopping for half a day or overnight; I have forgotten why.
In Colorado, at Pueblo, we disembarked for six hours. Dr.
Jordan arranged for a drive off into a waste place where a
real-estate firm had laid out and left to simmer the ground plan
of a city. Streets, parks, lampposts, tall stakes at the street

corners and little white stakes at the corners of the lots, everything complete on the grey plain, and not a building in sight.
No human beings either, except our little group and Dr. Jordan
enthusiastically picking small desert flowers and showing them
to us between his thumb and forefinger, telling us their names
and how many petals they had. Here we saw the prairie dogs.
They sat up on their haunches at the mouths of their holes and
stared at us. Here we saw cactus. Dr. Jordan told us its names.

We spent a night in Leadville, with mining camps and machinery on the slopes around. Ten million dollars' worth of
silver mined here every year, Dr. Jordan said. We thought it
a scrubby little Western town, but did not disdain expanding
ourselves and tingling with its crystalline air. We looked
around with delight at the snowy mountains rimming it and
up into the pure blue of its sky.

We climbed the Rockies. We went over the watershed. Dr.
Jordan showed us exactly where the drop of water could split,
one half to flow into the Atlantic and the other half into the
Pacific. We passed through the Royal Gorge, and found it lonesome, wild, barren, and tremendously useless. It glared in the
sun. We came to Utah and the Great American Desert. This,
I said, is the worst yet. "I don't believe," I said, "there is a
more desolate spot on earth." Dr. Jordan said, "There isn't."
In the night I lifted my berth curtain a little and peeked out. It
was full moon, which did not help my spirits at all, and grey,
pale, interminable landscapes, devoid of life, stretched off to
nothing. At the moment, the thought of our project was ice
cold and I wished I was home. Mother, crossing the continent
a few years later, had a different reaction. Knowing she was
bound for California, the land of perpetual sunshine, she joy-
ously threw her rubbers out of the train window in Nevada.

Green River, an oasis, held us for twenty-four hours. It had
a meek grass plot, a fountain turned on when the train went
through, three trees, a water tank, a hotel. We spent the day
in retirement, sat in our rooms with the shades drawn and

deliquesced in negligee. At evening the heat abated. The men plowed through the sand to the river for a swim but found the current too swift. We put on our clothes and went outdoors to breathe the winey air and experience with amazement the great globed stars spangling the hollow sky. We even put up our hands to gather some.

After Green River we climbed the Sierras, twisted down the further side from Truckee through snowsheds, and grumbled at their hiding the view. We could not account for the snow-sheds, but Dr. Jordan explained. At Dutch Flat we came out among the gentler ranges, and soon began to see the bare and molded foothills. In some places they lay crowded softly together beneath a plushy fawn mantle of dry grass in a way that reminded one of gigantic and recumbent feminine shapes; twin breasts smoothly mounding up, a great thigh curved, a crouched form melting into geography with long undulations. Something primeval.

At Auburn, where the earth is red, we eased down toward sea level. We came into the spreading valleys of the San Joaquin and the Sacramento, wide and flat out to the distant violet hills. We saw green of irrigation, the turquoise green of alfalfa, the tawny yellow of wheat fields at harvest, apricot and peach orchards weighted down with ripening fruit, figs purpling on the trees, cheerful little frame houses, brightly painted, in gardens of roses, pepper trees, the gay geranium, the blowsy, generous petunia, oleanders busheling with rosy bloom. Or, often, the little houses stood pridefully in the middle of their spacious orchards, the laden and propped-up boughs brushing their windows and doorsteps. It seemed a foreign land.

We came to Benicia. A ferry swallowed our train in sections and carried us across miles of salt water, *the salt of the Pacific*. We looked up at the cliffs of Benicia, and Mrs. Jordan told me there was an excellent girls' school there and Edith might be sent to it. We came to Oakland; another ferry; but now we sat upon the upper deck, forward, and thus was enchantingly revealed to us The Bay. I cried, "I don't believe there is a more beautiful water on earth!" Dr. Jordan said, "There isn't." The sparkling sunlight played over the waves in points and splinters, in flitters of dancing planes. The lovely blue harbor wound out among its capes and islands to the Golden Gate. We saw the Golden Gate. The dark sculptured Marin Hills brooded on the further shore. Shipping rode the water, shipping lay at the wharves. Slowly the ferryboat moved forward. Mistily at first, then clear and frank, the City's chequered pattern rose away to the sky. We watched it, "like a tall gold cliff arise out of the sea's wind-splintered gold . . . . blown by a wind, broken against a hill."

An attentive gentleman met us at the Southern Pacific station, Third and Townsend streets, Mr. Herbert Nash, secretary and major-domo in the Stanford household and former tutor of the boy Leland Stanford, Jr. He conducted us down the Peninsula on the train to Menlo Park, and there we found Mr. Stanford himself waiting to welcome us. The portly, quiet man greeted us all with dignity and graciousness, and noticed the little boys, saying that the long trip was hard on children. Escondite Cottage, he said, had been prepared, and he hoped Dr. and Mrs. Jordan would find it comfortable. A few cordial words, a few minutes' standing together on the station platform, and he bade us good-bye, entered his carriage, and was driven away. He, with Mrs. Stanford, he said, would see us again very soon. We were weary travelers; the trip had taken ten days in all; it was restful and encouraging to be thus thoughtfully received and so quickly put at ease.

Mr. Nash loaded us into a sort of carryall or small bus with two long seats running lengthwise, so that we sat facing one another; but the Richardsons left us to go to a house in Menlo Park which they were to occupy for the summer. There was mail, we knew, at the post office and we stopped there to get it. The three men began to go in and come out again loaded to the eyes with mail. They threw it in on the floor of the little carry-

Escondite Cottage in 1891

Frenchman's Lake in 1891

all, and our feet were more and more in the way—though certainly having the first right—until the whole bus-load of us, nearly in hysterics, took them off and put them in our pockets or perhaps sat on them; at any rate, our several pairs of feet disappeared of necessity, for the floor up to our knees was piled and packed with this enormous ten-days' accumulation. Leslie's habitual smile grew a trifle rigid, as though by inner mechanics, for he was the one who would have to deal with every bit of it.

The office was emptied at last; the postmaster came and stood in the door staring at us silently; the men clambered in on top of everything; and the carryall proceeded. The first notable object for our peering and curious eyes was the redwood tree beside the bridge over San Francisquito Creek. It was the "Palo Alto," the tall tree, which had given Mr. Stanford the name for his estate, an old landmark in the neighborhood and the only redwood on the Bay plain. Beyond the bridge we passed the wrought-iron gates to the Stanford private grounds. We branched off to the right from the highway, and by a field road crossed a vineyard, its vines not trellised as I was used to in Hector but snubbed off into low bushes, leafy and bunched with half-formed grapes. Beyond was the "winery," looming importantly; a row of chestnut trees; a grove of thick-foliaged oaks, dark and motionless; a sunny open space beyond with the Museum going up. Then at a dramatic gesture from Dr. Jordan we looked toward the foothills and saw *The University*, our goal, the source and end of our destiny. What—to me, excited, tired, wistful, homesick, full of fanciful imaginings and hopes— an anticlimax! My heart sank. It is a trite phrase, but nothing so well expresses the ironic experience common, alas, to mortality! For I had expected the University to be beautiful, imposing, adequate to high thoughts and noble purposes; and what I saw, some distance off across a dry, dun waste, was a low, bare line of buildings, plain and stiff, unrelieved by greenery, lying against hills of the same dusty hue, not an arcade or a court or the least mitigation of their commonness. They ap-

peared to me exactly like a factory. Of course it was the outside, the back, we were looking at, and court and cloister were
inside. One ought not to see his dream first manifested wrong
side out.

I made no moan; I don't remember that anyone said anything; we drove sketchily over the field, came into a road
announced by the President as Pine Avenue, obviously from
the pines along its borders, and so to our destination, Escondite
Cottage.

It was fitting that we should enter our new life through the
doorway of a myth, and that was the doorway to Escondite. The
long, low, white-painted house was called "Cottage" but it was
more like a chalet or a small one-storied villa. The windows
were narrow and long; the large front veranda was overhung by
an old oak tree growing from the neat gravel. There were pines
and pepper trees. There was a dovecote at one side secluded in
the foliage, and beyond that a good-sized brick building, the
library. Dr. Jordan told the story. Many years before, Peter
Coutts, "The Frenchman," had suddenly appeared from France,
bought a tract of land, built this chalet, and brought his family to
live here. He was a great man, swung great projects, laid out and
landscaped a large estate, ran a business with blooded cattle,
for which he built a series of long red barns. He planned a fine
chateau on top of one of the hills for his permanent home.
When we arrived, he had long been gone; for at some mysterious message he and all his family had disappeared so suddenly that "the children's playthings were left strewn upon the
floor." It was known that he went back to France. He never
returned, and Mr. Stanford later purchased his property, which
adjoined the Palo Alto ranch.*

Dr. Jordan stated that the house was modeled after the
Little Trianon, and that the lonely round brick tower to be

---

* The legend of Peter Coutts, "The Frenchman," was circulated in several
versions. An authoritative account by Dr. Edward M. Pallette, illustrated and well
authenticated, is to be found in the *Stanford Illustrated Review* for December 1925.

found a mile off in the hills was in imitation of a tower Louis the Fifteenth built at Versailles. There was a little lake close to Escondite, the banks stoned and cemented and Lombardy poplars planted on its margin. A tiny rocky islet, grassy on top, was there, and tied to the island a rowboat. In the field between lake and hills an arched wooden bridge stood in the grass, with steps to go up on one side and down on the other. We could see, in a small valley of the foothills, a grove of dark evergreens which the Frenchman had planted, brightened at some seasons with the wine-color of the poison oak. Here and there on the flat stood poplars; and short lines of them wound among the slopes and valleys. There were tunnels in some of the hillsides. The noble hill beyond the lake had the faint ghost of a trail curving up the side where a drive had once been laid out and on the sightly summit a group of cypresses and pines had been planted to surround the family mansion he expected to build.

When we came there were no doves in the dovecote, the Frenchman's celebrated Elzevirs had gone from the brick library where still a handsome globe and some leather-covered chairs remained. No little stream ran under the bridge in the fields where no channel had ever been dug. The lake was solitary; the rowboat had no oars. We walked through the dry tall grass up the faint trace of the winding driveway and came to the crown of the hill; looked off to the silver Bay and the dove-colored tumbled range beyond, and south over the Santa Clara Valley. We found no house there on the hilltop nor ruins of one, only a bare empty space turfed with dried grass, surrounded by evergreens. We listened to a meadow lark singing. The grass was grey and brittle under foot.

The jockey boys had a school in the brick library, arranged by Mrs. Stanford, who took an interest in them. When we came, the jockeys vanished, and the library served as the first administration office to the new University. In one of the red barns we found stored the furniture we had freighted from Ithaca. The unexplained brick tower, remote and buried in brush, became a favorite subject for the amateur photographer, who did not worry about how it came there.

So, in the late afternoon of June 26, 1891, our carryall drew across the gravel and up to this romantic place. We unloaded ourselves and our impedimenta and two weary little boys, and all trooped up the steps. Mrs. Jordan led. The door opened and we saw a Chinaman, Ah Sam, all in white, bowing and smiling. He showed us in. We saw the long hall paneled in redwood, and peeped into Frenchy rooms leading off on each side. The living room was hung with figured cretonne, its arm-chairs covered with the same. Long white lace curtains floated at all the windows. Each chamber had a walnut single bed, white-covered, plumply made up, and a tall walnut bureau. The air came in sweetly, smelling of pine and alfalfa. Mrs. Jordan indicated our room, and we shut the door and went at freshening up.

Ah Sam called us to dinner with gracious ceremony and served to perfection a sumptuous meal. A bouquet of pink roses the size of cabbages dominated the table—at which I stared, both fascinated and abashed.

"Roses don't have any smell in California," said the girl Edith.

Dr. Jordan, who never paused, had been outside exploring the domain while we freshened up, and came in late to the meal.

"There's more of this Aladdin business, Miss Jessie," he said, using his domestic name for his wife. "I've found a horse and carriage in the stable!"

We put the little boys to bed. Dr. Jordan and Leslie went off together to look at the Quadrangle, where the watchman would not let them in at first but was finally intimidated by Dr. Jordan's bulk, or perhaps by the very outrageousness of his pretensions. The rest of us sat outdoors on the veranda in the scented midsummer dusk. We talked a little in fragments, fell silent, and listened to the crickets. A small owl in the oak (a "squinch owl," according to Dr. Jordan) communed with the

night in a meek rustling moan comically inadequate even to the
sorrows of an owl. We were tired; we were bewildered, we
were glad; we thought about home; we sat quietly and wondered
what was happening to us.

A big carriage with beautiful horses and a burly coachman
drove across the gravel and stopped at the steps. Mr. and Mrs.
Stanford had come. They would not go in to be more formally
received but sat down cosily with us on the porch. It was the
half-light of early evening. We found them kind-hearted, unaffected people, carrying their large figures with simple poise.
She was dressed in silk or satin of creamy white, with lace and
jewelry, but seemed unconscious of her garments. He appeared
somewhat feeble, with his cane and a slowness in his walk. They
were grave, yet full of eager pleasure at our coming and at the
unfolding of their plans. We felt their urge and happy desire
to see Dr. Jordan's work initiated and to help him with it in
every possible way. Mr. Stanford was still a member of the
United States Senate; some called him "The Senator" and some,
old-timers, said "Governor," for he had been war governor of
California in the 'sixties. He seemed to us an aging man, feeling
his age, ready to be rid of burdens and care if he could successfully transfer his wealth, which would have gone to The Boy, to
those who needed it. We knew what he had said when their only
child died, that he would take the children of California to be
his children. We were sorry for him and loved him.

X

FIRST SUMMER

Mrs. Jordan seemed to fit the celebrated Spanish architecture of the University. She looked pure Spanish, dark eyes, olive skin, glossy, straight black hair done in a pompadour; but in fact, she was pure New England, from Worcester, Massachusetts —a piquant combination. She was capable, quick, and petite, executive by instinct; Dr. Jordan, a big, rambling sort of man, good as gold, did as she bade him, admiringly.

But it was he who, as the Adam to this Eden, went about naming things. The Frenchman's house he named "Escondite," "hidden"; an artificial pond where later the students built boathouses he called "Lagunita," "little lake"; the streets on the campus which developed—Alvarado, Salvatierra, Lasuen, Serra, etc.—he named them all, and years afterward the streets on the Hill, Dolores, Cabrillo. Somebody once intervened, when the President was away, and named a street "Aibonito"; but he changed it when he got back. "Aibonito" was not a word at all, he said, just a made-up term meaning hurrah-boys or such a matter.

The Escondite household, those first days, was large and its activities confused. This "cottage," the only dwelling on the campus, was most properly given to the President, and he had hospitably taken us in until we could find a lodging elsewhere. Albert Fletcher was also at Escondite, there being no other place for him. Ah Sam took care of us very well. We learned from Dr. Jordan that "Ah Sam" was Chinese for "The Tree," but he was addressed as "Sam" precisely as though christened Samuel. His queue had been cut off; that, Dr. Jordan stated, was because he was a Christian. I thought it a pity, religion or no religion; but Mrs. Jordan thought it much better for the kitchen. He was our first Chinaman, and furnished an early thrill when we spied him squatting at the door of the red barn eating rice out of a bowl *with chopsticks*. But servant problems began promptly, for he did not last long. He said he was not strong, and Mrs. Stanford had told him there would not be much work to do; but, "plenty work—I go." Afterward he went crazy. And what happened then is Mrs. Jordan's story, not mine.

Leslie did not seem satisfied with the four hundred letters yielded by the Menlo post, all to be answered immediately, and took it upon himself on Saturday to go to the post office for more. California was having a "most unusual" hot spell, thermometer 95 degrees in shaded house, 105 and upward outdoors. Leslie composedly walked to Menlo, two miles, in the glaring sun and two miles back, and arrived home with a high fever, not realizing that nobody ever gets sunstroke in California. We put him to bed over Sunday and he recovered. On Wednesday, July 1, he began his career as Registrar, and held entrance examinations on the Escondite veranda. Three candidates arrived: Miss Longley and her brother, who passed, and a nameless, forgotten one who failed. The next day, Francis Batchelder appeared, to take over the stenography and enter the University; he was a Cornell man who had just finished his freshman year. Leslie and he set up administration offices in the Frenchman's library, and Leslie held a second day of examinations.

All our faculty who had come on—it was only the Jordans, the Richardsons, and us—were now honored with a luncheon at the Reid School secluded in the lovely Belmont hills. We met faculty people from the State University at Berkeley, and school people from around the Bay, a genial company who pleased and warmed us by being just like ourselves. In the

handsome residence of the Reids we were comforted for our
exile when we saw over the mantelpiece the same Sistine Ma-
donna, the same photograph of Goethe on the bookcase, the same
old friendly books on the shelves. There was a clipped green
lawn outside with white clover in patches, and I amused Mrs.
Reid—herself an Easterner, but acclimated—by nearly dropping on my knees to kiss it.

Everybody was from elsewhere. "What part of the East did
you come from?" we asked when we met. A gentleman from
Connecticut, one of Mr. Reid's teachers, took me off behind the
bushes and showed me a row of little elms four feet high which
he said his father had sent him. He was proud of them, sub-
duedly passionate. "To *you*," the idea was, because he saw
my state of mind. I had seen no home trees and supposed they
would not grow in California; I was delighted and suffused;
and the gentleman, aware of my emotion, impulsively gave me
two of them, to be claimed and transplanted when I should have
acquired a garden of my own.

It was at Belmont, with its high sightly outlook, that our
attention was first called to Mount Diablo. It dominates the
Coast Range, beyond the Bay. "Do you know why it is named
Diablo?" Dr. Jordan asked. *"Because it is in sight from everywhere."* We laughed, and kowtowed to Mount Diablo. Now, in
these days, it has on top of it a beacon winking at the airplanes
—still perhaps in diabolic character.

Shortly after the Belmont party Dr. Jordan left for a trip to
San Diego, inviting us to stay with Mrs. Jordan until his return.
He toured the state "south of the Tehachapi"—we learned that
term—acquainting himself in two weeks with every city, town,
village, and crossroads; every college, school, church, library,
and hall of justice; every teacher and person of importance in
the south. He also learned the flora and fauna, the fishes of the
sea, and all data about the Missions. Later he absorbed the Bay
region and the valleys—industriously and with speed became
a Californian.

But I had to find a lodging for my family. There were no "stone cottages," and a later plan to house the entire faculty in the capacious men's dormitory, Encina Hall, had been played with but given up. Anyway, we could not inhabit Encina at present, for it was very much unfinished. Mrs. Stanford was superintending it. When she wanted a window or a porch taken out as soon as it was in, the workmen took it out and substituted something else as directed. Mrs. Stanford said it was impossible for her to know how a thing was going to look until she saw it. As they were building massively, this somewhat retarded the work.

I supposed that Mayfield was a neat little flowery village— I judged by the name, which certainly breathed this aroma. It lay near Escondite, and we might, I thought, find a boarding-place there. Albert Fletcher drove Louis and me to Mayfield with the Escondite horse and carriage. I was all hope and cheerfulness, but how soon dismayed, for the village straggled aimlessly about, sprinkled with small, one-story houses of the kind we called shanties in the East, and no style or promise anywhere. It seemed predominantly saloons; fourteen, I believe, with a few poor untidy shops. The rotund, jolly Bracchi, tending his bright fruit stand at the sidewalk with the assistance of a large family of dark-eyed children, and good Mr. LaPeire, whose grocery and whose friendship later became our sure reliance in our housekeeping trials, must have been there, but I do not remember that my grieved and clouded eyes that day discerned them.

We went to the one hotel; Albert made perfunctory inquiries at the bar. It was a men's place, and the men looked at me and the babe with as much surprise as I at them. We turned and went out, followed, I was sure, by wondering, if not worse, glances. We drove along the dusty streets and asked at the doors of houses, and learned that taking boarders was unheard of; why should they take boarders? And they shut the doors slowly, peering at us through the crack. Albert Fletcher seemed to think it might help if he explained us; so he said we had come out from the East to start the Leland Stanford Junior University. They said, "Oh, do you think Stanford is goin' to *start* his college!" We said we did; Albert turned pert and said, "Why not?" They laughed sneakingly and looked at us with pity. "Them workmen has been a-buildin' over there for years!" they said. But one pleasant-faced man at the door of a sort of half-empty shop was gracious; he felt sure he could accommodate us. The shop was so small and queer when we stepped inside that we could only wonder how. If we would agree to stay three months, he would run a partition across the further end, he said, and make an eight by ten room for us. He gestured it out, squinting at the back of the shop and doing phantom measurements with his arms. I told him I must consult my husband and I would let him know. However, Albert, outside, said it was impossible.

"You can't live all summer in a single room eight by ten." I replied that Dr. Elliott would only be there nights, and Louis and I could play outdoors most of the time.

"What would you eat? Shavings?" said he, for it looked like a kind of a carpenter shop.

In the end, the Richardsons at Menlo Park rented us a bedroom in their house, Francisquito Cottage, and we had meals at the Oak Grove Villa Hotel. Here for two months Louis and I were stalled in a bedroom and a graveled back yard. Mostly I sat on the gravel, supported by the trunk of an oak tree, and wrote letters home, or sewed on some unnecessary garment, or read in the books Leslie had bought me in the City—*Adam Bede* and Emerson's *Essays*. For some reason, none of us had brought books, not conceiving, I suppose, there was a spot on earth where books did not grow on bushes. While I thus thrillingly passed my time, Louis dug in the gravel with his toy spade, filling his toy pail with stones and emptying it out again over and over. He appeared satisfied.

We had to leave these quarters before the summer was over. We spent the remaining weeks in a terrible hole of a place, a room above an unoccupied store, where we went up a narrow, dark, clattering stairway and fumbled into a dim coop—but very high in the ceiling—with a great bed in it and a wash-stand. We set up Louis' crib, though the bed itself would have held five persons; and after that we had to dress and undress tandem, there not being room for both to move at once. The mosquitoes ate us up. They camped in thick patches on the outside of the rotten window screen and oozed in by detach-ments to suck our blood. The dark old garden below furnished fleas also, who came in riding on the mosquitoes' backs. Re-pelled from the bedroom, Louis and I would fumble down the stairway and, when we found the latch, exit upon the narrow, wooden, sagging porch; and on the top one of its two sagging steps I would sit down. Louis, having by this time a nice red wheelbarrow suited to his size, paced back and forth on the uncertain board walk, trundling it. I, having no wheelbarrow, sat chin in hand staring at two saloons and a livery stable across the road. In this lodging there was a parlor where I could stay if I did not touch anything (stipulated), and some-times when Louis took his nap I sat there on a pink plush sofa beneath a large gold-framed oil painting of a religious incident and breathed guardedly the antique air. I lifted the corner of the window shade enough so that I could read *Ramona*, lent me by the Mexican woman, our landlady.

Many things in our environment displeased me. The moun-tains were bare; our mountains at home were always covered with woods—Adirondacks, for instance. I did not care for the live-oak foliage; it failed to blow in the breeze like maple. I thought the palms pretentious vegetables. I hardly approved of the eucalyptus with its pink suggestive skin and carrying its clothes over its arms that way. The yellow landscape got on my nerves; the brazen sunshine hurt my eyes; I even objected to the wandering oaks on the foothills because they looked so like old apple orchards and weren't. I was shown Leland's cactus garden, and pitied him; what a flower bed for a child!

I had looked for a local welcome but found myself for the first time in my life a stranger. No millionaires tripped through turnstiles to make our acquaintance. There were no turnstiles, and if millionaires they lived invisible to us in rural seclusion at the center of great "estates," surrounded by foliage and for aught I know thorn hedges besides, like the Sleeping Beauty. They all had San Francisco mansions also, and Dr. Jordan said they went to the City to call on each other. I had a jaundiced impression of these neighbors. They were probably nice people like anybody else—only not aware of our existence.

Mr. and Mrs. Doyle called upon us. He was a handsome and distinguished lawyer and she a lady kind-hearted and companionable. I thought I should return the call. My tether was short, no longer than my little boy's legs; but I was a good walker, and it was time he was getting some practice, too. They said they lived "in Menlo," and the distance seemed not too far. But it was far enough, and the roads were dusty enough, and the sun was hot enough, and the child's patient but inadequate pace slow enough to exhaust us both completely, well before our journey ended. We arrived finally at the welcome coolth of the grove in which the Doyle home lay, and wound our way through the grounds to the house. A great feather brush hung at the side of the door, and I was pleased to see it. I dusted Louis down and then myself, and rang the bell.

The Doyles were amazed at our exploit. They petted and lauded us, comforted us with flagons, stayed us with apples (apricots). We had given them, I am sure, a grand idea of the stuff we University people were made of. Louis lifted up his drooping head and began to smile around at the company; and I, in response to inquiries, began to tell them how I liked California. They drove us in their chariot back to Francisquito Cottage, and we have never forgotten their kindness.

The Menlo physician, Dr. Charles, had a wife from the state of Maine and daughters growing up—the eldest, in fact, in a pre-bridal illumination and looking like Botticelli's Venus.

They were cordial, came to see us, and I believe were glad of us. That was one place where Louis and I could drop in and feel at home.

Captain Harkins, retired, and his wife came on horseback. An army man, the Captain brought a gallant welcome and, so far as he was concerned, gave us the keys to the city. He was Senator Stanford's friend, and conversant with his plans. The Harkins family was young and numerous; he had brought them here and built a house a few miles away, and intended, as soon as the University was started, to enter the children "from the kindergarten up." Entertainment rolled off his tongue. The son of a sea captain, he had enlisted in the Army as a boy, went through the Civil War "from end to end," was in the South during Reconstruction, had dealings with the Ku Klux. In 1870 he "happened to be" in Paris accompanying the French troops "in my uniform," saw the Tuileries burn and the mob storming it. "They killed every clergyman they could get hold of," he said. This was news to me. How startling! We were in Paris in '66, looked on the Tuileries. What if Father had been there in '70!

Being a cavalry man, Captain Harkins invited me to ride. But I had never ridden (except Old Katy); I had no riding habit; there was no horse. He would change all that. He would bring a horse; he would bring Mrs. Harkins' habit; he would give me lessons; it would be a pleasure. I could not deny him, although I am terrified of a horse when on top of its big, warm, undulating back. What if it should lie down and roll, as I am sure used to be in Old Katy's mind, or jump the fence into the field, or run away! The Captain came a few days later, without my horse, to apologize and explain the "deviltries" of his "little brown bronco." She had bucked with him. Failing to unhorse him thus, she planted her forefeet and kicked up her hind feet and ducked her head to fling him off in front. He stuck on. Then she lay down and rolled over (just as I thought); and this was conclusive.

"Now I ask you, is *that* a horse I can accompany a lady on?"

But he would come again. I demurred. Yes, yes, I must set a time. And in brief he came, mounted properly, leading my steed, and bundled under his arm Mrs. Harkins' long black calico skirt. I put it on over my dress for a habit. I must choose our road; I demurred, I was a stranger; yes, yes, I must choose. So at random I took the dustiest one in the neighborhood. My hair shook down and I had to stop and fix it. Though gently urged, I dared not go off a walk for fear the horse would take the bit in his teeth and run away. Captain Harkins, a perfect gentleman, made no remarks; but I think he was disappointed. I do not remember any other riding lesson.

I wrote home. Naturally I wrote home. I thought Louise had better come out and grow up with the country, just through with college and looking for work, as she was, I placed her presumptively as art teacher in a girls' preparatory school that was to be established—or I offered her room and board and home privileges in my house if she would come and help me with Louis and my (presumptive) housework, and she could meanwhile be taking lessons in portrait painting in San Francisco. Eddie, too; I planned for him. And there was a Presbyterian Church at Menlo Park, no doubt they would be changing ministers; Father might get that place. Mother, I was certain, would be free of hay fever out here, for with all the dust and sunlight I had not sneezed a sneeze. The air was like wine (I said), pure and bracing, and smelled so good. There were no thunderstorms. And no mad dogs running around in the street to bite you. No snow in winter; here winter is the green season, all the hills are green. Here they plant things *in January!* It does rain, in the rainy season, I am told, but only at night; daytimes it is always bright sunshine. Annually the sun shines 360 out of the 365 days of the year. You don't need fires to keep you warm—if cold, you go outdoors and sit in the sun. Or you exercise. So I beckoned, longingly.

My nostalgia for the woods never left me. I did not see any

woods anywhere, not the woods that encompassed my childhood, grassy, flowery where I walked, sun-flecked green boughs over me, where I could once in a while come on a mountain laurel with a few fairy blossoms like little pagodas carved of flesh-pink shell, once in a while under a brown broken log find the Indian Pipe made of snow-white wax, and see the cushions of jewel-green moss, and the solitary blue harebell on a rocky ledge over the Lake, and young slender saplings leafy around me. There were rumors of La Honda, but that did not sound like woods. La Honda was a "canyon"—a cold, dark gash in the rocks, evidently. I heard stray bits about the ocean and the beaches. No one went there. And if one did, they would not find the woods. I was convinced there were no woods west of the Mississippi.

My dear Man was too busy at the University to minister to my yearning, had not even time to become aware of it. But once, on a Sunday when he could for an hour emerge from the cloud that encompassed him, Leslie did hire from the Menlo livery stable a high-seated, small, uncovered buggy and a reluctant horse; and, after inquiry, we drove out toward the hills on a country road that ran past a little Catholic cemetery and took what we were told was the Sandhill Road to Searsville. All the covered buggies and smart horses were taken before Leslie got to the livery stable. The horse we had was the kind called "safe." What was Searsville? we asked. A reservoir, they said. But why "ville"? Oh, it used to be a town. It was now a reservoir. What became of the town? we inquired, thinking of Lost Atlantis, Sunken Bells, etc. Oh, the water came in gradually and the folks took their time getting out. Anyway, a promising mystery; we embarked for Searsville. They said it was a nice ride.

The horse did not think so. He poked and sulked, crinkled his skin derisively under the touch of the whip, and got his tail over the lines. His whole attention was concentrated on the effort to scuff up with his hoofs as much dust as possible in great, hot clouds. The sun smote us tenderfoots with scorn. The child sagged quietly between us, his feet dangling, and mine scarcely tiptoed the floor. The horse slowed, faltered; we feared he was going to drop dead and leave us alone to perish. But we toiled forward on our desperate quest among endless rolling fields, yellow, dry, uninhabited. We proceeded in silence, fearful, sad. We peered ahead but saw no Searsville, town or reservoir. We were evidently following an *ignis fatuus.* Suddenly together we exclaimed, "Let's turn round and go home!" Leslie pulled the beast around; he had dropped into a deep sleep, but the reverse pierced his stupid brain like lightning; he kicked up his heels, switched his tail merrily, and set off for his stable at a high-pitched racing trot tending to gallop. In no time at all we sped back past the little cemetery into Menlo and arrived in a whirlwind at Francisquito Cottage gate. Mrs. Richardson sat on the porch and greeted us pleasantly.

"Did you have a nice ride?"

"Yes indeed. Very."

I believe I was the only person who also served by standing and waiting that summer; all the others were as busy and aflutter as birds in nesting time. So was Leslie. He left me, with other faculty men, after an early breakfast at the Oak Grove Villa, and did not return until evening. The happy scholars walked the dusty roads to the Quadrangle carrying lunches in baskets, like schoolboys, chatting, I make no doubt, in the pleasant collegiate fashion, and—since no one in this country ever did walk except the tramps—they were called by the natives "tramp perfessers." Faculty members arrived week by week, leaving their families parked somewhere if they were wise; and many were young bachelors, carefree. There was no provision for anyone's housing, and they nosed around and found whatever shelter they could. The Oak Grove Villa Hotel took several. The David Marxes, Cornell graduates, with two small children, stayed at the impossible Other Hotel, since burned down, where they had for bedrooms mean dark huts in the shrubbery with fleas, and suffered from malnutrition. Professor Branner, also Cornell, State Geologist of Arkansas, put his family in San Jose, and they did not move to the campus until the next spring. Professor Anderson—Cornell claimed him too, in a way—left his children in Germany getting their schooling until we were better ready for them. It was he who long afterwards grew elderly, retired to Florence, and beautifully translated Dante. We had, by August, Woodruff to be our librarian. "Dr. Woody" Louis called him, though he was singular in that early group in not legitimately bearing the title. He tired of us, always was homesick for Ithaca I think, and soon went back to Cornell and became a law professor there for the rest of his life. Woodruff was a jolly person, droll in telling a story. In any company he was mayonnaise to the salad. He called on Mr. Stanford to talk about the prospects for the library, and reported back to us how they sat on the porch and Mr. Stanford adroitly "talked about the sparrows on the lawn!" I believe it was he who first heard the reputed remark of the Founder that he wished for the University a library "such as any gentleman might have on his shelves." Woodruff could make a good story, and I cannot believe that railroad builder and legislator, experienced and traveled—and he had been Governor of California during the Civil War and was in the United States Senate until his death—I cannot think he was, in the matter of college libraries, a complete ninny.

Before we left the East, Dr. Jordan, functioning as the Pied Piper, had induced two bright young college women to come out to California and organize a girls' boarding school "as a feeder to the University"; and they arrived in August, full of ambition, Lucy Fletcher and Eleanor Pearson, and put themselves in the President's hands. He and they ferreted out a place to start the school, an old empty mansion named Adelante Villa, standing on a mound in a grove of gloomy overgrown trees a couple of miles from the Quadrangle in the back country. It had a grave in the garden, with a ghost. Untended rose vines grew across the windows, choking out the light, and rats and squirrels gamboled through the chambers rolling nuts. The grounds were edged with willow brush and you crossed a wooden bridge over Los Trancos creek to get into the yard. All these creeks we met were bone dry, of course, but, we were told, would be raging torrents in the winter. The rooms of Adelante were high and austere, Victorian, the upholstered furniture dropping to rags; but it was large enough, and Lucy and Eleanor leased it of Mr. Stanford, got servants, and set up housekeeping. Quite unexpectedly to them, Adelante became immediately filled with boarders. The faculty, put to it for quarters and new men coming in all the time, went up the field and presented themselves as suppliants at the door requesting to be rescued from starvation. How could they be denied? For a month there flourished at the old ghost-haunted place a fine merry company, entertaining themselves in the evenings after work with music and juicy conversation. Eleanor Pearson had a salty tang, she was excellent at give-and-take; Lucy Fletcher played the violin.

The story of Adelante Villa, elaborated for us I am sure by Dr. Jordan, was circulated and worth it. Adelante was the summer place of a San Francisco lawyer, and his wife, an invalid, loved it. One summer she knew she was to die and so begged to be buried in the garden. It was done, the grave put under the oak where she used to sit; and her husband tended it and put around it a close hedge of cypress. But he lapsed; he married again; his new wife and her grown daughters could not abide the grave, quite too visible from the windows; and they induced him to cut down the cypress hedge. Then they burned it on top of the grave, and—the story went—the grave fell in! The man grew old and miserable and died; the women moved away; the place was abandoned; weeds overran the flower beds and vines tangled up the walls, and rats and squirrels took over, gnawing holes under the eaves to get in and build their nests. And the poor lady who had loved it *walked*. Many years later the earthquake demolished the house. I suppose the lady walked away into eternity, for one never hears of her now and not a vestige of the whole establishment remains on the quiet mound beyond Los Trancas among the trees.

This romantic situation was inconvenient in every possible way. The mistresses of Adelante had to go through the field road and across an extensive campus cluttered and torn with building operations, and by long detours around gates found unexpectedly locked, to get to Mayfield, far from their solitary base, and procure the food and daily supplies to run their family. They set up a horse and surrey. The horse was "Jim" and afterward belonged to Mr. David Marx, as everybody knows. The necessary boys to do chores and take care of Jim were sent out to Adelante from the source of all activity, the office at the Quadrangle—working students, of whom there were many. They were not very satisfactory, came and went vaguely as they drifted away of themselves or were dismissed, until the office sent a young fellow from Portland named Herbert Hoover. After that the ladies had rest to their souls, for he cared for the horse and did all the chores and performed every duty allotted to him with silent and perfect efficiency.

Lucy Fletcher was Irish, at least her mother was born in Cork. Her eyes were Irish blue, deep, with dark lashes, her hair dusky, wavy, dark almost to black. Madam Fletcher used to visit her, after the school was established, enhancing by her imposing manner, her deliberate portliness, and her gift of elegant language the prestige of her very popular daughter. She spoke as of the Court: "Come in," she said, leading us up to the furnace register, "I deplore the fact that I have no better welcome for you than this *inhospitable aperture.*"

The administration had moved to the Quadrangle from Escondite as soon as any space there was said to be "ready" for them. They had three rooms, one for the President, one for the Registrar, and the third for all the rest of the faculty together. The furnishings of this room consisted of some revolving bookcases and six roll-top desks, nucleus of the University equipment. The men grabbed the desks as they arrived, first come first served, and two could use one desk, if amiable. In a corner was a small table for Eleanor Pearson, representing the "Castilleja School"—Dr. Jordan had christened the Adelante school after a bright upreaching flame flower he knew on the hills. Outside these rooms—and indeed more or less inside, for the woodwork was being interminably rubbed down—gangs of workmen clattered about at all kinds of building and finishing. They hung doors and put on latches and set in windows and did some pounding and laid the tile pavement of the arcades and the asphalt floor of the Quadrangle. It was confusing. But the faculty were gay, and knew that chaos precedes creation. At noon they debouched into the arcade and ate their little lunches, sitting around on the curb. Mr. Batchelder brought layer cake, and all the others envied him. Every basket contained a small bottle of sour wine, by which they knew they were in a foreign land; not, however, Dr. Jordan's from Escondite; he nourished his big frame and vivid energy without stimulants. He thought they made you feel strong when you were not. Tobacco was obnoxious to him, and though he did not parade it the other men knew of this and for respect and love of him used to refrain from their pipes when he was in the room.

Public interest in the University had been steadily growing, especially in the state of California. The summer was enlivened by the coming of visitors with all sorts of axes to grind. Some of them wanted to sell things—pianos, parcels of land, hardware for the buildings, books—a university would want books. Leslie was approached with insidious proposals involving commissions but I suppose sternly replied "Get thee behind me, Satan"—at any rate I never saw any commission emoluments. A detective came hopefully surmising there would be work for him and suggested he establish himself on the campus. The University had an altercation with a city newspaper which offered to boom us and when turned down threatened blackmail.

Student applications for admission, not only from the state but from all over the country, poured in, so that the modest estimate of a hundred or so was outrun even before the start. A faculty of fifteen, it was evident, would be absurdly inadequate. Dr. Jordan was delighted. He bubbled, he overflowed; nothing pleased him like appointing new professors unless it was gathering in new students. August and September saw him with banners flying and the arriving faculty wheeling into march behind him with banzais. If they experienced some bewilderment at first, and looked around them at the unfinished scene and the bare rural setting with doubt, their suspicions vanished overnight before the moment's irresistible enthusiasm. Thirty faculty members instead of fifteen were on hand by October. Among them was Bolton; he came to teach mechanical drawing under Mr. David Marx, the engineer, and to establish here a famous art school rivaling the schools of Paris, only more up-to-date. The last item was concealed in Bolton's head at the time, he came to teach drawing, and did.

XI

WAH-HOO! WAH-HOO! L-S-J-U!

Wah-HOO! *Wah*-HOO! L-S-J-U! STAN-FORD!

Imagine our excitement when four hundred young men leaped from their seats in the sunny Quadrangle and bellowed out this their natal cry!

We were massed in chairs in front of the Quadrangle's entrance arch, enclosed to make an alcove. Those who had not been early enough for chairs stood up in the rear. Those who could not get within earshot of the speakers promenaded the arcades and made remarks for themselves.

Within the enclosure of the arch fell the rich folds of the Stars and Stripes. Feathers of pampas grass plumed up at the sides against the buff stone; a fringe of eucalyptus crossed the top, with five little Bear Flags of California fluttering among the drooping, curling leaves. The portrait of The Boy was elevated on the wall at the back, a serious face, seeming to look down upon us in a long meditation.

Grapevines garlanded the arcades, their purple clusters large, making you think of Joshua's spies or the Greek bacchantes, according to which end of your education got its overtones in first. Banners breezed from the arches. The long cloisters marched round the court much like the Piazza San Marco; but no ducal palace, no piazzetta, no campanile or immemorial doves. Flower beds on the asphalt, strictly curbed to circles, offered hopeful bunches of cannas, palmetto, bamboo.

The court at the rostrum end was packed. "In the early

morning the streets of San Jose and Santa Clara were alive
with vehicles carrying people to Palo Alto," the newspapers
said. Special trains ran up to the buildings on the freight
switch and unloaded large numbers of curious, eager men and
women. Every post, bar, fence, and tree on the surrounding
fields had its hitched saddle horse or a surrey or a buggy. The
enthusiastic people pressed through the entrance arches—all
gay with flowers and flags—into the Quadrangle, where chairs
had been placed for an audience. The President and the Trustees were on the platform; the Faculty sat in chairs on the
Quadrangle floor facing the people. Leslie and David Marx
were where I could see them by peeking through the ranks of
heads. The reporters were in a pen beneath the platform's
edge; the cameras were perched on the red-tile roofs or on
stilts here and there among our chairs.

Mr. and Mrs. Stanford came quietly from the shadowed
arcade into the alcove, stood there a moment below the dream-
ing Boy; and then the shout arose, the young men sprang up
and cried their lusty greeting *"Wah-hoo! Wah-hoo! L-S-J-U!*
Stan-ford!" The Founders dropped into their seats.

The chorus sang. I cannot remember seeing the chorus at
all; I imagine they were angels, invisible somewhere; they sang
"Glory Be to God on High." The Reverend Robert Mackenzie
prayed to God; the Reverend Mr. Stowe read the Scriptures.
The Senator, with Mrs. Stanford standing at his side, gave the
Founders' address. He outlined clearly and cogently their ideas
and their purposes, he spoke to the Board of Trustees, remind-
ing them of their future responsibilities; to the members of the
Faculty, admonishing them of their duties. And with a touching
urgency he counseled the students and told them of his hopes.
Others spoke. Dr. Jordan came last. We were sung to again;
a minister blessed us.

We broke up and went our ways. The noon sun was hot, we
held up our parasols and streamed out of the Quadrangle. Horses
were unhitched and carriages drove away. The special trains

waiting on the sidings got going. People who had brought lunches sat down under the arcade and ate them and helped themselves to the big bunches of purple grapes from the decorations. The Trustees and Faculty departed for the Stanford home, invited there for lunch. All but Dr. Elliott. He was obliged to rush back to his office and register students, which he did without pause or intermission, not eating or sleeping, for the next forty-eight hours—at least that is how I remember it. We had extremely nice celery soup at the luncheon and no doubt other things besides.

This was October 1, 1891.

Around the Quadrangle southward and westward lay the plain, greyish yellow, flat and empty, covered with dry grass, the residual grass of the wild oats. We Easteners called it spontaneously and unconsciously a "wheat field," we called all this countryside a "wheat field." You see why—it looked exactly like our reaped Eastern harvest fields with yellow stubble. In many places, especially on the foothills, the dark green live oaks grew; but the "wheat field" around the Quadrangle was bare of trees, and very wide, and very flat. The white flowerets of the tar-weed spread over the dun surface in a delicate froth and scented spicily the hot summer air.

Encina Hall loomed up impressively. Soon after our arrival at Escondite in June, "the Row" was started, a line of professors' dwellings, ten in number, projected on the flat over against the Hall. When the students came later and looked across the field, counted the houses—ten—noted their stylized effect, how they were the same size, the same distance apart, and all toed the mark alike, they exclaimed "The Decalogue!" We chose our house, the tenth, at the furthest end, having a great view of Black Mountain behind and in front the range across the Bay; and all those dreary weeks while I was standing and waiting, I knew that I was, in the end, to have a home again. The President named this, our street, which had not a tree or shrub or blade of green, or any sidewalk or road except the wheel-broken track in the blistered adobe—he named it "Alvarado Avenue"! I nearly fainted.

"But it is so *obviously* a *row!*" I exclaimed.

"It will be an avenue some day," Dr. Jordan said, but twinkling. He changed the name to Alvarado Row.

Into this end house, Louis and I moved a few days before the University opened. I say Louis and I because that was the way it was, although Leslie must have been there, too, the first night, when we slept on the parlor floor and through wide windows all open to the night breathed in the tingling air, dark and full of mingled cool fragrances. The mattress we slept on we borrowed from the David Marxes, who were settling in next door. We lent them blankets, which they lacked.

Our freighted things had been sent over from the red barn, and other articles had by that time come from the City, where I had bought them in frantic shopping expeditions. All were elegantly and permanently crated. The crates, mostly large, stood around the bare rooms the way crates do, putting themselves out to be inconvenient; and I sat around among them much more subdued than they, praying the Lord for help. Leslie, the natural box opener, was not there, as I have said. The plan was for him to send me from the office working students who would open the boxes and arrange the furniture. Fine! A boy came in at the open hall door, crashed around with a hammer, pulled out a table, and stood it up on its side in the gangway; splintered another crate, tore open and bestrewed the wrappages, and dragged my Great-Uncle James' mahogany sofa into the kitchen to be out of the way; split two boards from the flat case containing the great French gold-framed mirror— "Heavens, boy! Be careful!" The check to his industrious fury reminded him; he wiped his brow with the back of his hand, looked at his watch, turned and rapidly departed. I never saw any of them a second time. It was always a new boy, and he could never stay more than half an hour. In between, I waited—violently. Had Mr. Hoover been sent me it would have been different, I am sure; but he was up at Adelante taking care of the horse Jim.

Louis trailed around gently, his flaxen locks disheveled about his puzzled face, a little boy lost. No carpet on the floor, no high-chair at the table, no table—eating off a box, not in any dining room either. All the chairs were queer—doubled up together with their legs sticking into the air—frightful! Mother sitting on the bottom step with strange eyes, looking at one thing, then at another thing, then at the wall somewhere. He would go to Mother and speak to her . . . . but she only said, not seeing him, "mm-m-m, mm-mm-m?" Leaning urgently against my knee, he whispered, *"Let's go home!"*

All the ten houses were taken at once, as there was a shortage. The bachelors mostly went to Encina. One or two houses, in fact, held two families; and this would do, for they were two-storied, with several bedrooms, and comfortable. We were much pleased with ours. The redwood finish intrigued us, looking rich and warm with its clear varnish surface. All the Easterners fell in love with the redwood, a romantic lumber, although we were informed by Dr. Jordan that this was only *Sequoia sempervirens,* the true Big Tree of California being the *Sequoia gigantea.* We dandled happily around our three fireplaces, not expecting to have to use them much (and a good thing too, with coal thirteen dollars a ton) but valuing them for picturesqueness and literary associations. I myself had never seen a fireplace in action, for the old ones were all boarded up and the new ones hadn't come in where I lived, and we used stoves, black and ugly. The walls were tinted plaster, not papered as at home.

Mrs. Marx and I had thought we could have something to say about the colors on our walls, and Mr. Marx drove us over to have a try. So we began influencing the tinter, but he seemed astonished and offended at our interference. I had elaborated for our house a full color scheme, different tints for each room, all harmonizing. But this man said it was all to be one color, terra cotta.

"What! Can't I have one room different?" I cried.

"Now these haint no mansions on Nob Hill that we're puttin' up," retorted the man, getting mad and slatting his paint pail around.

"See here, you!" said David Marx, coming forward with a bang. "I'll have you understand these are ladies you are talking to." And he shepherded us away, the man with his tail between his legs, but growling. Terra cotta it was.

The bachelors went to Encina. Bolton went there on arrival and shortly fell ill with poison oak and lay abed two weeks with fever. He had gone for a walk, as at home. We had to give up going for a walk out here, what with a dried grass-seed, barbed like Satan's tail and named "stickers," and the tarweed which bedewed everything it touched with pitch, and the blinding sun, and no place to walk to anyway. Mother wrote from Burdett and, in her quiet way, insinuated into my ever conscientious mind that Bolton ought to be in a home atmosphere. I was now favorably installed in a nice home, said Mother, so what? Not that Mother would ever have expressed herself as "so what." We invited Bolton to domicile at our house thereafter. Other bachelors fell out of Encina presently when the University built Madroño Hall for them—first named "Lauro." But they did not like Madroño Hall either, and themselves put up and lived in what we called the Bachelors' House. It stood in the field across from Alvarado and later was moved along to opposite the schoolhouse, after there was a schoolhouse.

Encina Hall gave room and board to the students for twenty dollars a month; Mr. Stanford said that was all a student ought to be asked to pay. But Ariel Lathrop (pronounced A-*ri*-el), a brother of Mrs. Stanford's, was the University's business manager and during the absences of the Stanfords in Washington did as he liked. In the spring of 1892 he gave notice that the rates would go up to twenty-eight dollars in the fall.

Mr. Stanford telegraphed him that this would not do; Ariel paid no attention. The spirited youths of Encina also thought it would not do. The majority of them moved out and stormed Mayfield for lodgings when they returned to college in September. Some were taken into families there; some clubbed together and rented cottages and "batched"; some threw up shelters much like piano boxes; some lived in tents. They ganged cheerfully back and forth to classes in the Quadrangle and exulted in their liberty. "The wind of freedom blows" was the slogan, a good one, given us by Dr. Jordan—*"Die Luft der Freiheit weht."* But the rains came; the tents and piano boxes were drowned out; the mud between Mayfield and the Quadrangle was terrible. It was discovered and handed about that Ariel (whose offices were in the City) was no more; it was said that Charles Lathrop, a younger brother, reigned in his stead. The Encina rates came down to normal, the Encina youths gradually dribbled back to the Hall.

Poor Leslie at the University had dealings with Ariel but got along with him. We on the Row experienced him now and then, especially in the matter of our lights. Encina and Roble had candles, as Mrs. Stanford was afraid of kerosene lamps exploding and the electricity was late in coming. Alvarado also was wired for electricity; but the connections were not made, and we too used candles stuck on boards or into bottles and such lamps as we had. Then the light came. We turned it on at dark all over the house, upstairs and down, by two switches in the lower hall. We had never used electric lights before, and they told us the cost would be negligible. Glorious illumination! A few weeks later Ariel sent us word that the bill for lights would be twelve dollars a month, flat rate. We all immediately had them disconnected and stocked up on lamps, which, though reactionary, did us very well until meters were installed in the houses and we learned how to turn on one room at a time.

The Founders intended that women should be admitted to the University from the first, Mrs. Stanford shrewdly observing that if the men came first and the young ladies came afterwards "the young ladies might be considered as interlopers." A stone dormitory to match Encina was projected for them, as far off from the men's Hall as could be managed—the other side of the campus, with the Quadrangle between—and the blocks of cut stone lay ready on the site. But it could not be erected in time. A concrete "temporary" building (which is there yet) was rushed up instead, and the women students went into it in the fall.

More faculty houses went up on the campus. Alvarado was augmented at each end; and two new streets, Salvatierra and Lasuen, rapidly materialized parallel to it. When Louise, who came out during the first winter, was later married to Herbert Nash, she went as a bride to the house he built for her on Salvatierra, exactly behind ours, the two back yards separated by an alley. Ultimately Lasuen became the favored location for the palatial buildings of the fraternities and sororities. By then whatever squeamishness had existed about separating the sexes had gone—pouf! They were set beside each other, hit or miss, cheek by jowl, in some cases so close you could call good night from the windows. *Honi soit qui mal y pense!*

At one corner of the field, slightly away from the streets, the cluster of workmen's huts remained. The boys took them over, whitewashed them, and gardened them. Dane Coolidge asked Mrs. Stanford to give him trees, and she contributed Italian cypresses; he and his brother Herbert brought pines from the hills. The boys ran these buildings more or less hilariously as "The Camp." Boys lived here who were not the fraternity kind, and boys who worked their way, and those who had to eat only vegetables either from conviction or economic necessity—like the two brothers who subsisted on nuts and, having no money for shoes, went barefoot. The parents of these two sympathized with their sons and sent them for Christmas a hand-organ!

Almost from the first the fortunate possessors of real houses were besieged to rent rooms. But who ever heard of such a

thing? All the ten generations of my known ancestors, all my
family all my life long, we had never rented rooms, no matter
what. Our homes were always full with relatives and with
guests or anybody we wanted to take in; but how could one take
money for any part of our *home?* It wasn't done, and my house
was my castle, and all that. So one day I sat self-containedly
on my porch. A distracted-looking student came along the walk
and stopped. He looked at me hungrily. He glanced upward
and saw the two-story effect with obvious garret windows, turned
in and strode (he was that determined!) up to the steps. Had
we a room to rent? No, we did not rent rooms. But *wouldn't*
we rent a room? No, we never rented rooms. But, he said, he
should have to go away from the University if I did not rent
him a room. He had tried everywhere; there was no place;
except Encina, and the rent there had been raised; he was a
working student, waited on table for his board, I would not have
to board him—any kind of a room would do. He said he had a
cot bed if he only had a place to put it; he had a lamp, too, and
only needed a box to set it on . . . . I could but melt, and gave
him my attic chamber. I donated a chair and he carpentered
himself a table for his lamp. I bought it of him for fifty cents
when he went away. I refused to take pay for my room, which
was of no use to me at the time anyway; and he refused to
accept charity. We were at an impasse, finally compromised
by an agreement that for his lodging he should scrub the porch
twice a week, which he faithfully did.

When we came, "Palo Alto" was the name of the Senator's
estate and, more particularly, of his celebrated racing ranch
of blooded horses; and where the town now stands was nothing
at all but the plain running to the Bay, and one or two ranch
houses; otherwise mostly "wheat field." A coop of an agent's
office stood near the railroad track, and a slight open shelter
was the station, serving to flag a train now and then. A net-
work of surveyor's stakes, painted white, indicated the forecast
of a city. The literary street names were posted at the corners:

Bryant, Waverley, Cowper, Webster, Kipling, Tennyson, Melville, Everett, and so on. Yet it was two years, really, before people ceased shopping round all over the whole region and began seriously to build and populate Palo Alto. Mr. Stanford formally presented the name to the town; and the "Tall Tree" on the bank of San Francisquito Creek by the railroad bridge was adopted as its totem.

After the opening of the University the Stanfords were mostly away from the campus. They had many interests, and Mr. Stanford was a member of the Senate. They were at their Washington home in the winter. There was a short European trip in the summer of 1892, for his health, which was failing. The following winter he was in Washington but hardly able to carry on his usual activities. Yet the development of the University was their most vital concern.

Once, at least, the Senator had the great pleasure of receiving a group of students and of entertaining them at his home when in the spring of the first year some enthusiastic youths had the happy inspiration to call in a body and do him honor. It was an event always to be remembered by the boys, and the Senator was so pleased and touched that, it is reported, he felt and told his wife it was "the very best thing that has happened to us." The students were cordially welcomed into the house and taken into the library, where "they surrounded Mr. Stanford in a hollow square and gave the college yell." He talked to them about the University and what he wanted it to be. Afterward they all went into the dining room and had supper together with Mr. and Mrs. Stanford.

Mrs. Stanford, who was with us so much longer than he, was better known at the University than "the Senator." One of the girl students in a home letter dated 1896 from Roble Hall gives with charming frankness and appreciation the following account of a call at the Stanford home:

. . . . Helen Younger, Alice Colt, and I went to call upon Mrs. Stanford. She is apt to be home on Sundays as she is very fond of being here

for service in the Chapel. Our object was to invite her to the Roble
Thanksgiving dance or at least to use her name as one of the patronesses.
After our cards had been carried in by the Chinese boy who came to the
door, we were ushered through a little ante-room into the library. It
was almost twilight and the book-lined room with its heavy carved furniture was very impressive. Mrs. Stanford was writing letters at her
desk in the bay window and she received us very cordially and kindly.
We talked for about an hour and I sat where I had a perspective of the
library, ante-library, and the great dining room where the table was set
and made a very pretty interior. The funny part of it was that Mrs. S.
was so bound up in metaphysical thought, in memories of Leland and
her husband that I thought it would be simply impossible to mention
anything so mundane and frivolous as a Roble dance; the opportunity
came at last, however, and Mrs. Stanford seemed very pleased and appreciative of the attention and said perhaps she might come tho it was
a great strain upon her to meet people and especially people so near
Leland's age. When the lights were lit she showed us through the rooms
on the first floor and we followed her rustling silk-lined skirts with much
admiration. She took us around the long veranda and showed us beautiful glimpses through the trees and lawns, and was very hospitable when
we went . . . . she impressed us as being a very sorrowful, lonely
woman . . . . She dwells upon the personal thought of her loss so that
she lives in a future world where her conditions will be just as they were
on this earth before her dear ones left her sight . . . . She speaks so
affectionately of Dr. Jordan who evidently brings her no complaints or
worries and who has her utmost confidence.

The Stanford home, separated from the white-fenced paddocks and stables and barns of the horse ranch by a stately
avenue of eucalyptus trees, was approached from the University
by way of the upper edge of the Arboretum, along the chestnut
trees that bounded the vineyard, and by the winery. Its own
tree-shaded drive wound pleasantly along the bluff of the San
Francisquito and led to the highway close by the bridge over the
creek. The grounds, beautiful in themselves, were particularly
inviting to me because of the lawns, the irregular natural planting, and the homelike trees I found among the strange lemon
trees and oleanders. Vines embowered the house, a ranch house
built by a former owner and remodeled by Mr. Stanford into
something of a country mansion. The rooms were large, the
furnishings handsome and ornate. When at first we called on

Mrs. Stanford, she took us into the garden to show us the miniature railroad built for the child Leland. It was in a quite informal part by itself where there were trellises and gravel paths,
and it wound among lemon trees and friendly little flowering
bushes. She took us to another spot in the garden and showed
us a tomb, the plain brick building where the Boy's body rested
for nine years, until the Mausoleum was built. We read the
poem, "Haunted Ground," cut in its marble tablet.

We walked in the Arboretum. Mr. Stanford was affectionate
toward trees; the Arboretum was large, many acres, and had
all kinds of trees growing in it. It was to have been the setting
for a handsome family mansion adequate to their wealth and
the growing life of their boy. The spot for this house was selected and left vacant; and out from this site, through the Arboretum, ran a fan of avenues bordered with redwoods, cypresses,
and pines, the house to be the center of all. But it was never
built. We walked in the grove and looked up the silent empty
roads radiating through it, and saw at the center, remotely, the
granite Mausoleum with sphinxes guarding its doors.

The students have taken up the custom of keeping fresh
flowers always in the portico before the iron grill of the tomb
where the Stanfords lie. A pair, a boy and a girl, are appointed
each year, and every Sunday they go with flowers and leave
them there. But the radiating avenues are blotted out; one
cannot trace them now.

A tiny graveyard appeared after a while under the peppers
near to the Tomb: some little children gone too soon, a beloved
teacher, others. We must have a place to put our dead. But it,
too, is gone. There is nothing now among the pepper trees but
whispering grass, and quail, and a rabbit or a squirrel playing.

The second Commencement exercises were held in the Men's
Gymnasium, May 31, 1893. It was a large wooden building,
and with apparatus looped up on walls and rafters made a very
good assembly room. Chairs were ranked on the floor. Ever-

greens lined the walls far up, as far as the high windows which ran around under the eaves like a clerestory and let in the slanting shafts of the morning sun. The doors were open to the air and light. Flowers covered the platform wherever people did not have to sit.

The hall was full, with the graduating class together in front; and I sat not far away at the right of the aisle. The Founder was to speak. They had come from Washington back to their home here, and he was to speak. Mrs. Stanford was hopeful again; he was better, she said, he was like himself, bright and chatty, she said. He wished to see the students and address them, and was to speak on "What the University Expects of Its Students."

In the rear, at the door, a small group appeared. Mr. Stanford came in, a large man, unwieldy now, two men-servants bending toward him gently and helping him, supporting him under his arms. He walked slowly, heavily, up the aisle. The students clapped; but he went on slowly, step by step, laboriously up the aisle. Mrs. Stanford walked behind him, Mr. Nash giving her his arm. They reached the platform, climbed carefully the steps; and Dr. Jordan greeted them and placed them in their chairs. But the Senator did not speak. Dr. Jordan told us his voice was not strong enough, and he himself spoke for him on what the University expects of its children. Afterward Mr. and Mrs. Stanford greeted all who came up to them with their gracious cordiality, especially the graduates and their friends. A group of intimate invited guests accompanied them to their home for luncheon. Three weeks later, at Burdett, we heard of his death.

XII

EVERYBODY WAS YOUNG

EVERYBODY was young. Dr. Jordan, forty, our "elder states-man" and beloved leader. The Bible tells of a time when "Your young men shall see visions and your old men dream dreams." We had no old men, and before all our eyes the visions of youth were dancing. The men worked hard, with enthusiasm, devotion. Leslie came home from a committee meeting one night at eleven o'clock. I stormed. I declared I wouldn't have it:

"I don't believe in your working so hard. I never have and I never will. You no business to go back to the office evenings. The idea of your staying over there till midnight!"

"Only eleven . . . ."

"Bad enough!" (from the pillows).

"We had to decide whether to require Latin of all students before entering or only require it for certain courses." He spoke mildly. "It took some discussing," he added.

Everybody was having babies. I myself had a baby, a nice little thing named Christabel. Mrs. Pease, at the other end of the Row was pretty sick with hers, and declared she would go to *a hospital* for the next! It sounded desperate. The hospital idea for having babies was a novelty and we did not much like it. What were homes *for?* Imagine going to a hospital and bringing back to the other children a new baby, exactly like a pound of coffee or sugar! Our doctor came from Redwood— mine did—a good one, who arrived jauntily in a pearl-grey spring suit and a rose in his buttonhole. Our nurses—trained

213

nurses, if you please—came from San Francisco, and probably two weeks ahead of time, sitting around at twenty dollars a week, in case . . . . Mrs. Jordan's baby was born so soon after the opening of the University that the entering class adopted her: "Barbara Jordan, member of the Pioneer Class of the Leland Stanford Junior University." They purchased a silver set, mug, spoon, etc., with her honors engraved upon the pieces, and presented it formally in a velvet case. How proud and gay was the Pioneer Class of this notable addition; how proud and happy were Mr. and Mrs. President.

Barbara proved worthy of her unique distinction. She took hold of the world about her with her father's verve and acumen. Birds were her special delight. It was she who, as Dr. Jordan tells it, disproved in a flash some old philosopher's theory that the universe does not exist except in the mind. "But," says Barbara, looking around the garden where she and her father stood conversing, "it cannot be—*there's a squash*."

This charming and gifted child stayed with us only nine or ten years. You will see now the Pioneers' silver set and Barbara's collection of birds in the Jordan Room at the University, and a bronze memorial tablet with birds flying about it, which Bolton designed. When, many years later just after the War, we were collecting vast quantities of clothing at a vacant store in Palo Alto, to send to the children of Germany, Mrs. Green called me aside. She showed me an opened bundle that had come from Mrs. Jordan. She said, "I'm sure these are Barbara's things." We went over them together, delicate long white baby dresses and gowns, little sacques, gingham school dresses, old-fashioned, with full gathered sleeves and skirts, and bretelles. I knew I had seen her wearing some of them, for she and Christabel had been playmates. All were in lovely treasured order. Mrs. Green and I folded them together in a special package and put them with the thousands of garments going to clothe the children of Germany. We blessed them from Barbara, and let no one handle them but ourselves.

Christabel had double bronchial pneumonia at eleven weeks. The nurse had long gone; Nettie, the maid, had also departed. Until I got help we went for meals to a boarding-house which had started on Salvatierra. I was alone in the house with the baby; she choked up suddenly in her crib upstairs in our room. I could not leave her to call anybody; I looked out the window and saw Mrs. Marx below in her side yard and asked her to run for Dr. Wood, the University physician, living a few houses down the street. He came and gave ipecac, thus saving her from choking to death before our eyes that very afternoon; but we had a fight for it through the days that followed. Her fever was very high. Leslie, Louise, Bolton, and I divided the twenty-four hours among us into equal watches of six hours each; and she was never alone one moment. We noted every labored breath. We rigged an umbrella for a canopy over her crib and kept a teakettle of water boiling on a one-burner oil stove underneath; and for sixty hours she breathed, without cessation, the warm, steamy air. With no one to take care of it—the men had their University work, Louise had fish drawing to do for Dr. Jordan's scientific papers—the house got dirtier and dirtier, adding a sordid misery to our trouble. Then two big Swedish sisters who worked out by the day were engaged from Mayfield. Without asking a question or making a sound—I shall never forget how mouse-like they tiptoed—they cleaned my house from top to bottom, sweet and shining. They were then slipping away; but I ran after them to pay them. They would take no pay, I could not prevail upon them, they "wanted to do it." They spoke briefly, not saying at all it was because they were so sorry for us and the little sick baby. Perhaps I shed a tear there in the clean silent hall after they went; I was overwrought with anxiety and suffering, this kindness warmed and helped me. In my soul I kissed those two great Swedish sisters, those good women.

Dr. Wood was like our brother and friend. One would think the baby was his own. He came every day, twice a day, any time we called him, once in the middle of the night hastily, his trousers and coat on over his nightshirt. When she was enough better, we moved the crib downstairs into the parlor for greater convenience of nursing. Still she lay almost immovable, eyes closed, so quiet, every bit of her precious vitality conserved to fight the disease—she would not waste a movement, an extra breath for a cry. All the life force within her rose up and, moment by moment, battled death. Then, a day when she stirred a bit, she once put out her arm over the cover, she turned her head a little on the pillow. I was frightened! "Oh, she is worse—this restlessness! Go for the doctor—quick!" He came at once. He took her up out of her bed, gently; he walked up and down the room, back and forth; he looked down at her fixedly, walking gently back and forth. He laid her down in her bed, gently settled her, turned to us brightly—"*Why, she is better!*" he said. That very day she smiled at us, faintly, for the first time since her illness.

We sat on our porches a good deal. In the absence of trees or boundaries we had an unobstructed view right down the line of houses and could even exchange greetings from yard to yard. There was adobe in front—indeed, we were entirely planted on adobe, and we soon learned about it. My child went out to play in the field after it was wet up by the first rains. He soon came in hobbling like a dog with a sore foot, his poor little shoes caked with big clods of black mud, and asked piteously to be extricated. I took off his shoes and set them to dry behind the kitchen stove. We had mud at home; and we always dried it out and then brushed it off. But this technique failed; the adobe dried to *bricks*, that being its nature; I had to soak the shoes in a pail of water till the 'dobe turned to putty and could be scraped away; and the shoes were never the same again.

But adobe grew splendid roses. It was rich, unctuous, extravagantly generous, once you got on to its kinks. It gave us in time enormous Bartlett pears, honey-sweet, and peaches by the bushel. It grew us a passion-vine over the porch, lusty, aspiring to heaven by way of the roof, and bearing large spreading pink blossoms followed by oblong yellow pods about the size of young melons—though all this did not happen the *first* year, even in California.

At first we just sat there looking at the dry stubbly field in front and at the trodden stubble of our yards, and wondered what to do about it. We wanted lawns. Of course we wanted lawns. The natives hooted at us: nobody had lawns; oleanders and palms, cinders and gravel, and paths and cypress hedges— that's the way to make a garden. Lawns! Impossible. There is not water enough in all California to keep grass green all summer. Besides, we like the yellow color of the fields better. We Easterners stopped complaining in public, but our suppressed desires ate into our souls. Mr. Allardice (Mathematics) proposed we paint the whole strip of land which ran in front of the houses a nice green from end to end; but as he was a bachelor and irresponsible nobody paid any attention to him. When the rains came one family put in grass seed, and all the rest watched to see what would happen. Lo! it came up! It grew. It soon required mowing, like a boy with his first shave; and everybody was as interested as the boy's circle of relatives. Others sowed grass, and it all came up. After a while Leslie sowed grass on the whole of our place, front and back; and if, years later, it all turned from lawn grass to Bermuda, that was due to Mrs. Branner, who imported Bermuda grass for her back yard, next door to ours, because she wanted something that stayed green all winter and was hardy. She asked advice of Professor Dudley (Botany), and he said Bermuda. Ultimately all the lawns became that. Twenty years after, thirty years after, we fought Bermuda grass out of our lawns on the Hill. The entire campus ran to Bermuda grass, introduced by our dear and innocent Mrs. Branner. It was hardy.

Unanimous as to lawns, the Row had divergent ideas about the rest of the gardening, though Mrs. Earl Barnes, our natural leader from the moment she appeared, tried to blend us into harmony. She said, what was true enough, that we were a unit anyway, our houses and yards regimented by fate, and we ought to concert together some unified plan. Her fancy was a row of palms, one palm in each front yard. A few palms were planted—such is the hypnotic effect of natural leadership— but not by the Elliotts. Louise set red roses in the front and red geraniums under the edge of the porch. Louis and I made a vegetable garden in the back under the kitchen window, a square yard of lettuce and radishes. Louis asked if the seeds would come up flowers. "No. It will be something to eat," I said. After ten days the shoots appeared, and he came in from the yard with a smear of juicy green around his smiling mouth. "What have you been doing?" I exclaimed. "Eating my garden," he replied. Louise put in chrysanthemums and sweet peas, and a bed of marigolds. She said, "We must cover the ground." Roland, the Marx's small boy, came over one day in a fine frenzy and pulled up the marigold bed by the roots; Dorothy, his smaller sister, had kept them pretty well plucked off anyway, having a passion for yellow. Roland's mother imprisoned him in the house an entire day for this outrageous offense—it was Sunday, and I sat peaceful in Sabbath quiet, rid for many hours of Roland's *choo-chooing*—which always begot Louis' *choo-chooing,* and they two following one another around and around the yard in an endless trance of *choo-choos* pierced by occasional hoots, elbows working rhythmically. The Wings came from Madison (Engineering), and stayed with us until they found a place; and their baby, a fat youngster called Sumner, fell off the porch into the geraniums four times in the three days of their visit. The chunky Dorothy fell into the violets by the steps. Louise stuck the broken geranium stems into the ground and they grew again, but she said Dorothy was ruining the violets by so constantly packing the earth.

Louis played happily in the yard. Packing boxes lay there in confusion, and this was delightful. They could be any kind of thing and a dozen different ones in an hour. He was amused by the Chinamen's lingo and practiced doing it himself industriously. One day, seeming to feel he had achieved proficiency, he stepped up to the laundryman, Quong, and suavely addressed him *in his own tongue*. By permission he played in the "black dirt"—adobe—but the "white dirt," lime remaining from the buildings, was *verboten*. The black dirt before the rains was a gratifying coarse powder, excellent for shoveling into a red wheelbarrow to be dumped out again elsewhere; also good, in a bored moment, to scoop up and pour over one's head and shoulders; and one could comfortably wallow in it under the hot sun. He was allowed to travel across the field in front to the water tank that stood away there solitary, our supply of drinking water from an artesian well. It worked by steam, and a man was there tending it. Sometimes a professor would be at the tank with two big pails, or, if the chemistry professor, with a big container of heavy greenish glass shaped like a giant's enormous bottle. The professors hailed Louis jocosely, drew water, and carried it back to their homes. There was a litter of puppies once in the water tank shed.

Under the socializing influence of a playmate, Roland Marx, my son developed rapidly, Dorothy's occasional attendance at their play providing laboratory practice: They gambol in the side yard. Dorothy lumbers down the steps, joining them tentatively.

Louis (who has a peculiar horror of his bones coming out): "Dorothy, I will take your bones out." (Dorothy weeps.)

Louis: "Roland, shall we call Dorothy naughty?"

Roland: "Yes."

Louis: "Dorothy, you naughty." (Dorothy weeps.)

Roland: "You naughty." (Dorothy weeps.) When she cries so loud they are afraid somebody will come, they say, "Oh, no, Dorothy, you not naughty." She stops instantly. They begin all over again: "Roland, shall we call Dorothy naughty?" And so on.

But Louis got his comeuppance from the house on the other side of us where John Branner lived. John was some years older than my son, and scared Louis to death by making faces at him. He kept the child in a state of permanent intimidation by a simple strategy of booing and grimaces. Louis would come running into the house screaming that John "made faces at me!" as though he had been shot with a gun. It certainly did him no physical harm, those "faces," but children appear to have an aversion for the grotesque. Doubtless it excites their imagination. When Christabel was three or four years old, she sat on the lounge looking at the pictures in the *Bab Ballads*. Glancing up she inquired, "Did God make these pictures?" "Why, no, of course not," I answered. "Some man made them." "He was a bad man," she said in a tone of sober conviction. Once when I presented a child with a mildly comic mask, he repelled it with a sort of horror. Do they, perhaps, unfallen angels, recognize the Lucifer in distortion?

Our house had a bathroom with plumbing. Very elegant, for we had never lived with plumbing before, except an iron pump in the kitchen beside a sink which had a drainpipe discharging into a pail on the floor. True, the water "looked like mutton broth" and turned the tub and basins a dirty permanent yellow; but Mrs. Aber said we should not be upset over that. "Nothing," she said, "is worth the sacrifice of your equanimity."

The cellars, square holes beneath the kitchens, cemented up, leaked. I don't mean they leaked; the trouble was they didn't leak. They had steps down from the surface of the earth and old-fashioned sloping doors ("The prettiest girl I ever saw was sliding down a cellar door," Father used to sing). When it rained, the water gathered in a stream and flowed down the steps into the cellar and stayed there in a pond. It was not the water's fault, the place was carefully cemented, floor and walls, like a cistern. When the storm was over, perhaps my husband could bail the water out by the pailful; but if it was two or

three feet deep he despaired and sent for Everett Lesley, who
had invented a contrivance, and he came and siphoned us out.
For many years Everett Lesley siphoned out our cellar after
winter rains. And when we built on the Hill and someone left
a tap running in our basement there, and he was a respected
professor in the University instead of a working student, I tele-
phoned Mr. Lesley, with many apologies, begging him, for the
last time, to come and siphon us out. The good fellow did it;
that's the kind of a man he is.

We shopped in Mayfield for the simples of our housekeeping. It was a mile away, but I could walk it. I went one day
to buy a set of muffin tins. The small store was empty. I saw
the tins lying right before my eyes on the counter and waited
patiently to be served. No one appeared; there was no other
customer; the place was empty. I waited *im*patiently. I became
active and drummed on the counter; but no one came; there was
only a peaceful silence. The muffin tins lay there; I eyed them;
they were plainly marked at ten cents. Slyly I put my dime down
on the counter, lifted the muffin tins, and walked out. I felt like
a thief but escaped arrest. I suppose the storekeeper is wondering about the dime to this day.

I learned how to ask for potatoes in California. "Give me a
peck of potatoes, please." He looks at me meditatively a
moment; his face brightens: "Oh, you want two-bits' worth of
spuds?" "Two-bits" meant, I found, a quarter of a dollar instead of some negligible trifle—a "bit"! And they disregarded
the penny in the most off-hand way—like "here's a fiver and
keep the change." It surprised and dismayed me, for I was
never so circumstanced that I could pretend a penny was invisible. I asked the clerk for three-quarters of a yard of ribbon,
since that was all I wanted. It was ten cents a yard. "You might
as well take a yard," he said contemptuously; "you'll have to
pay for that anyway."

Mr. LaPeire, the Mayfield grocer, came every day for

orders; and blue-bloused Chinamen in couples brought fruit
and vegetables in panniers to the door. The panniers were
heavy baskets slung with ropes from wooden yokes, or poles,
across their shoulders, and running over with green and pink
and yellow—"Ni-i lettis," "ver' goo' stlawbellies today." But
heavy or not, whether you bought or not, the men trotted off
goodnaturedly under their swaying burdens and chanted melo-
diously their high-pitched cries.

Not until December was our adobe trail in front of the
houses given a board sidewalk. We watched with interest. "It
takes ten workman to lay the walk; and they hammer on the
average one nail in five minutes." Months later the road itself,
a mere rutted track left by the builders, was surfaced: "Twenty
chattering Chinamen in blue blouses and overalls making road
in front of the house, as sociable as so many sparrows; they
work leisurely, chattering Chinese all the time." We, from the
efficient East, always on the jump, always up to the minute,
found exasperating a nonchalance, a dilatory mood, a tendency
to dilute business with pleasure or with the easements of socia-
bility. We write home to our relatives: "When a man does
an errand out here he never walks to do it, but drives and takes
another man along for company. The bread man brings a small
boy with him to carry the loaf to the door while the man sits
and holds the lines."

None of us set up carriages; we walked mostly, went on
trains to our two cities, San Francisco and San Jose, and hired
from the Menlo livery stable at impossible prices when we had
to. An erratic and insufficient bus service gradually developed
when the town of Palo Alto was getting on the map. But in our
extremity there came a sudden burst of ameliorating bicycles.
It was the low wheel, just superseding the stately high one, and
we called them "safeties." All the men, Bolton and Leslie, too,
got them and learned to ride on the asphalt of the Quadrangle
or up Eucalyptus Avenue. Bolton's was all nickel, shining like

the full moon. He used to career around the country-side astonishing the natives. "They call me the Silver Rider," he
chuckled. A little later the women had them, too, and everybody went on picnics and expeditions into the back country.

It took some time for our domestic affairs to shake down
into a routine, circumstances being what they were. The Chinese cooks were rather beyond our means. Japanese "schoolboys" and full-time servants were to be had, and some of us
liked their skill and politeness; others did not relish them. A
lady from the Middle West declared with energy, "I don't like
the Japs—they bow too much!" The working students were a
resource. There were many of them, both girls and boys, glad
of the chance to earn; and often in later years we saluted as
faculty members here or in other colleges and as high trusted
officials elsewhere those who had been our cooks and housemaids
and student waiters—the word "hasher" had not been invented.

I had first a Japanese student. He soon departed because he
found that as he worked in our small, narrow kitchen the stove
was too hot for his head in front of him and the glaring western
window too hot for his head behind him; his head refused to
stand it and he left. Next came Florence and Della, two jolly
student girls, who shared the whole of the work between them,
four hours apiece. The plan was successful; but their schedules changed the next semester and they went away. Then I
had Nettie, a proper domestic, who did everything and gave
her mind to it, caring nothing whatever about being educated.
My sisters gradually came out and were with me, and though
they swelled the family they helped, too, and made things seem
homey. I gave the wash to the Chinese laundry, pretending not
to believe they sprinkled clothes by taking a mouthful of water
from a dipper and squirting it out through their teeth. Mrs.
Richardson discovered this by peeking into the laundry next
door to the Oak Grove Villa Hotel; she asserted he was sprink-
ling a tablecloth; but I never saw it myself.

We young housewives, educated women, married to our educated mates, started with one common ambition—not to get mired down under our housekeeping. Most of us wanted to "take" something, over at the University. One (but she had no children) began to study for her Doctorate. History courses were popular. Some took the writing courses—I did that. I took gymnasium also. There had been a gymnasium for women attached to Sage College, the women's dormitory at Cornell. There, twice a week, the girls took off their corsets, or were supposed to, put on an ankle-length, full, lined, grey-flannel skirt and a blouse waist, and did wand drill sedately round and round the hall. The advanced pupils had dumbbells. I think there were Indian clubs besides. But I, living at home, had to walk two miles up Buffalo Hill to college every day, and back, and was excused from gymnasium. Thus I had not these benefits, and so took gymnasium at Stanford. I had piano lessons of Mrs. Pease, and paid for them from some money I had from an article printed in the *Popular Science Monthly* recommending women to be content with the domestic sphere. What, you say, piano lessons! Did you have a piano? Yes. We were deep in debt; we had to buy furniture and all kinds of housekeeping supplies; living expenses were higher than in the East; we paid more rent; our salary was not enormous; and we invested in a piano! At least, we rented one, even before Christabel came, the rent to apply on purchase. What possessed us? Wind of freedom, I suppose. I could not play. We had had no piano at home; music did not run in the family; Father had a beautiful voice and sang a great deal, it is true; but yet he could *not* distinguish "Old Hundred" from "Yankee Doodle." However, I had always intended to have a piano and take lessons.

Adventure was in the air, here at the western edge of the world, where progress crested in foamy iridescence. Of course we need not be mired down by the housework; we intended to apply our minds to the problem. We did this in our several ways, busily. One of us got after waste motion, and tied a pedometer to the maid's leg to see how many miles she walked in a day doing the housework. Another adopted uncooked food—here in the land of abundant fruit, with almonds, walnuts, and olives hanging on the trees, and milk very nourishing, and bananas. Mrs. Aber advocated a diet of popcorn and spring water.

Our most pretentious experiment was the co-operative kitchen, conceived in theory and born of courageous enterprise. Seven campus families got together in powwows and elaborated a plan for one common kitchen with one cook (and a student helper) to prepare meals for us all at once. The powwows eddied furiously around the difficulty of getting the meals to the seven houses all at once, hot; for we had no idea of sacrificing the sacred privacy of our home dining rooms. It would not be hard now, for we know about nonconductors and asbestos; but then we knew only the tea cosy, and this, though we dallied with it, did not seem adequate. Finally we invented a container. A tinsmith in Mayfield made us seven of them according to specifications. The container was a large, heavy tin box with a strong handle at the top, a moveable shelf, and a door. In it were placed the several dishes of the meal, piping hot, prepared at the common kitchen; and a waiting student snatched it up and ran a Marathon to the house it belonged to. It must be the right house, because we had our own china. Somebody at the house received him and put the food on the table, which (we hope) was already set. The meal arriving thus like manna was peacefully eaten by the family sitting at home in seclusion, and the boy came and took back the empty serving dishes in the container to be washed and filed in the kitchen. We took turns bossing the cook and marketing, a week at a time; and Dr. Richardson's mother, a mathematical expert, kept the accounts.

The Kitchen ran for a year or two. At first we were gloriously inflated with our freedom from care and considered patenting our system. Then we began to think we were paying a price. This was not what we had intended. We had expected

that a real genuine invention would really and genuinely solve
the problem in hand, not offer us a bunch of new ones. Differences of family tastes and habits emerged, to everyone's
dismay. For what could be done when one of the seven ladies
grumbled that her table looked so *empty*, and she had to put
on private jellies, jams, catsups, salads, and cookies, to fill
out; and another grumbled because of turkey every Sunday,
which her family could not afford. And some detested onions
and others wanted them all the time; and some declared their
husbands refused to eat stew and others thought occasional
stew a necessity for moderate incomes. Protests were made
politely, jokingly, in our regular set powwows, and we tried
hard to accomplish suiting everybody. "But," we would say,
"you know you can have the menus your way when your week
comes. And the cook understands, and never does send you
boiled onions." The fact that little by little the monthly bills
went up and up (and Madam Richardson's figures were unmistakable) flabbergasted us. One kitchen, one coal fire, one
cook (plus a boy who got his meal for his help), and more or
less discount on buying in quantity, in place of seven cooks,
seven coal fires (at thirteen dollars a ton), and private buying
—our reasoning was perfect. But the bills went up and up.
The powwows grew even more lengthy and more entertaining—really quite a social function, where each one of us talked
in a sprightly manner about how her husband and children
reacted to this scheme (and other matters suggested by the subject) or, if the doleful type, deplored aggrievedly the difficulties
of domestic life. These gatherings became our clearinghouse,
our club, our avenue of expression. But they solved not our prac-
tical problems in the matter of the Co-operative Kitchen, and
presently it sank like any Utopia under the waves of experience—*spurlos*. The one idea, and that a heretical one, some of
us salvaged from the wreck was a suspicion that co-operation
was a fine theory but, practically, we ought to have hired a
manager to run the enterprise for profit.

Yet I would not allow myself to be mired down under the housework. Even after Christabel came, and I had thus two children, I would not. I decided to be the arbiter of my own destiny, privately, without co-operation.

I bought a patent dishwasher, and an Aladdin oven invented by Edward Atkinson of Boston—a grand achievement in the application of science to cookery. The dishwasher behaved like a perfect lady provided you used boiling water and did not expect her to clean egg off a plate with it. My dishes were washed in ten whirls of a crank, and dried themselves. They would have got out of the racks and put themselves away on the shelves, I am sure, if I had just known enough to repeat the proper formula. Aladdin Oven was a trusty slave, a complete success as a cook, providing you agreed he was to take his time. I did up the kitchen work with these mechanical helpers all by myself in no more than three hours a day (family of six) with ease and the éclat of mind triumphing over matter. I could loaf and invite my soul if I wanted to. But I never loaf. I am humiliated to confess it, but contemplation (oh, I fear!) bores me. What I did was to lay out all this extra time methodically (like in college). I practiced my piano regularly, finger exercises and "The Happy Farmer." While the baby took her forenoon nap I wrote "The History of the First Crusade." I went to my gymnasium class three afternoons a week, and anywhere else I wanted to go after three or four o'clock, when a sister came home to look after the baby. And I was *not* mired down under the housework.

XIII

THE UNIVERSITY SETTLES IN

Mrs. Jordan was New England; responsibility sat upon her with an easy grace. While we were racketing across the country on the train, she gathered "her ladies" about her (Mrs. Richardson and me) and unfolded her thought. The gentlemen would organize and develop the scholastic side of our adventure, and have their hands full at that. Our part would be to temper the scholastic with the social. We, she said, must plan occasions where professors and students could meet as the merest human beings and get acquainted. We must mother the girls, and indeed the boys, too, if possible. Let there be no formality, no barriers, everybody free and comfortable; and, remember, we are setting a pattern, starting university tradition for times to come. Everybody at ease with each other. And, yet, there *were* forms. I don't think Mrs. Jordan expected the "wild and woolly," or even suspected it; but New England and type were there and (but she was no prig) would delicately function.

Our first essay in social planning was naïve but effective, for by means of it everybody got acquainted. To this day "old grads" speak affectionately of the "Faculty-at-Homes" of 1891–92. The setup was simple and obvious. It consisted of ten houses close together in a Row, and Escondite Cottage, the presidential mansion, some distance off by itself at the end of an unlighted road. The faculty wives discussed the situation, agreed to co-operate, and as soon as the University opened sent out a printed card as follows—the numbers our house numbers:

228

President and Mrs. Jordan will be at home to the Faculty and students, at Escondite Cottage, on the third Friday of each month, from three to five and seven to nine.

The other members of the Faculty will receive in Alvarado Row at the same hours:

FIRST FRIDAY		THIRD FRIDAY	
Mr. and Mrs. Pease	No. 1	Mr. and Mrs. Wood	No. 6
Mr. and Mrs. Sanford	No. 2	Mr. and Mrs. Bryant	
Mr. and Mrs. Swain	No. 3	Mr. and Mrs. Richardson	No. 7
Mr. and Mrs. Jenkins		Mr. and Mrs. Howard	No. 8
Mr. and Mrs. Barnes	No. 4	Mr. and Mrs. Griffin	
Mr. and Mrs. Gilbert		Mr. and Mrs. Marx	No. 9
Mr. and Mrs. Griggs	No. 5	Mr. and Mrs. Elliott	No. 10
Mr. and Mrs. Miller		Mr. and Mrs. Todd	

These popular little parties served no refreshments. Why should we? People had plenty to eat at home, our domestic resources were restricted, and a continuous dropping in at one house and then the next and the next all afternoon and evening seemed not to implicate us in feeding our guests. The neat device of half the Row receiving on one Friday and the other half on another not only saved the students from plethora but gave the faculty people a chance to visit each other. The Friday when it was not your turn to be host, you happily functioned as guest. Informality was a necessity anyhow; but we kept an eye out for the intrusions of costume, caste, or rank. The winds of freedom—yet there *were* forms; and when a lady who was a sort of instructor among us took to wearing a white ruffled apron on the Quadrangle, she was "spoken to."

Mrs. Jordan arranged with the moon so that her receptions came in the light half of the month. The moon was much in our minds the first year, what with the mud, pitfalls, and the unlighted and uncharted pathways and roads of the campus. But if the clouds too much obscured the night, and the rain was too difficult, the Roble girls could borrow the lantern of the good-natured watchman for the mile between them and Escondite.

When they got there they might find the President in his slippers, feet up on the fender—Dr. Jordan could not be harnessed
and, besides, "Miss Jessie" indulged him more in those days
than later when we grew conventional and he had to be laced into
a dress suit. The Roble girls and Encina boys could sit around
on the floor and watch the fire while he told the tale of Peter
Coutts, or the Ghost Story of Adelante Villa, or how the grizzly
bears used to roam this region where now the campus is, or that
there were once *two* redwood trees on the banks of the San
Francisquito, twin landmarks for the whole countryside, and
many years ago one of them perished in a storm and went off
down the flooded stream to oblivion. The Coutts story was the
favorite, for the company was gathered here in Escondite itself
and could look around at the Frenchy fittings, the "tapestries"
with the "Little Trianon" flavor. We could go out next day
and gaze at the very bridge over nothing in the field, and explore
the tunnels in the hills, and take a walk to the brick tower the
Frenchman had put up "because Louis the Fifteenth had a
ruined tower at Versailles." Of its many versions, Dr. Jordan's
enchanting narrative of Escondite and the Frenchman was the
most satisfying. It goes without saying it was the most factually
inaccurate of them all; but a plague on factuality! He knew
how to catch butterflies without rubbing the plumage off their
wings.

When life became really established there were other receptions besides the "At Homes." Mrs. Jordan entertained the
faculty by itself. I imagine refreshments came in. But not
priggishness. There was a "nonsense evening" where we all
got up and perpetrated whatever silly stunt we had with us,
amid the genial roars of our comrades. Perhaps I did not recite
"The Dutchman's Baby," but if I had I would not have been
disparaged. Bolton, who could no more sing than Father, stood
up and caroled, solo, a funny song from his college days, and
Mary Roberts Smith prancing all over the piano trying to keep
her improvised accompaniment in key with his surprising varia-

tions. We had once a lovely masquerade party. I went as a French lady of the Empire, dressed in my white cambric Mother Hubbard nightgown which was girdled from indecorum by a wide elegant Empire scarf inherited from my ancestors, white cashmere with ends of gorgeous tapestry in red and black and gold. I had red morocco slippers, and my hair was high. Leslie made a great hit. As Father would say, "I didn't know he had it in him." For he went to the City and hired a gentleman's costume to match mine, and a wig and a small mask. Nobody could guess him, and when the mask came off and he smiled (enjoying himself) he looked so perfectly wonderful that I fell in love with him all over again. If gentlemen only knew the effect on a lady's heart of silver buckles, satin knee-breeches, embroidered "weskits," and swanky silk coats—and wigs!

When the ladies of Adelante moved to Palo Alto, which they did about as soon as anybody, and built them a house for their school, they gave dances in the attic and get-togethers in the halls and parlors, and were more popular than ever. Palo Alto was just beginning, the "faculty quarter" taking form among the oaks. They left oaks in the streets as long as they could, and the town looked sweetly umbrageous until traffic made its demands and one by one, reluctantly, amid growls and even curses, they cut them down and burnt them up for firewood. If there is one of that "Old Guard" left in the street, it has a red light on it; and thus we see that the joys of one generation become the dangers of the next.

On the Row, the neighbors met at one another's houses twice a month on Thursday afternoon to sew and chat and have a good time; a doubled-over sandwich and a cup of tea were passed around. We sewed, not for just "busy work," but because our children needed continually gingham dresses, and calico aprons, and blouses for the boys. No programmes; we improved our minds at other times; and certainly no stand-up-hats-on affairs. We aimed to enjoy ourselves. Perhaps this spontaneous habit was the origin of the Faculty Women's Club;

but hardly, for, when it came to that, we met in Mrs. Howard's parlor and deliberated with self-consciousness and responsibility as Founders. Where should the meetings be held? Well, at each other's houses, for there wasn't any other place—was there? Who should be included in the membership? A complicated discussion, ending by admitting everybody. What should be the name of this organization? Many suggestions came forth; mine was to call it "The Better Half," objected to by a literalist who felt that "the gentlemen might not like it." We settled finally on "The Faculty Women's Club," all of us charter members. The dues were to be negligible. We took our sewing to this club too, and took off our hats, and sat down, and enjoyed ourselves.

Some of us were asked to a luncheon by Mrs. Barron, a rich and beautiful lady living on a large estate just beyond Mayfield. The house was elegant, the luncheon sumptuous, Mrs. Barron quite perfect and unaffectedly kind. I wore my black broadcloth dress with white tucked chiffon vest, and, just for effect, added a small Eton jacket which I had made of red cashmere and lined with black silk. Mrs. Jordan liked it. She said to me whisperingly, "I'm glad you wore that jacket."

We appreciated Mrs. Barron's compliment and its aristocratic and wealthy flavor. We discussed what to do about returning the courtesy. A call, of course; but ought we not to entertain her in some way?

"I should never dare!" said our Mouse, trembling.

"I shall ask her to my house just as it is and give her the best I have," said our Lioness.

The students carried on as students do. The young ladies were a trifle demure under the eye of Mrs. Stanford and the Roble matron. Some of the young gentlemen were said to be "wild," and even "rough." I guess these terms in the 'nineties meant exuberance—which no one can deny to the Pioneers. The classic misdemeanor, trumpeted down the years, was the letting loose of a flatcar which stood on the spur track and running it down to the main line. What a stir! The newspapers headlined the crime and reported that it so incensed Mr. Stanford that only Mrs. Stanford's intercession restrained "the infuriated old man" from expelling the entire population of Encina Hall. I suppose this quiet, kindly gentleman, nearing his end, had never been infuriated in his life, and the faculty easily subdued the offenders.

Encina had student government, and roistered pretty much as it pleased. The boys hung out of the upper windows and dropped paper bags of water on people's heads, and dangled in front of the bus, on a fishline, signs such as, "Do you wear pants? etc." They made funny remarks out of the windows, too, at the passers-by, especially if young ladies from Roble. They smashed up their chairs, made "pie" of each other's rooms, and dropped dishes and furniture down the well of the stairway from the fourth floor so as to hear the smash. A "prof" living in that lively place was banged over the head with a pillow as he came out of the bathroom—"Oh, excuse me! I was laying for a fellow." The bachelor profs did not mind—merry fellows themselves so lately. The Hall did not mind the profs; invited them, so we were told, to their "feeds" whenever they had a box from home.

Lights went out in both halls at ten-thirty, and young folks were expected to be in early. Dancing entered shyly, tentatively; for mixed dancing was forbidden in the halls. Roble danced by itself, girl with girl, and Encina danced boy with boy. Roble presently staged a curious "mixed" party when half the girls dressed as men in borrowed evening clothes. But fraternities and sororities came in very early and houses were found for them. Quite uninhibited, they gave dances in addition to receptions and teas. In the second year there were "hops" at the men's gym, "mixed" hops.

Mixed calling was all right at Roble on Friday evenings. The parlor was in blue and pink, it was long and large, with a fireplace and "a pretty mantel at each end, and by each a pink

as well as a blue chair with large ribbon bows." The matron,
I suppose, sat in one of these obviously ceremonial chairs and
the young gentleman decoyed the young lady off into the corner—for the room *was* long and large.

The students tried to make an escapade of "stealing" grapes
from the vineyard. Going on a dark night in tremendous
secrecy helped; but as the professors frankly "stole" grapes,
too, and as the vineyard was open to everybody and not policed,
all this was not too devilish.

There was "booze" in Mayfield and also in Menlo Park;
but Mayfield was nearer Encina Hall. Those callow youths
who thought it part of growing up to be "hard-boiled" fre-
quented the Mayfield saloons. A group of them established a
special table with a cult and traditions, a table where they could
sit and slop their liquor and carve their distinguished names on
the top, and proceed to manliness according to code. I don't believe we had many bad boys, certainly not any degenerate ones;
and I suppose those who boozed in Mayfield came through that
phase like the measles and emerged into respected citizens—
that is, if they escaped being "taken to the edge of the campus
and dropped off." The town of Palo Alto was horribly Puritan,
for in every deed of property transferred there was a clause
that liquor should never be sold on those premises.

In March of the first year, our footballers went up and
trounced the Berkeley men. It ran, an electric shock, through
the State University, through San Francisco and the state of
California, through the entire country, through all the known
world, and it is probable Mars heard of it, and possibly it
caused extra spots on the sun. The State University had bragged
too much. The astonishing success and the immense prestige
of the new college had got on their nerves—they bragged bluff-
ily. They went around singing that "the glitter of that glamour
is no more!" And then we went up and walloped them—in a
special train festooned from end to end in flaming red, tooting
continuously the Stanford yell, the entire University, faculty

and students, bursting the coaches; our team, called "kids" even by their own captain, went up and played the game on the Haight Street grounds, and won!

Louis and I, who appeared to be the only people not taking the train, sat on our porch and saw them draping it in the brilliant red, saw the crowds streaming over the field to get on, and thrilled to catch the first *"Rah! Rah! Rah!"* of the engine whistle. Leslie left with them for the City but instead of attending the ball game went to the matinee and saw Joe Jefferson. He has regretted, he says, that error in judgment all his life. When he came home sedately alone at seven o'clock he brought us the news. Much later the special train drew in, still tooting the yell. There were three bonfires, and some feeble shouting, but the University was exhausted with victory and went, worn out, to bed. Bolton's description the next day was hyperbolic; but he swore to its truth: Lovina Ames had wept in the train from excitement and desired to swathe herself insanely in scarlet bunting; Roble was hysterical; the Encina men kept right on shouting and could not stop, although nearly voiceless. And the faculty were croaking and limp—next day they had to whisper their teachings to the class.

It was really almost too impudent when, a few weeks later, our baseballers went up and walloped the baseballers of Berkeley! This time the returning victors, besides bonfires, did a nightshirt parade under the windows of Roble and painted the little Palo Alto station red.

The Founders were planning a noble church building, and a site for it had been left in the arrangement of the Inner Quadrangle. Meantime one of the lecture halls was fitted up as a chapel. At one side of the platform with its simple reading desk Mrs. Stanford had placed a small organ, and a small screened-off corner served as a vestry. Several large oil paintings, excellent copies of great religious pictures in European galleries, gave the room beauty and dignity. For twelve years this was our place of worship. Then, in 1903, the great Memorial Church went up in mosaic, stained glass, and stone. And three years afterward, the earthquake cast it down to earth in ruins.

Mr. Thoburn was our saint and leader, a man so close to our hearts, so inwoven with the inner life of the University people, students and faculty alike, that when he died—so soon after his coming to us—and Dr. Jordan rose to speak of him at a memorial service, the president was unmanned by emotion, stammered, choked, stopped, and turned about helplessly, and someone else on the platform took his manuscript and read it for him. Mr. Thoburn was a Methodist minister preaching at Mayfield and, later, on the faculty; but in fact he was an archangel, probably. He could say such things as, "Anyone who has seen a mother has seen God." Many years after his ministry to us, a friend of mine told me this experience: She was one of our moderns who, well brought-up, had not clung to the church, supposed herself agnostic, if not an atheist, felt no need of a "God" or interest in the subject anyway. But once she was in trouble. She happened to make, at that time, a routine call on an acquaintance; and this person, a beautiful young woman, sat nursing her baby. Suddenly she looked down at her child with a different gaze, intense, abstracted, spiritual, the look of love.

"At that moment it all came over me"—my friend could hardly command her words here—"I can't express it—I was overwhelmed by a revelation. I *saw God*. I knew He was there. . . . . I was not thinking about any such thing—it just came . . . . that wonderful look she gave the baby!"

When she told me this I remembered what Mr. Thoburn had said.

Although he was our spiritual leader, Mr. Thoburn was not our official minister. We had none at the time. Our chapel pulpit was supplied by eminent clergymen of all denominations, many of them from the East. Our own faculty members "preached." Leslie did so at times, and he had the chapel arrangements as one of his executive duties, assisted by a committee. Mr. Mott arrived during the first year and stirred us up about Christian Associations, but the students themselves had already organized a joint Association of men and women. This indigenous form flourished a while with brilliant and devoted supporters but was later modified into two branches, and the Young Men's and Young Women's Associations, formed. Parents wanted a Sunday school, if children were not to grow up heathen in this outpost. An informal Sunday school sprang up for the little children, with volunteer teaching. For older people, both students and faculty, certain Bible classes were held in a Quadrangle classroom, or in the home of the leader. As the village and town of Palo Alto developed, churches were started there and church buildings put up. When our children got old enough to profit, as we thought, by the regular religious training of a church we gave up our long and fruitful habit of attending at the University and joined the newly organized Palo Alto Congregational Church. There our young ones grew up to be regular attendants, belonging to the Sunday school, the choir, and all, and they each joined the church in due time, quite voluntarily. We sat back, contented parents. Having trained them in the way they should go, we expected them when they were old not to depart from it. They are not very old yet, but, alas, now married and with children of their own, they have certainly departed from the churchly habit of their youth and heredity. They and their children are satisfactory to us; we think we have done a good job to have started them in life. What is the matter with them about going to church we don't exactly know. Maybe I do not attend as regularly myself as when we had children to set an example for.

Palo Alto soon developed its own churches, schools, a women's club, men's clubs, and other organizations. Zealous mothers got the public schools started, classes at first being held in private houses. The women gathered a handful of books, commandeered a room somewhere, and began a public library, open at certain hours with the women taking turns as attendants. Castilleja, and later the Harker School for Girls, gave an extra tone to the studious atmosphere. In a few years the town and the whole neighborhood around it came to be an educational center with not only the public schools but many private ones of different sorts, and in Menlo Park and out in the foothill country several fine institutions carried on by the Catholics. The University seemed the center of all. The Catholic College sent its young priests over to take our courses, and an occasional pair of nuns from Santa Clara, voluminously robed and coifed in black, paced our cloisters on their way to lecture halls. Every child in the schools expected of course to go to the University. Bracchi's children did so, and the children of Jasper Paulson, our original livery man; and the school work was molded to the University's standards. The State University at Berkeley grew steadily in numbers and influence from the moment of Stanford's arrival. With Dr. Jordan as leader and inspirer, the work of the Leland Stanford Junior University stimulated and benefited the whole of California, and we saw coming true in a larger way than he could forecast Mr. Stanford's aspiration that his wealth should bless the "children of California."

XIV

THE CHILDREN

MY IDEA of a special car was the kind that presidents and ambassadors ride in; but the special that carried us East immediately after the 1893 Commencement did not turn out that way. There were several faculty families going home for the vacation, and our men thought to economize by joining together and chartering a car. It was a ramshackle derelict salvaged from the junk pile; and we lived cooped up in it for many days, and what we saved in money we lost in self-respect. There were hordes of our young children along, that was one reason for having our private car, and indeed there was a sheet-iron stove in the vestibule where we could heat their possets. My alcohol lamp the porter would only let me use in the iron sink. The porter was not too attentive, thinking us of the emigrant class, no doubt. Yet when Louis knocked the marmalade jar off the seat and the porter came and cleaned up the mess, I saw Leslie pass him a fee, handsomely. Several ladies had their infants' diapers to wash in the toilet room, and they hung them out the windows to dry, except when going through cities and the porter forbade.

Christabel disgraced our family and tore the nights to shreds by wailing hour after hour for her "bangy." It was a disreputable little crib cover, soft and folksy, whose corner she wobbled up against her nose while she sucked herself to sleep on her thumb—and I had left it at home thinking this a good opportunity to break her of the habit. Heavens! Don't ever do

239

a thing like that, young mothers! You underestimate the tenacity of the human will. Every night on that long, hot trip, in that crowded car, she howled steadily behind our green curtain, with cries of "bangy," until exhaustion set in and she was overtaken by sleep. Substitutes infuriated her. I wobbled up her own afghan, the train blanket, her father's overcoat, and stuffed them into her hands and stuffed her thumb into her roaring mouth; but my agitated attempts to rectify a terrible mistake met with only anger and repudiation. I suppose none of them smelled right. She never gave up—we learned afterward, as we grew better acquainted with Christabel, that she never *did* give up—but in Burdett became gradually pacified to a new bangy which she wobbled against her nose while she sucked herself to sleep on her thumb as heretofore.

Very soon after we got home the news came of Mr. Stanford's death. I was not startled; it was not unexpected. I remembered his long period of ill-health, his ominous feebleness at Commencement. California was far away, the life there almost a dream; I was at home again with Father and Mother in the Banker house, the aunties down the road at the other house, the four girls, Gertrude, Zaidee, Harriett, and Bessie, in their teens, making a gay group to visit with. We were the returned wanderers, explorers, heroic pioneers, and adventurers, the center of attention, everybody delighted and curious. I was therefore too blissfully preoccupied with myself and my babes and the pleasure of the renewed familiar life to notice, at once, the significance of the death of the Founder. But Leslie understood. When we were all so merry together he sat silent. "Why were you so sober?" I asked him afterwards. "Thinking about them at the University," he replied.

There, at the University, everything suddenly stopped. The large properties forming the endowment must be probated; there was a business panic; Mrs. Stanford was advised by her counselors to close the University, at least until she had something more to pay salaries with than the monthly allowance granted by the courts for her private housekeeping expenses. I am not writing a history, this record is only what I know from my own living experience, but the account of this crisis given by Miss Bertha Berner, secretary to Mrs. Stanford, and her biographer, so expresses and confirms my personal impression of Mrs. Stanford and of our President that I may quote it here and agree to it. "Yes," I can say, "they were like that."

"After Mr. Stanford's funeral," Miss Berner writes, "Mrs. Stanford spent two weeks quietly, in an effort to form a plan for proceeding. . . . . When it was proposed by her business associates that she close the doors of the University she said: 'And do you think I believe that my husband's carefully laid plans can wholly miscarry?' Dr. Jordan hoped she would have the courage to continue; but felt he must not urge her." When, her mind fully made up, she sent for him and told him the University would go on, "the large man knelt and kissed her hand, both with tears in their eyes." Miss Berner saw this. She adds: "They were deeply moved, and when they had recovered their composure they began at once to make plans for carrying on the work."

I am not writing a history of those years; others have done it, and told of Mrs. Stanford's beautiful, careworn, steadfastness and of Dr. Jordan's loyal co-operation and unfaltering faith. The United States government complicated a situation already sufficiently precarious by bringing suit against the Stanford properties; let some wiser person than I explain what they did it for. The court stretched the monthly allowance granted Mrs. Stanford for her private running expenses and winked at her applying most of it to University needs instead. She reduced her own ménage as far as possible; she sold her valuable jewels to keep the University in funds. New buildings, new equipment, new faculty members, expansion of all kinds, was suddenly halted and for seven years kept at the anemic minimum which would still support life. *But the University went on.*

Not only the two leaders, Mrs. Stanford and the President, but the entire faculty did their part. They were already fused into unity by the bright flame of the first creative years and by Dr. Jordan's radiant initiative; and not one of them, either, was in this adventure for his own private profit. They stood by Dr. Jordan, they stood by the University. Gritty and unaffected, they just took in their stride seven years of denial and shortage in all departments, hopes gone glimmering, expectations abruptly canceled, and for everybody, even the least of the instructors, a ten per cent cut in salary. So we, the families who had to live—and merrily we did it, on docked incomes, when they had been less than sufficient before—we helped, too. And the University went on.

Our own salary was not too tiny; but we had afforded a move across the continent and had set up afresh in a new place, we had afforded pianos and babies (another came along in here, David), and we had helped our home people at need. We were in debt and seemed to go right on being in debt. I'm sure those who had money invested in us and received their interest regularly never worried. Neither in general did we. I was an experienced economist—born and bred in a brier patch! I knew the exact worth of an egg and how to do without it, hygienically. I could and did calculate the cost of each meal, and of each dish of the meal: Meat so much, and I knew all there was to know about preparing cheap cuts to be good and nourishing. The dessert so much, and no more, and I knew plenty of them within that limit. But one day my nerves did get fractious and I worried, for the moment, because of our financial obligations. I walked along the Row to tell Mrs. Barnes about it, our counselor and friend. We sat down on the lawn in her front yard and I unfolded my tale, and plucked at the grass and dribbled it through my fingers abashedly as I confessed to her that we were *in debt!*

"Why, poor child," said Mrs. Barnes, "we're all in debt; didn't you know that?"

Perhaps I ought not, but I rose up on wings of alleviation and walked home completely rehabilitated.

Those years, long and troublous to the University, sparkled for us with the children. Christabel, especially, dances through them. She went to Burdett with us (disgracefully, as has been told), and during our first leisurely summer there fell in love with her grandmother. After we came back, she was being constantly discovered writing to her grandmother quite long letters. On the porch floor she sat, earnestly covering an envelope with scribbles. Scribble, scribble, scribble: "This is going to be a letter to my Bamma—I hope," she said. Scribble, scribble, scribble.

Dr. Branner, elder statesman with our President, passed on the boardwalk every morning at a certain moment going to the Quadrangle (and those who arrived for his eight o'clock geology class at two minutes after found the door locked). He called to Christabel friendlily, and she counted on it. Once he said: "I'm going to Europe next week. What shall I bring you when I come home?" "A bear," she answered instantly. And a bear he brought her six months later, a carved wooden bear from Berne.

She went up the Row to the Griffins' house—they had no children and were fond of ours—rang the bell; the door was opened by Mrs. Griffin, and Christabel sweetly presented her with one of my silver teaspoons. "I will give you this," she said, and lovingly smiled. Mrs. Griffin, with exquisite tact, thanked my child, accepted the gift, and restored the spoon to me privately with explanations. That lady deserved children of her own.

She yearned to carry umbrellas in the rain. "Umbrelloo-o" she called it, with fine appreciation. Nobody would hear of such a thing, though she tried us all. She would "get wet." Absurd! When you carried an umbrella expressly in order to keep dry! "The sharp ends of the ribs would stick into her

eyes"; this was too frivolous for notice. She must not even
"fuss with it" when she found it stretched and shiny, a magic
tent, drying on the floor of the back hall. The precise, spring-
ing ribs, the round black dome, it would exactly fit her for a
little house, and she must not "fuss with it!"

On a drizzly, windy day she blew down the walk to her
father crouched on the lawn pulling weeds, and requested him
nonchalantly to open a big family umbrella she had brought
from the porch. He replied, jocosely, with appropriate and
lively gestures, that should he open this umbrella for her "the
wind would blow her over the house!" Dr. Abbott (Law) then
came by, accompanied by his Lois, and stopped to chat with
Leslie. Lois, a much older child than Christabel, was carrying
jauntily her small umbrella. Christabel, behind her father's
back, asked Lois in a polite and confidential voice please to
open hers; Lois obligingly did so and placed it in her hands.
A shriek! The two men whirled around. The wrestling umbrella tore loose from the wrenched, horrified child (expecting,
of course, to be blown over the house) and dashed gamboling
across the road to the field beyond. Leslie spared one swift
glance at his daughter crying wildly on the sidewalk and set off
to catch the crazy thing. They raced, he soon clogged with
adobe, the umbrella impeded by coquettish pauses and tacks.
Yet it was a good race. Brought up against the bleachers by the
gymnasium, the umbrella was captured and subdued, and Leslie
had won. That evening, Christabel sat on the floor before the fire
warming her toes. Her father, also warming, stood leaning
against the mantel; and I, who had glimpsed him through a
neighbor's window down the Row, asked to be told why he was
running across the field by the gymnasium that afternoon without his hat. He looked down at our child.

"It was all because of Christabel's disobedience."

This awful sentence was delivered straight at her, with sol-
emnity, by an adored parent whom she considered, with reason,
her perfect lover and complete bond-slave. It was too much.

Overwhelmed, she dropped her blonde head upon her breast and burst forlornly into heartbroken sobs. We could but laugh, the woe so large, the child so small! Leslie gathered her up and carried her off to bed, as usual.

It seemed the Wise Woman, or whatever your mythology names Dame Experience, had her eye on Christabel, who would learn in no one else's school. The day she ran away in her nightgown the Wise Woman obviously took a hand. I was away from home, Louise in charge. The children were put to bed for their detested afternoon naps, undressed. We undressed them because it was safer. Her mother absent, the winds of freedom blew Christabel promptly out of her bed. Marguerite Beauty was left in it, firmly covered up and told to be a good girl and go straight to sleep. Christabel tiptoed to the door, opened it, listened, tiptoed out and down the stairs, finding bare feet providential, slipped noiselessly through front hall and back hall, listening, and out upon the little back stoop. The beautiful green lawn lay before her all over the vast back yard. She descended the two low steps and stood in the cool tickling grass. Then—horrors!—some one was behind her; steps, a voice; Aunt Louise *was after her!* Electrified, she ran, picked up her nightgown, ran like Eve across the grass. Louise pursued. And the Wise Woman entered invisible, placed a bee on a head of white clover. Christabel's naked foot, flying, trod upon the clover, the bee (and who could blame it?) *stung.* Thus once more my child, following the gleam, was cruelly curbed to reality.

On account of Christabel's adventurous disposition, I procrastinated about taking her to church. Louis had begun early, behaved properly, and liked it well. There were the big pictures on the wall to study; there was singing, and the organ, and meeting your friends, and the Sunday atmosphere of specialness, a little wonderful, a little awesome in a nice way. I could not tell how it would strike Christabel; I waited for some reassuring maturity. Mother always said "children outgrow a lot of things." I was waiting for a while until she should outgrow her incalculableness.

But at four-and-a-half she went with the rest of us to church as a Christian child should, and found there much to attract. She had a "Sunday dress" (these were not yet obsolete), red, which was, naturally, her favorite color, and a red fez to match. She walked hand in hand sedately with her father down the whole length of the Row, on across the enormous expanse of the Quadrangle to its very furthest bound where was found the Chapel, with many pleasant people going in. Seated, she could smooth my kid glove in perfect silence and secrecy, and smooth Mrs. Griffin's silk dress on the other side in delightful surreptitiousness. She could turn the hymnbook leaves, slo-owly one by one, though her mother objected to this and she herself was annoyed by the whisperings the leaves *would* make, turn she never so softly. If she dropped the hymnbook she was scandalized, not from morals but from artistry, for she understood decorum and had no intention of being noisy in church. Her handkerchief was silent; she remembered it. She pulled it out, spread it flat to see how big it was, rolled it up into a ball to see how small it was, took off her fez, draped the handkerchief over it neatly and placed it on her head again with care. The white flaps hanging down each side of her cheeks gave her an Egyptian effect; she leaned back against the seat, now quite spent and flaccid, a martyred child. All this was amusing to others of the congregation besides Christabel.

Once by some unfortunate miscalculation of mine she and Leslie preceded Louis and me to church and sat up in front, across the aisle and two seats ahead of us—where I could plainly see but was helpless to control. During all of what happened she never once looked at me, and she appeared to be unaware of my existence. Her father, ever imperturbable, early abandoned the notion of checking her activities and composed himself to pay attention to the sermon. It was long, and she had time for all her repertoire with encores; imagine my uneasiness.

Uneasiness? Nay, panic, when Leslie, the king-pin of chapel arrangements, was announced to "make a statement" after the minister was through and sat down. Calm and Olympian, he *left that child alone in the seat,* and ascended the rostrum. Christabel, who had been frankly bored at the last, now revived and looked about her. She began furtively to hitch; she hitched slowly and with apparent deference to the other end of the seat; then after a pause and a smile around at her friends she hitched back again. The statement went on. She cast confiding glances about her, but not at me, sidled stealthily into the aisle, pussy-footed forward, and coyly mounted the low edge in front of the rail; turning, she stood below the reading desk and faced the congregation. Mrs. Stanford sat exactly opposite her a few feet away; she bestowed on Mrs. Stanford a pleasant smile. The people were now paying more attention to his daughter than to Leslie. She became apologetic as she stood, and began looking as though ready to sink through the floor with bashfulness. How could I (she seemed to think) have got into this conspicuous position—what *can* be done about it! She could still emit feeble smiles, however, apparently responding to those in front of her. Another mother sitting near me turned and gave me a laughing look. Louis at my side was astonished and troubled. Leslie kept on with his statement. (If it had been I there above her in the pulpit I should probably have leaned over and hissed.) In her humiliated mood she put out her arm along the rail and laid her head languidly upon it, her face turned shyly toward her audience. Slowly she raised it again; gingerly she stepped down off the ledge, glanced right and left sociably but with perfect restraint, wavered back to her seat. The statement drew to a close and the meeting dissolved. As we came out, I with her hand firmly in mine, the laughing mother told me not to punish her: "She didn't mean any harm." And Mrs. Stanford shaking hands with me turned off my apologies, saying she thought the child looked "very cunning"; and a professor friend of Christabel's patted her head indulgently and said *he* thought her a "pretty sight *anywhere*." Ever in cahoots with the public, how could my daughter be disciplined, save by the occasional indirections of the Wise Woman?

Our children reverenced Mrs. Stanford, the great lady who always appeared in elegant garments of velvet and brocade, fringed and flowered, and very impressive bonnets, she tall and large, yet bending down to them graciously and kindly, not noticing their awe. They knew who had created the Quadrangle and all our little world. Louis gave me a paper on which he had been seriously writing one Sunday afternoon, asking me to keep it for him; and this I have done for some forty years. The paper runs:

> Mrs J. L. Stanford wife of
> Mr. L. Stanford the founder
> of this university (stanford U)
>) her husband died and
> she is founder now.
>
> she KISSED me
>
> (Date April, 29, 1899.)   sunday
>   coming
>   home from
>   church
> my age 10. years old
> my weight 63.½ lbs

I have had three mystical experiences in my life, each momentary but as distinct and unmistakable as any impression received through the senses. One of them concerned David. He slept at night, when a few months old, in a tiny hammock swung across our bedroom, and swung high for my convenience in caring for him. At four o'clock in the morning, in a profound stillness, I suddenly woke—a touch on my spirit. I was called, certainly. There was no sound. I rose up in bed and instantly in the faint dusk saw the hammock sagging; at that moment the knot was slipping. I sprang out and secured the rope in place again which, if I had not wakened, would have given way and dropped the sleeping baby to the floor.

David was a wind-harp to joy. The sun shone through our eastern window and roused him in the morning; he sat up in his crib, silent, with shining eyes, and fell into a rapture, quivering with it from head to foot. Just so he quivered when he saw the ocean for the first time from the high cliffs of the shore. He was no more than two. "Otun! Otun!" he cried, trembling with excitement, and we could not lead him off to the cottage but he must be turning back and stopping to look again in half-fearful wonder and delight. We called this thrill "David's tremolo."

Stars intrigued him; so did angels. At three he understood things, and looking at the night sky remarked sagely, "Stars b'long to Papa." He was regretful when his father told him George Washington was the father of his country; "Then it wasn't you?" he said. Leslie, superintending his dressing, once spoke to him very severely about dawdling. David clouded over for a grieved moment, then gaily recovered with: "That's the way I shall talk to my little boy when I grow up and have a little boy!" He asked of course the usual disconcerting questions, such as, "What makes the days always go forwards and never go backwards?" "What makes the sun stay up?" The last he answered satisfactorily himself, when I confessed that *I* did not know what made the sun stay up. He chortled and said, "It stays up 'cause it don't come down."

"Did you ever see God?" he asked me. What a spiritual nature my son has, I thought.

"No, David."

"Ever see an angel?"

"No" (still swelling with pride.)

"Ever see a tame Indian?" (A mother deflated.)

"I suppose the evening star will be especially bright on Christmas Eve," he said as he walked on the campus one night in December and looked at the spangled sky. "Do the angels still sing in Bethlehem?"

In a philosophic mood he had "thought Jesus was just goodness—but I knew there was a God." A pause; then, doubtfully,

"Is Jesus real, or is he just goodness?" "Holy! Holy! Holy!" which his father sang to him to go to sleep on gave him not only a favorite pleasure but food for reflection. "Though the eye of sinful man Thy glory may not see," it ran.

"Why can't man see the glory?"

"Nobody but good people can see the glory. 'Sinful' means bad. Bad people can't see the glory."

"Where do bad people go?" (vividly), *"down the pipes?"*

David did not affect mechanics; he could never have invented an airplane. At five he went hopping around the bedroom, half-shod, crying out his vexation at having two feet—"I *wish* I only had one; I do hate to button my shoes so!" It was the joke of later years to try to get him to work in the garden; the spade, the hoe, he avoided automatically. In college, he came home growling that his psychology course was involving a study of the physical brain. "Don't you want to know how your brain *works?*" we asked, and got the reply—very pettish for David, who was the soul of good humor—"I don't want to know how *anything* works, so it works!"

But in childhood he greatly desired to fly; not in a machine at all, but by his own power. "I have wings on my feet!" he cried, and went flopping and leaping all over the place. As he flopped he asked me would his arms turn to wings if he kept on long enough. In view of the evolutionary process I could not flatly say no but warned him from expecting it too soon. He did not believe me. He went on flopping at every spare moment, sometimes exclaiming, "I'm going to fly!" and sometimes, "I'm flying! I'm flying!" Lionel Lenox, his playmate, a realist, got very tired of it. It was dull for Lionel. The pear trees were in bloom one day, like tall snowy brides on the green lawn, and the roses in a spring riot. The boys went out to play. David took off down the back steps like a bird, leaped across the grass, bounding, running, bounding, and beating his arms. "I'm flying! I'm flying!" he shouted. Drearily, discontented Lionel trailed after him, quite a ways behind: "Da-a-avid! Da-a-avid!"

he called. "You *can't* fly!" Well, he couldn't. But David never owned up to it. Lionel was beaten to begin with.

But these youngsters must be educated; the University showed no intention of undertaking it "from the kindergarten up." We very early established one or two tentative kindergartens, and after them a miniature primary school. These were all managed by parents in powwow and paid for out of our already depleted pocketbooks. The Engineering Department lent us a room. The most celebrated of our first attempts was, I'll be bound, a forerunner of the modern "progressive school"; for the little pupils were to do as they chose and not be forced into a Procrustean system. Consequently Knight Jordan (this is the celebrated part) chose to make his exit from the schoolroom by the window, sliding down a board, instead of by marching out through the door. I could never see the harm in this— I loved to skip through the low unscreened windows of my childhood—but so many thought otherwise that the "experimental school" idea was discarded.

I suppose we would never have had the enterprise to start on those radical lines anyway but for Professor Earl Barnes. He began at the beginning and taught us mothers to keep babybooks and record with dates and supplementary information the appearance of the first tooth, the first smile, the first word, the number of words in the vocabulary at one year (if any), at two years; does the child speak plainly or merely "garble a few extracts?" (*Mem.:* Never talk baby talk to your infant. This is as bad as rocking it to sleep.) These notes would later be correlated with the teacher's observations and theories and thus a new and superior science of pedagogy emerge—the laboratory method. It sounded good. The book I kept for Louis ran to two volumes, Christabel's a scant one; and poor David got a mere gesture, mostly blank pages. But that was my fault—I just fell down—not anything to do with the noble science of pedagogy.

Dear Ora Boring appeared about that time. I saw her first at my front door, notebook in hand, asking modestly, like the gentlewoman she was, if she might make a few notes on my children's reactions to the color element: she was taking one of Professor Barnes' education courses. Oh, certainly! Louis and Christabel (little guinea pigs) were brought in from the sandpile and stood, big-eyed, in front of the strange lady on the lounge. She showed them strips of colored paper and asked them which they liked best. Christabel preferred bright red. Louis preferred bright red. The reactions were written down. Ora thanked me for the loan of my offspring and returned to her class. Dear Ora! Her lovely life and friendship were with us through the years.

I must here make a parental footnote *re* laboratory method. For we found the children frequently slipped out of the formula, as the soap escapes from the hand in the bath water. As when I taught the infant Louis that the earth is round, "like a ball, not like a plate," and he proudly recited it to Leslie at night: "The earth is round like a ball not like a plate," then spoiled it by immediately inquiring: "When will the earth go Back East?" And later, when he was old enough to properly assimilate information from the *Geographical Reader*, Louis showed this same obtuseness. I read aloud to him—and he seemed pleased and appreciative—the chapter on "Mountains," with its clear account of the different ways in which mountains are useful to human life—condensing the rain, forming springs which become rivers, nourishing forests, and so on. When finished I began to examine him from the list of questions at the end of the chapter: "Now Louis, what are the uses of a mountain?" "To look at and to climb," was his prompt reply.

The engineers were soon obliged tenderly and regretfully to turn our kindergarten out, needing all their rooms for themselves. We remembered our legal privilege of free schooling, and inquired what district we were in. Mayfield. Impossible on several counts. Could we then be set off into a district of our own? Impossible ruled the Boss of Mayfield—who could not be blamed for wishing to keep hold of the tax money allotted him for the campus children. Mrs. Stanford was none too cordial to the proposal. A mess of difficulties had to be cleared away. It was done, after much powwow in all quarters, and a campus district set off. Then we found we could not have a schoolhouse because the state refused to build on leased property and the University was prohibited by charter from selling its land. Mrs. Stanford objected to a schoolhouse anyway. Professor Green and I, as trustees, traipsed around the campus day after day trying to find any hole or corner where we might insert an inconspicuous school, and found nothing except an unoccupied room at the "Camp." It was a whitewashed shell, which might do if we could enlarge the window and somehow close up the cracks in the floor. But I was all for a tent, instead, remembering their adequacy in the case of a circus. Mr. Green doubted a tent: it could not be kept warm. Oh, yes; two *big* oil burners; it would be much easier warmed than that barn of a clapboarded place in the Camp.

Mrs. Stanford then suddenly came round and proposed to build us a schoolhouse herself, which solved the problem completely. She did so, had a neat two-room building erected on Salvatierra, and adorned it with a cupola and a bell. Charles Lathrop, the University Business Manager at the time, for the school water supply provided the dirty water from Searsville. At our loud protests, he answered that he could not put in the good water (we had it in the houses, for drinking) as the children would just waste it! Yet from this tribulation also we were presently delivered. A teacher was obtained; our children were marshaled, and we became no more "experimental," but an ordinary American public school. Ordinary? Yes; but look at our Termans and Cubberleys, and the beautiful great Education Building. Perhaps a little seed was sown when Earl Barnes set us to keeping baby-books, and Knight made his contribution to the laboratory method by tobogganing out of the window.

XV

OUR RELATIVES

MY BROTHER Bolton, wondrously elate, strode into our sitting room at 10 Alvarado, his hands full of a large cream-colored, paper-bound book; with a magnificent gesture he flung it across from wall to wall. It unfolded as it went and fluttered down in a long strip of gorgeous color, panel after panel, the landscapes and seascapes of Nippon. Bolton it seems had acquired Hiroshige's "Upright Tokaido Series," a perfect copy, pristine, evidently just from some aristocratic godown where for a century it had been treasured until necessity and commercialism had fetched it out across the waters and into the stock of a San Francisco art dealer.

The color prints had been discovered a while back when some Parisian artist on the Left Bank took home a piece of cheese he had bought and found it wrapped up in a lovely picture, dishonored and in tatters, like Cinderella. About the time we came West they were just beginning to be brought to the shops from Japan, and Bolton saw and loved them. He was canny enough to find out when the ships were expected that carried them, presented himself at their arrival, and saw the cases opened in the storerooms. For this alacrity his reward was to be given first pick by the dealer and "any one for a dollar." As the "Upright Tokaido Series" comprises fifty-two prints, he may have paid for the whole book five dollars or so.

"See what I got!" he cried that day and threw out the glorious strip and fell back completely englamoured.

For a time Japanese prints engrossed us all, Bolton's enthusiasm spreading. He amassed them, brought them to us, exhibited them in public and in private, expounded how they were to be looked at, and scolded us when we looked at them wrong. When I got used to the conventionalized faces, the lack of shadows, the disconcerting oddity of bands of color used decoratively and for no other purpose at all, I began to enjoy them and ended by taking them intimately into my soul. I learned to discount the eye and respect obscure perceptions nearer to the springs of truth.

The art of the Orient was new to us and endlessly fascinating. We went up to San Francisco's Chinatown as to a fair—it was more Oriental before the fire and its rebuilding after that with plate glass and self-conscious roof lines. We loitered in the tiny dark shops, disorderly and full of treasure as a bandit's cave. We said "there is nothing like it in Hector"—Aunt Lida's classic phrase. We bought small curios for a dime or two-bits, nodding Mandarins, a doll-sized teapot, a translucent porcelain cup thin as a shell, lacquer trays and jewel cabinets, and trick boxes made of sandalwood which we forgot how to open when we took them home to give to the children.

"Look," said Bolton, turning a brown earthen vase lovingly in his hands, "the print of the maker's thumb!" And there it was, faint but significant, a communication from mind to mind.

The Art Department of the University blossomed out early. Bolton staffed it from the East: Arthur Clark, his Syracuse chum; Lovina Ames from Burdett and Zoë Fiske from Ithaca, both former pupils of his. The life class unfortunately was soon eradicated; for a kind gentleman one day conducted Mrs. Stanford unannounced into the studio. Startled, she saw the seated circle of boys and girls gravely intent on drawing the human figure from the model—nude. She got out as soon as she could and promulgated an order forbidding life classes at the University forever.

Perhaps it was inevitable that Bolton should fall in love with Lucy Fletcher, she being the most beautiful thing in sight. They were married in Castilleja parlor with our family and a few friends attendant, and Father and Mother who had by then come out to California from Burdett. The wedding was strictly characteristic. Bolton managed everything. He directed where people were to sit or stand; his own hands laid on Lucy's dusky hair the chaplet of white star-flowers he had made, the minister who read the ceremony which Bolton had composed was brought by him from afar for the occasion. Afterward he carried off the bride (like a cat with a captured mouse) for a two-months' honeymoon in the high Sierras, where they camped and tramped and lived their arduous solitary days according to his plan. We have no reason to doubt the sympathetic co-operation of the bride—else why did she marry him?

Bolton went up a mountain passionately. He pursued it, explored it, experienced it, mastered it; for there was Beauty to be won. He conquered the Sierras. He studied their vast intricate contours, the rock formations, the torn trees at timber line, the snow fields, the solitudes of the crest. Some of his exquisite drawings appear in his lithographs done long afterward at Woodstock. A peak in a Sierra range is named for him: "Mount Bolton Brown." An odd name for a fact of nature, yet, remembering Bolton, not so bad.

Father was hurt not to perform the marriage ceremony. "I would have married them with any form they wished," he told Mother, privately. But Bolton could always misjudge Father. He thought him "bigoted," and Father was about as bigoted as a morning-glory. Being by now a "free"-thinker (I say "by now," but it was doubtless congenital; you recall Boltie sitting obstinately in church with his hat on), my brother indulged quite angrily, like most radicals, in assaults upon the creeds of other people.

Father was, I suppose, brought up in what is called the Puritan tradition, though I cannot associate his parents, my grandparents, with its popular disparagements. He loved "the Church," reverenced its traditions, was devoted to his ministerial calling; his nature was affectionate and religious, and he had no rebellion in him. Besides, one did not go through four years of Yale College in the 'fifties and three years of Union Theological Seminary "preparing for the ministry" for nothing. But Father was also a scholar, a broad-minded one, clear-eyed to fact, imaginatively aware of implications and overtones; and his reading and thought were unimpeded and far ranging. All this did not make a silky mixture, but he managed it. He wrestled it through.

"What is the matter with him?" I asked Mother, who always knew; for it was Sunday, in Ithaca, and Father had looked woebegone and had finally stepped into the yard and quietly "puked"—it used to happen to him that way at moments of internal struggle.

"It's the Unitarian minister at the Chapel" (the University Chapel where we heard all the prominent men from Dan to Beersheba, and Father enjoyed them all). "Your father wants to go and hear him preach but thinks he ought not because of his being a Unitarian." Yet in time Unitarians became as other men to him.

The theory of evolution worried people terribly in the 'eighties. What if it *should* be true that we were descended from monkeys! The monstrous idea taking the place of the dignified and sacrosanct story of Adam and Eve in the Garden was hard to stomach. Nobody then was pointing with pride to the poor monkey who had pulled himself and descendants, with no help from the serpent, up from the beast to manhood. None said "I'd rather be him than Adam." (Though *I* consider Adam a weak sneak who pulled us all down with himself to perdition, where we still are.) And Father, too, like other people, was fastidious about ape ancestry. But, characteristically, he wrestled it through. One day, in Ithaca, where in the purlieus of a college openly branded as "infidel" we had the discussion always resounding, he came and stood before us, his bearing grave, almost ritualistic, and said:

"I have accepted the doctrine of evolution."

I, young and unreflective, had not so much "accepted" the "doctrine" as come by it unconsciously, in a twilight sleep as it were. I might have said a gay amen to Father's credal confession and a sort of "Come on in, the water's fine," but one could not be that casual in face of his gravity and his look.

Father and Mother had left their goods boxed in Burdett and followed their children to California. They savored the move romantically in the spirit of adventure. On buggy rides Father would insist that we let him out to hunt by the wayside for gold-bearing rocks. He would gather promising bits of stone, wet his thumb in his mouth, and rub the surface earnestly, peering for the precious glint. Many glints he found, and we used to go rattling home with treasure in abundance rolling around the buggy floor. The Spanish and Indian remains interested him. There was a crumbling adobe not far from the Quadrangle on the banks of the San Francisquito; how he prowled around it in the high grass, and mooned over it, and told us with verve that adobe bricks must be the same essentially as those made by the Israelites in Egypt.

One day when Mrs. Gilbert was making me a call Father came tramping in—when he was excited, he *tramped*. He carried a strange greyish bag or bundle which he dumped heavily on the floor.

"Bones! Bones!" he exclaimed and emptied the bag.

Bones they were: dingy, half-rotted, in broken shards, nothing very large, no skulls, but arm bones, ankle bones, knuckle bones (I suppose, though not an anatomist), and there they rolled scattering out across the sitting-room rug.

He said, gustily, he had collected them at the Indian diggings a few miles to the south of us in a field off the highway. Everyone knew of it. The students and their professors went there on bicycles to study archeology. Father had gone alone on his bicycle, poked about, turning up the soil with a stick, found some loose bones, got interested and "collected." Having no way to carry them home he had taken off his underdrawers (the field is entirely private), knotted the legs at the ankles, and filled them with bones to the waistband. But now, as he talked, his afflatus began to give way to a chastened sobriety. He began to look not gay but serious. While Mrs. Gilbert strove to control to decent limits her hilarity, Father turned doubtfully to me: "Nellie, it has just occurred to me I've been *robbing a grave!*"

His delight was gone. He bundled the bones away and would have nothing more to do with them. They stood around a while neglected, then were stored in the garret. Years later the garbage can received them. But by that time Father had left us for another world and doubtless made his peace with heaven.

At first our parents lived with us at 10 Alvarado but were much in San Francisco, where they would take a small lodging and devote their days to dockwalloping and the exploration of the city. Later they built a charming house in Palo Alto, designed by Arthur Clark and Louise. The walls were paneled with lustrous redwood untouched by stain or varnish. Between sitting room and dining room was set a satiny, deep-orange column, the stem of a madrone tree brought by Bolton from the mountains. Bolton and Arthur Clark found the burnt bricks for the fireplace, waste bricks pounced upon and cherished by artists for their accidental clouded colors and patches of irridescent glaze. A large white-oak wept beyond the little lawn in front. Mother planted violets and smilax by the little porch and a row of iris at the side, preferably pure white, but she also allowed some royal purple-and-blue ones.

In 1901 Bolton and Lucy with their three children moved back to York State. Bolton co-operated with Mr. Whitehead in founding the art colony at Woodstock, Ulster County, set up

a business in Japanese prints in New York City, applied himself
to oil painting, published a book about it, and did some beautiful pictures in that medium. Later he took up lithography,
made himself an expert and authority, lectured and wrote on
the subject, and taught it. His skill was marvelous, his industry
prodigious, and his pursuit of the perfect Beauty enthusiastic
and tireless to the end of his life.

In June 1902 Harriett Henrietta graduated from the University. At the Commencement Father had been asked by Dr.
Jordan to pronounce the benediction. He sat on the platform
at the left. The graduates one by one came up the three steps on
the right-hand side, received their degree and their diploma
from President and Registrar, and crossed to the flight of steps
leading down at the left. Everybody wore the scholars' gowns.
It was very imposing. Leslie of course was Registrar and
handed Harriett her diploma; she passed across the rostrum
and there at the top of the steps sat Father. *He rose as she
passed and kissed her.*

"She smiled at me—I would not have done it if she hadn't
smiled at me," he told us afterward. "I thought of all the other
fathers and mothers there," he said.

The next day Father went on the train to San Francisco and
took the ferry, intending to call on a friend in Berkeley. He
sat on deck at the rail; the sunlight danced on the blue waters
of the Bay; he could look off and see the Golden Gate, the
sombre Marin Hills. Suddenly he fell forward on the deck,
his spirit left the body, impulsively; it was like him. The attendants who ran to lift him found his face serene, untroubled.

Mother said he was wakeful the night before, talked of Harriett and of the Commencement, of all the children. "Now
there is only one more," he said; for Bessie was still in college.
Mother had the gravestone inscribed: "He walked with God
and was not for God took him."

Those two wore their unworldliness unconsciously, like a
used garment. Once while they were staying in San Francisco,

Father had a strange seizure in the night. Something went wrong in his head—it was queer, it pained, it whirled, he was ill. He got up and insisted on dressing and going out; he must have the air, he must walk. Mother could not stop him, and they dressed and went out together into the night streets of the city. They walked and walked; he rambled in his speech; he refused to go back to the room. They took Market Street, up and then down, and at the Ferry turned and came back. She tried to guide his restless steps to their own corner, but he would not turn in. A policeman encountered them returning over and over to his beat and spoke to them kindly. He took them into a drugstore and gave Father a drink of water and made him sit a few minutes and recommended a sedative. Toward dawn Mother got him to the Third and Townsend station and so on a morning train home to us. He was ill a few days, but easily and completely recovered. Then they went to the city, hunted up that policeman (Mother had taken his number!) and gratefully presented him with Moulton's edition of *The Gospel of John!*

Father feared not death: "Whatever happens to us at death, you may be sure it will be *natural*," he had said to my mother; but he was skittish about the dying and the approaches of decrepitude. As he grew older he warily refused to hoe in the garden, to go regularly to the post-office: "I've seen so many old codgers settle down and peter out hoeing in the garden and going for the mail," he said. This used to seem funny to us because of his obvious and indestructible youthfulness. His alert muscular body was stalwart, undecayed, his voice rich and full, his buoyant activity and vivid interests never flagged. He studied, read, and wrote every day to the last. And, when he was gone so suddenly, on the little table in Mother's sitting room where he used to write lay his manuscript neatly put together in a pile as he always arranged and left it when he stopped for the day. He was revising his book published some years before, *The Life of Society*. But I care most about another book of his, *The Divine Indwelling*.

XVI

OUR PLAYGROUNDS,
MOUNTAINS, SEA

Our most memorable vacations were not our trips East to visit our families, although we crossed the continent with the children occasionally, but our California play times in the mountains and by the sea. Especially Pacific Grove, then a sleepy little place near Monterey with a pine woods rising up back of it and tall, thin pine trees dribbling down through its gold-sand streets and its flower-bosomed yards to the rocks and the cliffs of the ocean. On one side of it around a headland lay the blue harbor of Monterey, full of small boats with white little sails, and fish nets in brown piles on the wharf. On the other side, if you walked the bluffs and passed the lighthouse, entered the grey dunes where the grey donkeys wandered and rested themselves under the evergreen scrub, you came to the wide half-moon of Moss Beach, exquisitely solitary. The water there was caught back ever by shallows beneath. Its languorous snowy scrolls edged incessantly up the silvery sand and incessantly, with glissades and netted foam, slipped back away. Driftwood came in there, and one could pick up shreds of it and make a little fire. Aunt Lida did that, and then she scraped out the spent coals and embers and sat down in the hollow to get warm—the sea-wind blew in free. There were places where the sand under your feet gave out a low whispering hiss or kiss with every step. In a moment it ceased, you were past the spot,

Chinese Fishing Village near Monterey. Reproduced from a line-and-wash drawing by Bolton Brown

you hunted back for it with your feet, and found it, always the same never anywhere else—"Singing Sand." Cousin Henry Bolton visited all the Singing Sands on all the wild beaches of the world and took home samples in bottles to his laboratory at Columbia University; but for all his examinations he could never find out what made them sing. And they did not sing in the bottles. The sun at Moss Beach behaved strangely when, big and red as though angry, it went down at night. It swelled out like a football; it became a squash; it attenuated into a band; it assumed a vase-form elegantly; it got back to a disk and squinched itself up in the middle as if with colic. I suppose my Cousin Henry knew what made it do so, but I do not. We were seldom at Moss Beach for sunset anyway.

Point Jo was as far as we ever walked the Beach, its farthest confine. An old Japanese man lived there among the rocks like one of the Hermits of Egypt. I think he sold an abalone shell about once a week to somebody. Our nearer way to Moss Beach was through the pine woods instead of over the bluffs and dunes, and bound to be interesting. The "butterfly trees" might be hanging full of brown butterflies clustered and vibrating like swarming bees, every bit of the tree covered and alive with softly throbbing wings. There would be the buffaloes off under the trees, browsing; and we peered at them in wonder, huge primeval dark creatures, and hoped they would not lift their great heads and notice us. Between us and Monterey on the shore was a miniature rocky settlement that we called "Chinatown." Its dainty beach was closely surrounded by crags of tumbled rocks bursting out into the ocean. Bunched together thickly on the rocks, up and down, perched wherever a ledge or cranny allowed, was an extraordinary huddle of weathered shanties where the Chinese fishermen and their families lived. The cobbled-up little huts were propped from tumbling off into the ocean by all kinds of sticks and poles and slats set in competently where they would do the most good. Early in the morning the white-winged little boats, toys on the great water, went out in a fleet, and returned with the catch before midday. I have been there watching from the rocks above when the boats came in. A strapping big violent woman, her black hair in a rough, hard twist, ran down the pitching trail from her doorway, shouting and gesticulating her orders. The boats sidled up; one by one, she seized the prow and yanked it up the sand; the boatman tumbled out and ran to and fro, and did this and that, excited and willing, just as she cried out to him to do; thus he got his shining slippery fish unloaded with skill and speed. She bossed the whole business. She ran about that wee crowded beach with shouts and warnings; she tugged and wrestled the boats, she grabbed and slammed the fish, she kicked the stones out of the way and jumped angrily over snarls of bladdered kelp. This was obviously the She-King of the village and equal to the office. It is all gone now. In its place, very clean and ugly, no poles or huts any more, the Marine Laboratory of Stanford University rears its four-square form.

Pacific Grove itself had narrow steep streets running down to the rocks and the water; they were of clean yellow sand and dried out marvelously quick after winter showers. Along them, close together in tiny fenced yards, stood old, usually empty, cottages, transformed to romance by the gorgeous perfumed smother of shrubs and flowers that wantoned from doorstep to roof, from house walls to gate, out along the paths and running away to the gullies of the coast. The place had a decent hotel, some shops, some churches, a museum housed in a small wooden octagonal building. The room within was dim and dusty and a dried swordfish hung from its ceiling. There was a pleasant park with a fountain. The children wove the fountain into all their days and plays; for some nameless artist had made it all of cement and rough stones piled as you would find in a fairy field, and in the crannies and on the little stone perches sat and peeked and ran little stone mice, and stone squirrels, and a lizard, and a stone bird or two twisting its head down toward the trickling water; perhaps a stone bird would hop down and splash a minute in the little shallow basin below. The park had a croquet ground, made of packed clean sand; and old men sedately played the game all day with long-nosed short-handled mallets of a local style.

A place not for the rich and proud; for them Del Monte flourished just over the hill. But certain people liked it and went there year after year, summer or winter, when the children got edgy at home and required to be "unlaxed." The cottages were for rent; a Manda or an Emma brought from the home kitchen could keep house in these miniature domains and have time besides to gather shells with the children.

We liked the wild coast and the golden beaches cuddled small at the foot of the rocks. The storm waves, the billows of the equinoxes, came in unhindered across a thousand miles, blown by the winds, pulled by the moon, and dashed over the highest rocky crests and promontories with thunder and foam. We liked the ebb when the tide, receding, left dark, wet reaches of slimy rock over which the glistening brown weed ruffled and great citron bulbs twisted their snaky tails. We hunted there for iridescent abalone shells and purple starfish, and lobster claws like carved ivory, cream-and-pink tinted, and bright "pretty-stones," and everything tangled in the citron, the wine-red, the lettuce-green, the brown-and-purple seaweed. The ebbing water curled back lazily and lifted the spread of floating kelp like a breathing bosom. We liked the tide pools left in the cracks and hollows at the ebb, sparkling, crystalline. An inch-long fish would limber through the fairy moss-plumes in a grey flash, his backbone plainly visible through his translucent flesh. An inch-long sea-cradle, pure sky-blue, would lie tilted against a stone, the cone of a small white limpet beside it. A red crab would hesitate and twiddle among the stones and dart out of sight in a dim crack. Impudent hermit crabs, gangsters, popped in and out of lichened fissures, dashed, crazily careening, over the floor of the pool; and on their backs went bouncing along the stolen shells of the snail, slowest of animals! A comic spectacle!

Leslie was not always with us at the Grove; we sometimes left him to run the University and get his meals "out." He had the dog and the cat for company, Ponto and Brice. Ponto, our handsome Irish setter, could raise more dust digging into a gopher hole than a Kansas windstorm. He plunged at it furiously with clipped shrill yelps, and in two thrashing minutes almost buried himself; then suddenly he would stop, back out, and sneeze, looking sheepish. Brice got his name from Dr. Branner, who happened along the street when Christabel first adopted the shivering, crying kitten abandoned at our door. "What shall I name him?" she called out, and our neighbor instantly answered "Brice." This cat grew into a large and beautiful lazybones, pampered and patrician, with a broad glossy black stripe down his grey-tiger back, caused, the children said, by our stroking him so much.

A flourishing correspondence enlivened our separations. We hoard letters in our family; so I have them all here before me, in envelopes, but of course minus their postage stamps on account of juvenile collectors.

I beg you to suffer a bunch of Christabel's letters—for a "skip in your walk." They will detain you but a moment and I shall not be skippish long, the next chapter is the earthquake! And after her will come—if you allow—quotations from others, the old letters lying here before me as I write. These open the door to the past as no mere transcription of a memory can do.

Sunday, Jan. 5, 1901

DEAR PAPA,

Did you get my letter. It is very rainy day. This morning we went to Chinatown but it rained before we got there. David is sik, that is he has a earache. My cold has all most gone. I have just come home from coffee beche and I found a coffee bean. "send 614 kisses for Papa," he has been in bed.

Louis is in Monterey with Mr. Thomas in a boat. Amanda found 4 coffee beans

With love from Christabel

Sunday, Jan. 6, 1901

DEAR PAPA:

Louis and I have not played checkers in a long time. How are you I am very very well. I will have to tell you a story. Once there was a little girl and she was very very good and her little sister was very very bad and her mother had to go to the city and her sister had to take care of her.

To be continued in the next number. Louis is making a "S" for his sweater.

David is teasing Mama to read to him.

Ante has just come home from the station she took her bag there early it is pouring and we are all in the house

With much love from

CHRISTABEL

PACIFIC GROVE, Jan. 7, 1901

DEAR PAPA:

The weather has cleared all up and the Sun is shining. Louis has gone to see if the tide is low. Mama is all right. David is better but not well, he says "I send papa "b,a,a,t" I will finish my story. When her mother got home she could not find either of the girls. She called and called and at last the good girl came and said that a good fairy had her and at the end of a month she would bring her back. At the end of the month the good fairy came back with Mary the girl. and she ran to her mother and said she was good so she was good ever after.

from your loveing daughter

CHRISTABEL ELLIOTT

PACIFIC GROVE, CAL., Jan. 8, 1901

DEAR PAPA:—

I will have to write a very short letter for it is after my bed time.

We went down to Lovers Rocks with Mama too and the tid was so low that Louis went way across to the other side.

hurried from

CHRISTABEL

PACIFIC GROVE, Jan. 9, 1901

DEAR PAPA:—I fairly danced for joy when I got your letter.

David is much better. Tel Grandma that we will be very glad to have her down here.

We did not have any rain but a little shower yesterday morning. how is ponto and brice? how are you?

from your loving daughter

CHRISTABEL ELLIOTT

PACIFIC GROVE
Jan 10, 1901

DEAR PAPA:—

I found another coffee bean down on third beach. I am better but I had my breakfast in bed. I am anxious to know what the name of Louis' book is. Could you send my Christmas cards down. I was called away in the middle of my letter for my dinner now I have had my dinner I think I can say a little more. David was carrying the dinner away and there happened to be a cup cake on a plate it was for Amanda and David was found eating it. With much love from

CHRISTABEL

PACIFIC GROVE, CAL.
Jan. 11, 1901

DEAR PAPA:

I beat Louis in a game of checkers today. It is pour down rain all day. David is sleeping soundly in Mama's room.

Louis has gone off in the rain to Chinatown beach. I am sitting in the sittingroom writing to you. I enclose something nice.

1. Little children love one another. St. John
2. Little things are little wings to bear little souls to heaven.
3. Be gentle.
4. Solomon says spare the rod and spoil the child.

With much love from Christabel

P.S. I enclose a letter for Aunte.

PACIFIC GROVE, Jan. 14, 1901

DEAR PAPA:—

I have sat down to write to you and I do not no what to say. Sunday we went to the Episcopal church and we saw the Peterkin family.

Solomon John was the best one among them The waves are not as fine as yesterday. We caught a horned toad at we think it is a horned toad. Ask Miss Pollock how young horned toads look.

With love

from

CHRISTABEL

P S The wind is very high. C.E.
I found a nother coffee bean
I enclose a stag. [Drawing enclosed.]

PACIFIC GROVE, Jan. 14, 1901

DEAR PAPA:—

The waves were very fine today and I have just come home from the Point. One of the waves dashed way up over the Point. I got your letter and I will be very glad if Grandma and Auntie will come down here. How is auntie? I hope that you are better are you

I wish you were down here. The male last night was late (I mean yesterday) but I got your letter as soon as I could.

With much love

from

CHRISTABEL

PACIFIC GROVE, Jan. 18th, 1901

DEAR PAPA:—

I found to coffee beans since I wrote last. I have six altogether.

To-day we went to Moss Beach and when we went to go home we saw the great buffalo and Mama was afraid and we cut through the woods. Louis has got eleven coffee beans and Amanda has 17 coffee beans. Mama has just got your letter and I am so glad Grandma and Auntie are coming down. You say that you have left the Inn, how is Mr. Hodges place?

Mama has no coffee beans.

With much love from

CHRISTABEL

P.S. David sends 1614 kisses to you and Aunt Harriett.

Sunday just after supper
of the 20, 1901

DEAR PAPA:—

I found two coffee beans over on first beach rocks and we have not found any at coffee beach.

Amanda has 31 coffee beans.

I asked David what he would like to send to you and he said "To kiss for wawa."

It has rained all day. Louis went to the Episcopal church and Mama and I went to the old ladies home and we cut thru the woods and came out the place were there blackberrys last year. Write soon.

With much love
from CHRISTABEL

PACIFIC GROVE, CAL
Jan 20, 1901

DEAR PAPA:

I found a nother coffee bean. We have not gone very long trips except to Moss Beach and we are going to Monterey to church.

We are all well. David to.

from

CHRISTABEL

My daughter, looking over this manuscript today, explains to me the strange coffee-bean obsession: "Why, Father promised me a penny for every coffee bean I found." And this clears up some other points I did not understand. One letter says: "Christabel wants to know if you can be depended upon to keep your word," and another asks if "Papa will send the penny down here?" But even my daughter herself has forgotten whether her father paid up or how many coffee beans she found.

"Louis is happy and companionable," says a letter from E.C.E. "He brings in wood, goes for the mail, and locks the doors at night . . . . He remarks, 'Somehow when I am away from Christabel I like her so much,' " she having that time been left at home. Again: "Louis says 'Papa's letter seems to comfort me more than anything else. It is the *gem of the trip.*' " Louis' letters are not numerous but very informing; for instance, this of December, 1899:

. . . . Just think where I have been! You will not guess. I have been to Point Lobos with a party of eight. Mama did not go because there was not room and I should not have gone if a lady had not backed out. We went with a dutchman he showed us lots of historical things he showed us the oldest frame house in California. He said it came from Sydney, Australia; and he showed us a tree where an Indian was hung for murdering a priest and he showed us a house where a German Count was killed. And he showed us the rudder of the ship that brought Napoleon the Great to St Helena. And he showed us the battlefield that the last battle of the mexican war was fought and we saw the trenches. All this was on the way over there We stopped at the Carmel mission and saw the grave of Junipera Serra.

We had a lovely time. tomorrow the english battleships are going to come into the harbor and are going to anchor at Monterey and we are going to see it. With much love, from Louis.

We went to see it, all letters home chronicle the expedition. England was at war; the ships were painted black; and so we saw them slowly rounding the Point, when we with all Pacific Grove crowded down to the rocks: two warships stopping to coal at Monterey. One was named "Warspite" and the other we forgot to find out its name.

CHRISTABEL

. . . . Well, can you believe it, we went to see the warships! This morning at ten all in the rain and by ourselves—no man along and how we wished for one!—That is, we did in the street car as we went over. It seemed such an adventure for women and children. However, as usual all the paths were made straight for our feet. We were taken from Monterey wharf, along with another party, in a rowboat and decently landed on board the "Warspite," H.M. firstclass battle ship, I judge, with the other ship, whose name we forgot to learn, and which was a second-class cruiser, lying near. A minor official with a cocky cap like a rowboat turned upside down was detailed to show us about, and shown about we were, stem and stern, bridge and conning-tower, upstairs and down— down—down. darker and darker, mysteriouser and mysteriouser, until he told us we were fifteen feet below water line and there was still a storeroom below us! The total outfit (over 600) were of all grades from the little fourteen-year-old sailor boys in bare feet, up to the Admiral himself, whom we did not see. Everyone spoke with the British brogue, except one or two who spoke Irish! The worst of it was that our boatman went back to Monterey and took the occasion to go get his dinner and so we waited and waited and waited, our guide dutifully attending, until we were tired of the Warspite and she of us, and when we finally got home it was two o'clock. Christabel will remember the occasion to her dying day, for with dancing eyes she ate a mighty wedge of mince pie, presented her by a youth of our party, who bought it (and more) of some scullion of the Warspite's back kitchen.

The children behaved perfectly and are now playing warship all over the woodshed and precincts. I went out a moment ago and said to Louis in a military tone "Bring in three sticks of kindling for the sitting-room fire." He smiled appreciatively and presently in came Christabel (arrayed in his old overall Dewey suit) with the wood. I said "Tell Louis it isn't very soldierly to tell somebody else to do what I commanded *him* to do." She looked up at me reproachfully—"He's the Admiral!" I might have known it of course, just my stupidity!

Dec. 15, 1899. . . . . What a time the English are having with the Boers! Louis is more than ever persuaded of the final victory of the latter—"just as we did in the Revolution." Do you suppose it is not, after all, Anglo-Saxon destiny to rule all creation? Did I tell you I saw on that British man-of-war "England expects every man to do his duty" inscribed in golden letters upon a great snow-white steering wheel? It stirred my blood. Also, as we rowed up to the vessel we saw the veritable lion-and-unicorn coat of arms handsomely done around the bow, and above in the front of a covered portion (what stupid phraseology!) were the three plumes of the Prince of Wales with "Ich dien" below, as big as life. Of course I know these things are realities. Yet having such a lifelong familiarity with them only through literature gives you a tendency to be surprised at finding them anywhere else.

The big tumultuous waves that some days came in all day along the rocky coast engaged our respectful attention. The letters teem with them so that I hear them again, booming and foaming, flashing white in the high air at Lovers' Point, at the ragged cliffs below the railroad, at Chinatown Rocks; we used to trail the coast on the cliff path looking and listening and saltily breathing in the tremendous experience.

[1899]

. . . . Harriett and I were out all the morning at Lovers Point and along the shore . . . . [The waves] were bigger than anything I ever saw here, and just kept right up hour after hour. The sky was beautiful too, with clouds, and blue, and rainbow after rainbow as various bits of showers came by. As we all sat in the lookout house one wave slapped up and dashed Louis in the face. He looked so surprised and as though he would like to be indignant if it had been anybody else but the ocean. . . . . An old man around here distributes tracts and today he gave one to Louis. Louis showed it to me and appeared to be mystified by the episode, so I tried to explain. I said he had given me one. (I did not use the word "Christian") Louis remarked "He would not need to give them to—ladies, he would know they were—Christian." A nice bit of instinctive gallantry . . . . Sunday. I went to church this morning. About nine o'clock Mother began to get ready and said she was going to walk to Monterey to church. It looked so lonesome to let her start off that I reconsidered my plan of spending the morning at home writing letters, and went too. The day was lovely, calm, bright and quiet, and we went along at the swinging pace of two miles an hour. Arrived at the neat Presbyterian edifice we went in, fifteen minutes early, and looked over the S.S. books in the bookcase. They seem to have improved the quality since my time, for here were *Alice in Wonderland* (!), *Lady of the Lake*, a fine edition of *Pilgrims Progress* . . . . Then the minister, having previously shaken hands with us and others, preached us a fine hearty sermon cast in a strict Presbyterian mould of (1) Original Sin, (2) Redemption, (3) Liberty, but proceeding so clearly from his own robust manly faith that you liked both the speaker and his expression . . . . We walked home (as I had piously dropped in the plate the dime that was to have paid Mother's streetcar fare) and arrived at 1:15, hungry enough for the dinner on the table. Harriett had been to the Episcopal church meantime and David abed. Now again there has been a partial dispersion, just about to complete itself by Manda's joining Harriett and David at the Point. It has clouded over outside but the day is still warm.

In 1899 David got his first sight of the ocean. The letters of that visit are full of him. He was just past two years old, beginning to talk, but with more intelligence than vocabulary.

November 24, 1899 . . . . As to the trip, David was full of ecstacy. When he got so he could speak (San Jose or beyond) he began to chortle of "de cah" and "*ni* cah" and "*ni pitty* cah" and cah and *cah* and *cah!* He could not believe in his good fortune. When we got out at the Grove he stopped on the platform, turned, stooping, and looked *under,* in among the car wheels, then lifted himself to me with a radiant smile and exclaimed in a tone of complete satisfaction "Cah!" It *was* a car. I was *in* a car. It was a *car.* . . . . He would not sleep on the train, though I put him on the seat and sat on him (he howling) for half an hour, and so he is very sleepy. He has been immensely interested in it all. He helped me unpack industriously and, besides, threw a lot of valuables out of the window one by one. . . . . David is fascinated by the "otun." When he saw the big waves yesterday he was much excited and for lack of a better name calls it "moon," which I thought delightfully appreciative. It perhaps impresses him as the engine does—so much noise and power. I drew his attention again and again to shells and seaweed on the sand itself but he looked round the corner of me at "otun! otun! *ni* otun!" entirely indifferent to lesser wonders. . . . . Of course he protested and cried this morning when brought in for his nap . . . .

December 6, 1899. David insisted on going to the ocean this morning and as no one else seemed inclined for it I took him. The day is bright and snappy and the waves something tremendous. . . . . We sat on the rocks a long time watching, David apparently enjoying it as much as I did. He remarked "Happy otun" several times. Of course he did not know what he meant but doubtless he meant it all the same and it sounded very nice. Coming home we sighted the train making its toilet and nothing would do but we must go and see it. We sat a long time on a platform at the depot watching with just as much delight as at the ocean, until we got so sleepy that our head dropped on the Mamma's shoulder. Then she up and said we must go home, which we resisted sturdily, and she carried us in her arms back to the bath-house. There we looked at the waves some more, and then, finding a bit of rope, we merrily played horse up the street and so arrived inadvertently at home.

. . . . David has learned "pittaty" today, just like an Irishman. If you can find a picture of a steam engine or a train of cars as big as a house you can present it to David for Christmas. I most rashly showed him in the *Review of Reviews* the train which heads the advertising pages devoted to Travel and Recreation, and by consequence he grew so enamoured that he pored over it all the time to the exclusion of every other pursuit. He tore the covers from the book, he rumpled all its pages and completely demoralized the advertising department in his elephantine devotion. Today I wanted him to go to the ocean, he refused and continued to wallow lovingly over the "cah-cah" on that enchanted page. In desperation I seized the book—he howling defiance—cut out the picture and pasted it on a big white card and presented it to him, all in the jerk of a lamb's tail. You should have seen his mystification and delight. *Now* he could go to walk, for the card could, and did, accompany him, and the *Review of Reviews,* by thus giving up a little finger, as it were, is saved in its general body to better uses. . . . .

. . . . As I came out of Steiners with my purchases—half a doz. eggs—I heard a familiar roar and here was Harriett with David *rampant* clutched in her arms. I confronted him and you should have seen his amazement. . . . The trouble was she had taken him into a store and he had wished to spend the rest of the day staring at a big iron train of cars on the counter. Indeed he had demanded them with his autocratic "cah-cah!" Hence the fracas.

Two years later, December 1901, David, being four, is still enamored of the sea.

. . . . You can't make a man with a muck rake of David. We provided him with a paper bag this morning, which he carried along gladly, but he gently shed all suggestions that looked toward putting shells in it. He dawdled with utmost pleasure. He threw a few stones into a few pools—when I directed his eye to the pool and provided the stone—made about four sand mountains, and ran up and down with the waves a very little bit. For the rest he sat about upon the rocks with me, and when I looked to see if he were bored, he would be gazing absorbedly at the near or far waves. He had a good time.

. . . . The sea was tremendous, waves dashing into foam as high as Lovers Point . . . . Louis glued himself on to the rocks at Lovers Point, Christabel soon wearied, got cold and went home to Manda, while David and I walked slowly along halfway to Chinatown, stopping and looking at every point along the way. . . . .

. . . . This morning being lovely and bright we all started out together . . . . and spent the morning dawdling to Chinatown and back. This afternoon Louis and Manda are out, David asleep, Christabel happily playing with the treasure trove we brought home this morning. She has made a kelp doll strikingly like a dark-skinned baby, and washed all her white limpets, and is now searching for a bottle to put them in. . . . . The waves were fine all along that beautiful beach (Moss Beach), trampling in in long, long foaming, breaking rolls. I got again the impression I have had there so many times, of white plunging sea-horses, dolphins, Neptunes and all. . . . .

. . . . David is not sentimental. He insists that the kisses appended to your letter are *bicycles!* . . . . We have been munching toast for breakfast and now are getting warm by the grate fire while David and Manda do up the work. . . . .

The children and I have been to the sand-hills and the children are now full of sand. It sprinkles out whenever they walk. . . . . All able-bodied persons went to church today and have just returned. The nice old Episcopal minister was the same as ever and the church and Window and the service as satisfying.

David, it seems, had a virulent cold and became very naughty. This was most unusual: "David is as cross as Sam Patch, 'bad-bad-boying!' everything from me to the marbles, howling unless I hold and rock him, and storming over every little thing. . . . . The other children view this sad development with astonishment and dismay. Louis asked 'Do you think he will stay so?' " In the next letter his cold gets better but not his temper: "I cannot understand his naughtiness. I called him to me today and asked him seriously what made him behave so.

"D. 'I do' know.'

"Me. 'Why do you talk that way and act naughty to Mamma?'

"D. 'I do' know. . . . . 'cause I don't want to.'

I thought this rather a clever analysis of the situation."

. . . . It rained and blew great guns last night. Today it rained off and on but everybody got out between showers. The house is now full of wet things drying. Harriett and I walked briskly halfway to Monterey. Manda had the children on First Beach a long time, the tide very low. . . . .

. . . . Thanks, thanks for the reading matter. The children seized upon it with avidity of starvelings. They have read the Rollo books through and through and have actually been driven to the Bible of late— a pity! . . . .

E.C.E. is very much involved just here in a discussion about the way the life of Jesus should be presented to children. She is reading to Louis and Christabel a chapter a day from a certain life of Christ which she thinks very good indeed, but it falls down in spots. For instance, "The Temptation": "The Devil tempted him."

"Did the Devil tempt him?" Christabel interrupts.

"No. There is no Devil."

"Then did God tempt him?"

"No. 'The Lord tempts no man.' "

And the reading cannot go on; everything hangs in suspense while E.C.E.—"lamely and unpreparedly"—explains her idea of the Temptation. "And it could have been so easily handled," she thinks, "by using a suitable phraseology." Even the Scripture itself is difficult at times. Louis reads aloud from St. Luke: ". . . . Joseph, his supposed father"; looks up, "Didn't they *know* he was his father?" and that startling question has to be laid before Louis can read on.

E.C.E. thinks children should be given "a satisfying, rational, and heroic picture of Jesus which would of itself suffice to nullify doubts and confusions as they grow older." They should read the Gospels themselves, making what they can out of them; but then, besides, they ought to be supplied with a *Life* written for them and free from dogma and theology and also from the limitations of time and place. It hasn't been done. E.C.E. thinks she will have to write it herself. (I hope she did.)

A letter from E.C.E. dated 1898 contains what she calls "a rhapsody" of Christabel's. Christabel at this time cannot yet write, but she certainly can dictate.

. . . . I wish you could have seen her while she delivered it. She stood in front of me rolling it off at top speed and in an oratorical tone, her eyes full of a fine frenzy. I could hardly dissuade her from continuing on indefinitely. Louis demanded to hear it so I read it to him and she stood by with an expression of frankest admiration on her face, glancing at him from time to time to see if it impressed him properly. (I think it did, for he said soberly, "That's a fine letter.")

"Dear Papa, A story you want? Well here's one. Once upon a time there was a giant, both big and strong. He had two little other sisters who were big and he sent them to get food. And the smallest sister brought a big bear, and the man loved bears most and so his wife cooked the bear and he ate, and thanked the girl and gave her many golds, and so did the wife. This is the end of my story. Oh, yes indeed.

"I was very glad to get your letter and the story was a nice story. I liked it. Pretty soon I will give you a poem about the sea.

> The sea is red
> And so is my head
> And locks and curls
> Are in the sea
> The rain is falling
> And it will come
> *P'tong* upon your head.

That is the end of my poem.

"Please, Papa, if you can, send a sugar-cake and my tray. My tray I need 'cause I haven't got my pin-cushion. Wasn't that a story that I just writ—a great big giant he was at least—and so the story was nice. Has Louis written a letter to you? I hope he has. I'm going to write to Aunt Mary soon. Mama said she had to make a cap for her middle finger because it got so dirty by the ink! We've found lots of shells. I hope the next time I write I'll send lots of shells to you. Yesterday—or I don't know what day—we found a great big horse skull and we're going to bring it home in the trunk" (Perhaps! says E.C.E. in parenthesis.) "How is Brice? I am going to write him a letter and here it goes. You read his letter to Brice.

"Dear Brice, How are you? Are you lazy any more? I hope you catch lots of mice.

> Brice
> You are a tyce.

I'm going to write Brice a poem. Here goes for one.

> Brice
> You would have tyce,
> But catch mice
> None you do.

That's the end of my poem for Brice and so is it the end of my letter for Brice. Anyway if he can't understand it tell him that I wrote him a poem and a letter. My Mary is all right. How are you? Good bye and several kisses.

> CHRISTABEL ELLIOTT"

Out of these visits to Pacific Grove with Leslie at home grew up a literature. Leslie sprouted poems and tales for the children in absence, and the children sent him back responses in kind. It was natural. In our set everybody wrote. As the children of railroad builders play at railroading and the children of gangsters play—I suppose—at gangstering, so with half the faculty publishing books all the time our children played at literature. Their fathers, too, bent down and made play literature for them. Dr. Jordan did the *Book of Knight and Barbara,* "corrected and illustrated by the children"—as the title-page reads. He wrote *Matka and Kotik* to inform them about his seals, and a jingle book for Eric—*Eric's Book of Beasts.* Dr. Branner, a Southerner, wrote out stories he had heard from the Negroes—*How and Why Stories.* Anna Comstock wrote all about insects, *The Ways of the Six-Footed;* and so did Vernon Kellogg with his insect book for youngsters. The campus children published a paper, *Little Nonsense,* which I think—the file lies before me—must have been subsidized by the editor's father (George Branner was the editor), for it is decently printed and the format quite unexceptionable. It sold for a dime. I believe the Jenkins family had a paper of their own, named *The Shooting Star,* which the Jenkins children peddled at the faculty offices on the Quadrangle. And later, after the campus schoolhouse was built, the children put out a paper called *The Red Tile Screamer.* Its first issue stated frankly in the prospectus "the purpose of this paper is to see if we are able to publish it every month."

Leslie's literary efforts give home news in piquant form; Brice's character comes out vividly:

Dear Louis,

When Brice was working at his meat
A strange cat came and snatched it
I saw the deed, though from the street,
And with my trowel matched it.

He went like shot but soon came back
For nothing much could scare him
While Brice in terror ran away
And starts yet when I'm near him.

Brice is handsome, playful, domestic, and aristocratic. But I really fear he is P-u-s-i-l-l-a-n-i-m-o-u-s. Even when he is hungry he will let one of the Hodges' kittens take his meat right away from him. That kitten isn't afraid of anything. He rushes right up and grabs the piece of meat, whereupon Brice growls a little and looks uncomfortable. But the kitten eats the meat all the same. Today Brice jumped to the very top shelf in the pantry after meat. I slapped him soundly and he was awfully ashamed. He felt so bad about it that he wouldn't eat the piece I afterward gave him . . . .

Christabel (her father's only girl) came in for fanciful attention. She was called "Bellehilda" when good, "Brunekilt" when bad, and "Willie Jones" when she wore blue overalls to play on the rocks. The communications from home admonished her to proper conduct:

> The Princess Bellehilda is good as gold
> She always does as she is told
> And never pouts or frets
> At anything she gets—
> A fall on the rocks, a cold in the head,
> A thorn in her finger, a call to bed,
> Or asked not to romp or tease any more,
> Or to speak softly and not slam the door,
> She smiles and she curtsies and says at her ease
> "I thank you," "You're welcome," and of course
> "If you please."

Sometimes we received simple fables like the one about the whale who maintained that the ocean was a better place to live in than the land. "Don't you see," he said, "those mountains and great trees that stand right in the way if you should wish to move about, and how inconvenient if one should happen to want a drink of water!" And again we got a "Gogo" story, an astonishing tale about "Rollum-Bollums," or tigers:

Once upon a time there were two tigers—this is a brand new story— and one said to the other let's go up on the mountain and hunt go-goes. All right, said the other, and away they went. But that morning a band of go-goes had said Let us hunt tigers today. And it came to pass when the tigers got to the mountain they put their heads right into a trap which the go-goes had set for them. So instead of having any breakfast they were sent to San Francisco to be in the circus where they could be looked at by boys and girls.

Dear Christabel
I fain would tell
Some tale about the go-goes.
Or lions wild,
Or dancing child,
But time would fail to do so,
For unless I quit
And haste a bit
The clock will strike for midnight
So now farewell
And sleep you well,
Tomorrow brings us sunlight.

We also had political screeds:

Rah! Rah! the whole establishment!
McKinley will be President!
Tomorrow is the very day
That Cleveland takes himself away
And when you read this little rhyme
Just after Thursday's dinner time
McKinley will be President!
Rah! Rah! the whole establishment!

And next day—

McKinley now is President
(I've already mentioned this event
But never mind that incident)
And so it is expedient
To raise our caps obedient,
And in this new predicament
Await the whole development,
Without a grave presentiment,
McKinley being President.

These writing fits were not confined to Pacific Grove; we were subject to spells of inspiration at any time or place. Once we wrote limericks for three days on end and nearly went crazy. (Such as: "There was an old dog named Ponto, Who said at night I don't want to Go to bed in your shed Till I'm fed some more bread, That illogical dog named Ponto.") Another seizure was Alphabets:

A is for Alphabet which we are making,
They are not at all useful, but then they are taking.

.   .   .   .

C is for Christabel, dear little girl,
Queer little Christabel's hair doesn't curl.

D is for *Don't,* which Christabel said,
And burst out a-crying and laid down her head.

.   .   .   .

F is for Fox who lives in a box;
This rhyme is not true but then it will do.

G is for Goat who scampers about,
He hasn't much tail but gets on without.

.   .   .   .

L is for Louis who cried just in here
Because he must stop making Alphabets queer.

M is for Mamma who still scribbled on
And sat making Alphabets when he was gone.

I is for Indian and also for Ill
J is for Jack and also for Jill
K is for King and also for Koke
L is for Louis who Laughs at this joke
Q is for Queen and Queer and Quick
R is for Haystack which Britons call Rick.

Louis, our eldest, wrote a book all by himself. I have it here neatly done in pencil (we did not allow ink at this period) with a designed title-page which contains, besides the title, the author's full name, a sort of printer's device, and the publisher's imprint—"Published by L. D. Elliott, Stanford University, California." Over the page is the notice of copyright with date, and again the name, but given in a third form—"L. Elliott." The title reads "Odds and Ends," ornamentally printed. There is a proper Table of Contents, listing five pieces of a fictional character, stories or narratives, which follow in painstaking script. I may add, modestly, that "This Book is Dedicated to Mrs. Elliott."

Christabel used to sit before me every morning on a hassock and learn poetry from my dictation while I brushed and combed and braided in tails her long blonde hair. She got a repertoire of more than thirty poems in the end. But she tells me she cannot remember one of them now. Another maxim smashed. We are admonished to fill our children's minds with memorized good literature—poetry, the Bible, and all—and it will be a charm and a safeguard to them through life. But there's what my daughter has just testified!

Nine times we went to camp at Peters Creek among the redwoods, twenty miles back over the Santa Cruz Mountains and down to a secluded untouched spot by the stream. We had a cold spring to keep our food in. We built shelves into hollow redwoods for a pantry and a library and established a campfire site. Leslie would cut a heavy longitudinal wedge out of a redwood log, polish off the two surfaces of the cut, and there we had a permanent bench with seat and back complete. The children learned to fish and swim. We trailed the wilderness for miles around, sometimes saw a deer, seldom a human being. Once we had a mountain lion passing near our camp at night. His lonely cat-call came faintly to us at intervals, then nearer, then behind us on the slope. But there it stopped, for Leslie issued from our tent and stirred up the fire to flames. The other people came in from their mattresses under the redwoods and stood in the firelight and talked about it with excitement. Ponto through all the commotion lay in a curl near the blaze, eyes shut, perfectly motionless, pretending slumber—*scared to death*. Nobody saw the mountain lion, but a faint paw track was discovered near the spring in the morning.

Leslie and the boys, when they were older, went bicycling or tramping on trips, with knapsacks and sleeping bags, fishing tackle and rubber boots, or whatever, depending on the nature of the expedition. Bicycles were a nuisance going up a mountain, though even then they could carry the baggage; but riding down was gay. You braked with your foot, perhaps; but that was hard on shoes; so a better way was invented. You cut a tree branch and tied it to the rear and braked with that, lickety-split, a terrific dust cloud, and the wheel bounded down the steeps triumphant. Yet it had to be stopped. It frightened the teams on the road into fits, endangering the lives of their drivers; the State of California made a law that bicycles should not be braked with tree branches any more. And that was that.

In early days we walked, for fun, for exercise, and to get there. For fun Leslie and I climbed afoot up the La Honda grade and down the La Honda grade to La Honda deep in a redwood canyon, sleeping the first night at Ham's Mountain House on top of the ridge. We expected to board the stage at La Honda; but when it passed us I was feeling so ambitious that we continued under our own power. We got to Pescadero at nightfall, twenty miles from Ham's, and slept at the village hotel. In the morning we wandered to a small, hidden, cave-like beach celebrated for the jewel pebbles washed up there. We hunted jewels on our knees with absorption, as one must; found them sparingly, small and precious; and carried them away to cherish—moonstones, agates, onyx, jasper—tiny and precious. We walked the bluffs to Half Moon Bay and back home by stage to Redwood over the mountain.

We went another time by the pipeline through the woods from Pacific Grove to Carmel and thence down the Coast as far as the Little Sur, where we turned in up a lovely gulch and slept that night at a remote resort named (of course) Idlewild. It is a long, high coast; rocky, broken by headlands where deep redwood canyons come down from the hills and jut out their steep banks into the sea; a lonely country, almost uninhabited, the road, in those days a stage road to the Big Sur, rough, dusty, and perilous. We took the stage, an open primitive vehicle, for part of our way back and were carefully shown by the driver the places on the bank where stages had gone over and fallen to the rocks far below. A cheerful method of entertaining travelers! We had few adventures. The fog drifted slowly in puffs and banners among the crags and up the open slopes to landward. We felt its damp and coolth delicately on our faces. We looked down to the sea beaches, small and secret among dark cataclysmic rocks; we saw the endless white surges beating against the cliffs. A field at the landward side ran up to the sky, a buckwheat field in blossom, fragrant and with bees; against the blue sky on the ridge stood its long line of crimson stems topped with white bloom in a froth.

Yet I remember an adventure: cattle clattering and bawling, tossing and heaving, a rank smelly multitude crowding the narrow road, billowed with dust and herded by rearing cowboys on horses. Twice this horrid encounter happened to us. The first sent me over the fence, and I crouched on the ground beyond fearsomely peeping through until they had bawled and tossed out of sight. The second time they came round a bend too suddenly—they were upon us, they would trample us to death, or toss us to heaven on their horns! But mercifully the road there divided into a small triangle to get round a stump in the middle of a bush. I desperately penetrated the bush, and sprang upon the stump, and the awful ruck of the herd streamed around and past me on each side, near enough for me to touch their lolloping flanks had I wished, which I did not. I forget where Leslie was both times—not protecting me.

XVII

EARTHQUAKE

W E'VE WON the suit!

At 11:30, March 2, 1896—"raw, windy, rainy, very cold," reads my contemporary account, "with snow on the mountains east and west"—the fire whistle blew. It sounded odd, startling. "People were rushing out of the houses and toward the Quad. Suddenly we realized that the whistle in a raucous bungling fashion was striving to give the Stanford yell! Someone cried 'perhaps we've won the suit!' "

We had. A busman brought the news; it was later verified. We rushed to the Quadrangle and so did everybody else. The place was in riotous confusion. Classes dismissed themselves, tore out of their rooms at the sound of the whistle; and their teachers raced after them. Mrs. Barnes' history class was just assembling in the Chapel; the crowd took possession, and Dr. Jordan addressed it as a mass-meeting. Some engagement elsewhere cut him down to a few minutes, and he left by crawling out of the window of the tiny "vestry," the multitude being too jammed to allow his reaching the door. The meeting went on, led by Sheldon, the president of the Associated Students. "Terrific cheering accompanied by bass drums and cymbals." In fact they broke the drum head with the madness of their beating. Sheldon confessed he had no authority but announced there would be no more classes that day. "Hail, Stanford, Hail" was sung. Meeting dissolved and men held hats at the doors for funds to buy fireworks.

The University then paraded in a ragged, shouting, tin-horning procession around the arcades. The flag was hoisted. A suit of clothes with "We've won it" was hung on the bulletin board. The anvil in the blacksmith shop was fired, fire whistle kept on blowing the yell, the Pioneer Class paraded the Quad howling

> Za! Za! Zeer!
> Za! Za! Zeer!
> '95! '95!
> We're right here!

The freshmen and sophomores staged a rush over a broom. Bolton on the street in Palo Alto heard the whistle, saw people running out of the stores with stepladders and bunting to tack up, saw a bus with flags going double-quick up the avenue to the University, learned the news, and turned round to carry it back to Castilleja. Arrived there he wrapped around himself "about thirty yards of red-white-and-blue, star-spangled banner stuff" and ran in on Lucy, who thought him crazy and strove to calm him down. In the evening crowds gathered at seven in the Quad with "terrific" hubbub, din, and shouting, red tam-o-shanters, red banners, red sweaters, red streamers, red tin horns, red Chinese lanterns on bobbing poles, cannon, pistol shots, anvil booming, a monstrous procession surging about and frequently tramping *as* a procession through the arcades. A mass meeting at Encina Hall with speeches and afterward fireworks.

But though the government suit was now decided and in our favor, the money shortage continued, the estate being still unsettled and in the courts. Mrs. Stanford and Dr. Jordan carried on with a beautiful courage and firmness; and the University, handicapped, continually lacking books, apparatus, and other equipment, and salaries docked, went right on with its proper work in loyal support to the President and the Founder. Dr. Jordan called that hard period the "seven pretty long years."

At last in 1900, seven years after Mr. Stanford's death had left the heavy weight of responsibility upon her shoulders alone,

Mrs. Stanford saw all the legalities of the will concluded and the endowment freed for use. A long unfolding future lay before the University. She knew that in it the Founders could have no living part. The one remaining contribution possible to them was to supply in good form the buildings which the developing future would require. The plans had been made with Mr. Stanford's approval; she threw herself now with characteristic energy and eagerness into the work of carrying them out as he would have wished. The eight buildings of the great Outer Quadrangle were erected, laced in with each other and with the Inner Quadrangle by a very beautiful arrangement of courts and arcades, and surrounded entirely by a broad, paved colonnade and cloister. Steps and terraces led up to the long front, and at the center an imposing sculptured arch opened into a graceful forecourt and entrance to the Inner Quadrangle. The road ran from the terraces first around a circle of greenery and then straight to Palo Alto through the Arboretum, one mile. Quarters for the Engineering, Chemistry, and some other departments were put up in the same general style of architecture at locations outside of the Quadrangles. Additions were built to the Museum, which was dear to Mrs. Stanford's heart because The Boy had been a collector and the Museum already housed the collections he himself had begun. A bountifully equipped men's gymnasium and a large library building were contracted for.

A site had been planned and left in the Inner Quadrangle for a church, which the Founders designed to be the center and heart of the University. They were religious people, and the experiences of their life had deepened their sense of the spiritual implications of existence. Now Mrs. Stanford desired above all to build the Church and to build it after the sumptuous design which had been fully considered and determined upon when Mr. Stanford was alive. It was to be their most significant message to the students of the future and the highest symbol of their hope for the mission of their son's Memorial; and she had been left to carry out this aspiration alone. She saw the Church finished and dedicated in 1903 and it had for her then a double significance. The shining, glowing mosaics spanning the façade, the glowing, shining mosaics covering the inner walls, the pictured glass of the windows, the massive pillars of the aisles, the rich curves and colors of the shadowed transepts, the fine wood of the roof, the marble flight of steps up to the whiteness of the marble altar, the chancel's golden bay, were the lavish expression of her affection and devotion to son and husband both. On the façade of the Memorial Church one reads the inscription:

Memorial Church
Erected by
Jane Lathrop Stanford
To the glory of God and in
Loving Memory of her Husband
Leland Stanford

In February 1905 Mrs. Stanford died suddenly in Honolulu. The Outer Quadrangle was finished; the Church was finished; the Gymnasium and the Library were under construction and were finished soon after her death. The solid material structure of Stanford University stood on the campus against its circling bench of hills—green in winter, yellow in summer, with oaks— as the Founder had dreamed and planned. She had seen his dream fulfilled in form, and was satisfied that it would stand thus in its substantial beauty for centuries . . . . In April 1906, in less than one minute, the earthquake shook the University into ruins!

Five o'clock in the morning, Wednesday, April 18, 1906, it was breathlessly still, half-lit, I was awake. I drowsily heard the chimes in the Church belfry ring the four notes of the first quarter. Immediately the earth shook and roared. The bells fell down with the belfry through the Church to the ground and rang no more.

An inveterate annalist, I sat down five days afterward and wrote, dated, and signed the account which I give you here, hardly changed by a word:

I was shaken furiously in my bed. I stared at the stovepipe bouncing back and forth in and out of the pipe hole. A picture swung outward, flopped around, and swung back again against the wall wrong side to. Leslie remarked: "The real thing." With the thought "the children" I sprang up, lurched across the rocking hall and plunged into the boys' room. A large cabinet full of playthings solemnly, with dignity, lost its balance and fell over toward David's bed, splintered its door across the back of a chair, and there rested. I threw myself beside David, still asleep, and had time after that to do a lot of shaking and to reassure him when he waked up whimpering. Louis was sitting half out on the edge of his bed looking sleepy and surprised. Leslie staggered to Christabel's room and found her bed moving across the floor toward the door. Then the jar and roar stopped suddenly and the pale light looked silently into the disordered room. One would say it was five minutes—it was less than one.

At once cries came up from outside "The Church tower is gone!" "The big chimney fell!" "The new library is down!" We rushed downstairs breathing in soot and plaster; saw the bookcases thrown down, the floor piled with tumbled books mixed up with masses of plaster and with soot from the fireplaces. We ran outdoors and saw the bricks from our chimney all over the lawn, ran into the road and saw a cloud of rising dust over the Quadrangle, a mangled wreck where the bells in the tower had chimed.

We got into clothes and joined the groups of campus people coming out of their houses and hurrying toward the Quadrangle. It was a sort of a procession at last. A tall young man, very serious, wrapped in a blanket over his night shirt, was marching across the field from Encina Hall and I wondered why he did not stop to dress. We grew more and more astonished as we went. The stately stone power-house chimney which rose behind the Church and nearly as high as its tower lay a great pile of broken stone; it was whispered that the night engineer was beneath it. His body was recovered some hours later. We went through a gap of ruined arcade into the Inner Quadrangle. There were large wandering cracks in walls, the grey dust was still afloat about us. We stood before our ruined Church. The spire had fallen. The whole glowing front where the mosaic of The Sermon an the Mount had been lay in fragments on the ground. The rose window with its little beckoning Christ was gone. We gazed in through the hole at the shining pipes in the organ loft.

About the time the sun rose we came to the façade of the Outer

Quadrangle and with an awestruck crowd of neighbors looked at the pride of the Quadrangles, the Memorial Arch. It was absolutely rowdy, on a titanic scale. Its sculptured top was knocked off—like ashes from a cigar; down its sides ran jagged fissures almost to the foundation; the roof of the archway was cracked and the adjoining arcades were crumpled up in heaps on either side. An enormous wedge of masonry hung down at one corner ready to fall off, which it did the next day.

A marble gentleman whose perch is on the second story of the façade had advanced a step but paused without jumping. Mr. Agassiz, similarly situated, had pitched down, rammed his hard head through the concrete pavement, held his neck stiff, and stood thus imbedded to the shoulders exactly upside down. His upturned boots quaintly supported his neat square shelf which had come away with him. His hand was gracefully extended from his shoulder; a student stepped up and shook it. "Quaker Oats" (known as Benjamin Franklin by the more respectful) had fallen on his face, like Dagon. Johann Gutenberg lay in the field below his cairn of stones snapped off at the ankles, his shoes left neatly standing on top like the slippers at your bedside.

The new gymnasium and the new library, great stone structures not yet occupied, were shattered into incredible mounds of debris, fragments of wood and of stone, ragged walls, broken stone columns, twisted girders. Both were complete wrecks.

Leslie had left the house before I did and made for the dormitories. At the physics corner he met running boys coming back from Roble Hall who reported to him that the chimneys had gone down and damage was done at the Hall but no one hurt. He turned and followed the running boys to Encina. The chimneys there had fallen and broken through the roof, taking the floors with them to the basement. Four students had been carried down from their rooms and were under the ruin. A line of boys were feverishly grabbing up armfuls of rubbish and passing it back to others, who flung it out of the way, so to uncover their buried mates. They unearthed one boy, then another crouched under protecting timbers not much hurt, dragged them out and laid them on the grass. A third was loosened from the wreckage unhurt. But the fourth boy was dead.

At Roble Hall the falling chimneys carried the third floor down.

"Where are you Ruth!" a girl called hysterically to her roommate as the floor cracked in two and the roommate's bed fell away down with the broken-off half. Ruth, landing far below, rose, dusted off the plaster and called back,

"Just down here in the parlor."

"The third floor has gone down into the parlor!" the word went round Roble. "Thank heaven, now we'll have some new parlor furniture!" cried a frivolous miss. At the edge of one gaping hole a door jammed and the girl within called that she could not get out. Instantly

Rose Window of the Memorial Church,
destroyed by the earthquake

Memorial Arch, destroyed by the earthquake

a little mouse of a thing miraculously possessed herself of a hammer, ran along the quivering floor at the edge of the chasm, pounded in a door panel and pulled the prisoner out. Another girl came out of her room through the transom. Then they all ran downstairs and reported in good order in the lobby.

A student in Encina Hall sat on the edge of his quaking bed and thought "This is the end," but did not attempt to escape until a tank burst somewhere and flooded his room, when he cried *"A tidal wave!"* and ran for his life.

That morning we did not realize that many of the buildings were not badly injured; it seemed to us everything was gone, and we said to each other as we went home to get something to eat: "The University is in ruins." Mrs. Johnston hailed us as we passed her house; she was giving everybody coffee.

Presently a boy went from door to door with the message that Mt. Hamilton had sent word to expect another shock at eleven. This was afterward found to be a fake but was dramatic at the time. [As the Mt. Hamilton Observatory had the biggest telescope in the country I suppose we thought they would be informed!] We took down our pictures and the big mirror and moved them and ourselves into the back yard, where we sat waiting on the lawn in rocking-chairs. Sure enough, at eleven we were gently jarred. At three, still on the back lawn, a smart shock gave us the opportunity to see from the outside our house jiggling ponderously. The Chinese cook at Roble Hall heard that Dr. Jordan was predicting more shocks and asked (reasonably): "Why he not tell us about the first one?"

We had scarcely time to realize our own situation when rumors began to come that San Francisco was shaken to pieces and on fire. By afternoon a murky cloud rose in the northwest which we did not understand. A Japanese said they always had an atmosphere like that after earthquakes in Japan. But it was the murk of the burning city. The air for two days was hot and breathless. Telegraph connections were broken; trains did not come in. Automobiles flew up the highway and brought back the news. There was no getting word in or out. On Friday an automobile started off with seven hundred telegrams from the University to find an office where they could be despatched. Oakland was in connection with the East but the office had already such an enormous number waiting to be sent that they refused our lot. Our men went on to Sacramento by train and found seven thousand on file there awaiting their turn. Sacramento, however, received our messages, sent them by rail to Reno, where they at last got on the wires. Our messenger brought back from the Sacramento office three thousand telegrams from eastward which he distributed as he came. Today, the 23rd, telegrams are coming in from the East dated the 18th and 19th.

[The isolation of the earthquake area for days caused, naturally, great confusion and distress. Poor Aunt Julie in Texas envisaged complete devastation. She sent Mother a letter, which arrived two weeks late, containing a sheet of blank paper, a stamped envelope, and a small stub of lead pencil, hoping thus to re-establish communication—if Mother still lived!]

On the campus and in Palo Alto a patrol was organized at once; the Quadrangle and dangerous buildings roped off and guards placed to keep away thieves and the plentiful idiots who would risk their lives to pick up a souvenir. [Leslie went to his office in the Administration rooms of the Inner Quadrangle all that summer with a pass.] Until Sunday, when it rained, the campus lived and slept outdoors. Slight tremors continuing, sometimes a more important one, making us very skittish. With all chimneys down and no lights but candles, and the houses a chaos of fallen plaster, the lawns and gardens were preferable. [Dr. Branner, our eminent geologist, said the slight shocks were of no consequence and there would likely not be another big one in forty years. Nobody believed him, except his family, who went to bed in the house as usual the very first night, the only people to sleep inside on the campus!] So we fixed up our cots and pallets in the yard among the fruit trees and rosebushes. All up and down the Row after dark you could hear the low tones of domestic conversations beyond the hedges and the children getting to bed.

On the streets the fraternity boys rolled up in blankets and slept. Excited young people sat around bonfires and chattered half the night. We heard the booming of explosions in the city—fire-fighting, with water mains broken and the Fire Chief killed by a falling brick. Two nights, before going to bed on the back lawn, we went out and stood in the road and saw the great red glow in the sky northward behind our ragged Church tower, the light of a city on fire.

Encina was unsafe and the boys made for themselves coverts in the shrubbery lining the road to the Hall and named it "Easy Street." Along its length were placards admonishing you not to walk on the grass, not to talk too loud, *please* not to pick the flowers; you were gently requested not to smoke. A fraternity house was practically demolished and the inmates established quite elegant quarters on the tennis court. Along one backstop ran the beds, coyly draped with lace curtains. The other backstop, hung with rugs, became the dining room wall and bore a large label: "Wieland's Pale Ale." An unmoved Chinaman squatted there before an improvised stove built of bricks from a fallen chimney. Their walk was labeled "Daisy Avenue," and their reeling house placarded with treasures from (apparently) many a Hallowe'en—"House to let. Enquire within," "We build to suit," and so on.

Relief for San Francisco was organized as soon as Wednesday. "300,000 people homeless" ran a message from General Funston, "famine imminent unless vigorous measures be taken." We knew the Red

Cross and the entire country would spring to relief, but with railroads crippled and communication cut we feared their help would be delayed. Little Palo Alto with its own chimneys down, stores wrecked, streets cluttered with fallen walls, joined with the University people in a mass meeting Wednesday evening. Mr. Carey, the butcher, donated five hundred pounds of meat; it was cooked in the night by Palo Alto women in the kitchens of the Congregational Church, and sent up with other provisions Thursday morning by train, the first load to get to San Francisco over the repaired railroad track. Los Angeles started a load on Wednesday, but it was stalled by injured tracks south of us. From Wednesday on, relief work occupied everyone. Headquarters at Palo Alto were open day and night; places were offered for refugees; bedding and clothing were collected and sent up. [I contributed the last remnant of my York State wardrobe, a set of all-wool, double-breasted, Jaeger union suits, high-necked, long-sleeved, ankle-length. I bet some woman sleeping cold in the Park was glad of them. I did not want them any more anyway.] The bakeries turned out bread, bread, bread, endlessly, and it was sped to the City in truck loads. We were expected to eat as little as possible here at home. Late Saturday a call came down for clothing for women and children, *especially infants.* Sixty babies had been born since Wednesday *in Golden Gate Park alone!* Every mother on the campus and in town rose up early Sunday morning to ransack the house for baby clothes and old linen. There was no going to church; we worked all day. I think there was no church, even the ministers too busy to preach. All day we made up kits marked "Mother and Child," a few necessities, rolled up in a warm wrap for a babe and fastened with a big safety pin. Many truckloads went to San Francisco Sunday and Monday.

In the city martial law had of course been immediately proclaimed and General Funston from the Presidio in charge. All the tents the United States Army possessed were either there for use or on the way in. Thousands of refugees were cared for in the cities around the Bay; thousands left on trains as soon as they could with free transportation to any destination, however distant. Camps were set up in all possible places, the sanitation regulated; there was no epidemic and little sickness, though the babies kept on arriving. The homeless crowding the camps and the parks and the hills were cheerful, preserved order, cleaned up their streets, and washed their children's faces. "Even the children did not cry," an eyewitness declared.

Now, less than a week after the tremendous disaster, not only are all those who fled from the burning streets cared for, but the great thoroughfare of Market Street, destroyed nearly its entire length, is cleared. Automobiles busily traverse it. Car lines have been repaired under incredible difficulties and are resuming transportation—free. Shattered sewers and water mains are getting mended rapidly, many now in use again. The lights are coming back. Thousands are at work clearing the ruins hardly cold. The great department stores are advertising to meet their employees at once; business houses advertise new, temporary, quarters and are doing business "as usual" with prices normal. The Mint is unhurt and the government has made its stores of coin available here as soon as the vaults are cool enough to open. Banks issue reassuring statements and expect to open in temporary quarters as soon as their safes and vaults are cool enough to be examined. Contractors and builders have announced they will not advance prices.

The burned-out newspapers, now printed across the Bay, report enthusiastic plans on a vast scale for a new and magnificent San Francisco. The city considers itself in amazing luck to have this unprecedented opportunity for carrying out extensive improvements long needed but almost impossible heretofore. Better buildings, earthquake proof and fireproof; finer streets, more parks. According to the press headlines "San Francisco will arise like magic, greater than ever before," "San Francisco's loss is the greatest in history. The fire caused a greater monetary loss than the fires of Chicago, Boston and Baltimore combined. We shall beat them by from twenty to fifty million and what's more it looks as though we would get more insurance than all of them besides!" This is the newspapers' boast. "Pompeii isn't in it," crows one excited person. "I saw all that was worth seeing in Pompeii in an hour and today it took me three hours to walk across one edge only of the burnt portion of San Francisco!"

So far the contemporary account. At the campus Dr. Jordan announced at the first that classes would be excused *until the end of the week,* which was very like Dr. Jordan, peace to his gallant, golden soul! Later in the day, after damage had been investigated, he announced the University would be closed for the remainder of the academic year. Suitable arrangements were made about the seniors' credits. They had of course no Commencement in June, but it was held on September 15 and they received their diplomas.

A few days of excitement and uncertainty, of waiting for money to go home, and then the campus emptied of students and the work of repair and rebuilding began. The incredible rubbish was soon reduced and disappeared, a lot of it went, I do believe, to fill up the Frenchman's Lake, which has been gone for so long now that nobody believes it was ever there. The Church was seen to be such a wreck that it was later taken down to the foundations and rebuilt, after the original designs for the most part, but with a steel framework. The University was able to reopen in August. The students returned, Stanford carried on. An earthquake could not daunt us.

In 1913 Dr. Jordan retired from the presidency, after twenty-two years of service, and was appointed Chancellor of the University. He had become deeply interested in the question of world peace and had begun to take an active part in efforts to promote it. In 1910 he was made Chief Director of the World Peace Foundation established by Mr. Edwin Ginn of Boston, and in the years following, on leave from the University, had visited Europe, Japan, and other countries in peace work. To this work he now wished to devote his "declining years."

Our dear Dr. Branner, who told us darkie stories, and named our cat, and remembered to bring home from Switzerland the little carved bear for Christabel; who had been Dr. Jordan's intimate friend and co-worker from the beginning and his chosen vice-president, Dr. Branner was named to the presidency. He accepted the office dutifully but would consent to hold it only two years, when at sixty-five he would himself be eligible for retirement. In 1916 a younger man, Ray Lyman Wilbur, Stanford '96, took his place.

In 1913 Louis, after graduation at Stanford and a year at Cornell, had a position in the government chemical laboratory in New York City; Christabel was in college at Stanford; David in the Palo Alto High School. That year Leslie took a six months' leave. We shook our shoulders free, rented our house, put our daughter to board at Madroño Hall, and went East. David we took with us and in the fall deposited him in St. Louis, to stay the winter with his Uncle Edmund and Aunt Mary and go to school.

We visited our relatives and friends in York State, toured New England by trolley, hunted up the graves of our ancestors in Connecticut, and perused the records of ancestral deeds in the historical archives of Massachusetts. We spent a month in Brookline with Zaidee, who was traveling librarian and organizer for the state of Massachusetts, with headquarters in Boston, and visited my dear Margaret Whiting and Ellen and Margaret Miller at Deerfield. Of them more anon, for they are steeped in indigo and madder and embroidered all over with pretty flowers and flourishes in the old Colonial style. You may not know what I mean, but wait a while.

In December we helped Louis and Helen Nagel make their wedding. It was at Yonkers, in the parlor of the minister. The bride, arrived the night before by overland train from the West, fetching her wedding dress (made by her mother in Los Altos) and packages of wedding gifts in her suitcase. Helen was a Stanford girl, a college mate of Louis', and came alone across the continent to be married. We were glad to be there to give a family touch to the occasion; and the minister's wife and sister made much of the party and gave us the unexpected courtesy of cake and lemonade after the ceremony. They admired Helen's courage and independence and praised her. Leslie and I took the bride and groom to a little restaurant, the best I had been able to find, yet rather naïve, and we had a bridal luncheon. The chicken was delicious. The colored man and wife, the proprietors, played up to the situation, waiting on us with delightful airs and manners. Everything was provided just as I had ordered, complete. Then at the very last, after placing dessert and even finger bowls, they brought in *toothpicks*, not nominated in the bond!

Now, having married off our Louis, I had better do the same for our Christabel although it was three years later. She finished college, taught a year, married a Stanford man, Dr. J. Harold Williams, and went to live in southern California. She is surprised to find that her children are "city children." One

of them being taken to the country gazed entranced at a brook
and exclaimed: "They let this brook go just where it wants to!"
As for me, I never get over being surprised that *my* children are
Californians. It seems queer to me when we really belong root
and branch to York State. But you would not think so to hear
my children talk.

XVIII

CONCERNS AND DELIGHTS

We built a house in 1908. We had occupied 10 Alvarado Row seventeen years, meantime choosing sites all over the fields and hills as we walked or drove about the country. For like all bourgeois Americans—I suppose we are bourgeois, though the exact meaning of the term is not clear to me—we desired to plan and possess our own homestead. So when the University opened a new tract on the campus and we could build on a fine little hill not very far from the Quadrangles, and have oak trees and views, and have big gardens among the slopes and dells of the first of the foothills, we ran and snapped up the very choicest location of all. It was a shoulder which dropped abruptly down to lower levels on three sides and thus assured free of interference our distant outlook. We saw not only the Bay and the range beyond it and, on the other side, the Santa Cruz Mountains, "backbone of the Peninsula," but looking northward we saw the Belmont Hills, sprinkled at night with necklaces of stars, and at night also we saw the twinkling ranks of the lights of the Bay cities. Through a field glass we saw the Ferry tower. We saw the great soft white fog creature curl over the mountains from the Pacific, and then we knew it would be cool. We saw from our big sitting-room window the sun set in splendor beyond a far horizon.

Having waded up the hills all summer through the dry grass to our knees, planning and superintending, and the road not yet made, we got into the completed house three or four days before Christmas and ambitiously undertook a Family Christmas Dinner. Mother and Bessie came up from Palo Alto. Louise was present; and Harriett with Herbert Coolidge, her husband, and their children; and all the five Elliotts. And I cooked the turkey, as I always did cook the turkey. It was in the Aladdin oven; the family sat in the sitting room foamed about with tissue paper, looking at their presents. The tree was green and tall and sparkly in the corner. The new fireplace all alight merrily purred. Then, alone in the kitchen, I set the house on fire. I went to peek at the turkey: I lifted off the heavy door of Aladdin and set it on the floor—*wrong*. Over it went *flop*, knocked down the kerosene lamp which was the oven's heater, and instantly the flame licked mocking up the wall. What possessed Aladdin, who never did such a thing before in all the many years of its useful life! One appraising look at the wicked little snake slithering up the wall, and I knew it was beyond me to control it. I went and stood in the sitting-room door and shouted to the company:

"The house is on fire!"

Everybody stared.

"Oh no it isn't," said Louise.

"It is!" I stamped my foot.

Herbert Coolidge sitting on the hob dumped a child from his lap, grabbed up a rug, and leaped to the kitchen; he smothered the flame instantly, really a case of abortion. We finished the turkey in the coal range and collected thirteen dollars insurance for damage to the rug and the wall.

I suppose the Hill would never have been settled up as it now is, homes and gardens covering it nearly to Mayfield and, indeed, with its settlement running out into the foothills beyond, except for the automobile. But the automobile had to win its way. It nosed in at first almost unperceived, an oddity, a plaything, a "horseless carriage" to be laughed at by men and regarded with terror by horses—perhaps with prescience. Dogs were at once driven crazy by motor vehicles, and nobody knows why, although Ouspensky affects an explanation in his *Tertium Organum*. He lays it to Time being a Fourth Dimension, or something like that. I remember our going down to Palo Alto to see "the" automobile (our first), which flourished around in the neighborhood of the station showing off for several days. When they came into actual use and traveled the highways at twenty-five miles an hour, old ladies called them "Devil Wagons" and whoever experimentally rode in them was looked upon as daring. But, indeed, in those days the cars did use to suddenly explode as they sped. I assure you they did: we read about it in the papers.

Naturally Mrs. Stanford would not have devil wagons about. They were forbidden on the campus. She herself was conveyed from place to place in the imposing family coach, and the imposing family coachman drove. The horses were beautiful creatures. It was the ancient and honorable custom; kings had gone around in coaches (now in museums) with beautiful steeds attached: "a coach and pair," "a coach and four"; even Cinderella had once a coach to ride in; and chariots, with horses, were as old as Pharaoh. So she was to the end of her life conveyed in her coach, and her own horses drew her along. This Stanford carriage, to which we were accustomed in all its old-fashioned formality, with its shining brown horses, its solemn old driver, the portly dignified Senator and wife sitting erect behind; and, sadly, Mrs. Stanford later alone; this carriage long afterward came to be sold at auction (an obscure everyday affair) and the carriage was bought, we heard, by Bracchi the fruit man of Mayfield, "for his wife," he said. So automobiles were forbidden. Yet no one could stay them for more than a few early years; presently an exclusive road for them was opened; it led from the highway across the campus to the home of our business manager. No horse-drawn vehicle might traverse it, and no motor vehicle might turn a wheel on any other of the campus streets. This was law, unalterable. When the Vice-President of the United States, Mr. Fairbanks, visited Stanford, he and his party were obliged to alight from their cars at the corner where the auto road crosses Alvarado and walk down the Row to the house of Dr. Stillman, who had invited them to dinner.

Our transportation in early days was various and sometimes quaint. There were buses, with erratic schedules but serving for those few who could not walk or bicycle. Some of them were huge enough to carry a whole picnic, like the celebrated "Marguerite," and useful in such a case. In time a trolley ran up from the highway and connected us with Palo Alto. And finally the autobus came in and the trolley rails and poles went out. Drivers of autobuses are commonplace fellows, chatting gossip with the girl who plants herself behind his ear; but in those magic days we had a tout, a campus guide, a bureau of information, in our rheumatic old driver of buses, Uncle John. He knew everything and much besides. "Them's *ancient liberians*," he stridently declared to his wondering tourist load and directed their gaze to the row of six stone statues standing on top of the Museum against the sky. Me he pointed out quite similarly one day as he drove down Alvarado: *"That's where the Register lives; and that's his wife there settin' on the stoop."* His astounding ballyhoo flowed out in a raucous bellow and none but the totally deaf could miss it. I heard him myself as I was walking down the Avenue to Palo Alto tell a party of astonished strangers that the Senator gave The Boy a million dollars on his twelfth birthday to spend as he pleased, *"and he give it all away to the poor."*

Other novelties besides the auto won our notice, and later possibly our approval and patronage. Would you believe there was a time when the campus knew not the telephone? And when at last they were brought into the University offices their use was suspiciously restricted by the management lest the campus ladies come in to order their groceries through their husbands' telephones. We were very green in those days. We did not know there was a way to see your skeleton right through your flesh. When we read about it in the papers we said "Pooh, pooh," and laughed.

And we laughed about the flies carrying germs. Christabel was having a light case of diphtheria. I had come down from the sickroom to get a breath of fresh air on the porch. Mrs. Green, who lived back of us on Salvatierra, came round the corner of the house and sat down on the steps. She asked after Christabel. Then, with an apologetic half-laugh, as though she were merely passing on a bit of rumored nonsense, she said:

"They say that *flies* cause diphtheria."

"Flies!" The idea seemed comic, the little innocent creature ("Baby by, here's a fly, Let us watch him, you and I"). I laughed too, superciliously.

But only the next day Dr. Will Snow came and asked politely if he might catch some of our flies; we gave him permission; he did so in the back yard, took them home to analyze, and *found the germs on them!* "Streptococky" I think. He reported to us, seriously. It was a great enlightenment, after we got over regarding it as a joke.

Yet, though green, we were intelligent; we also felt our responsibilities. The discussion, for instance, of Women's Suffrage reached even our academic seclusion, touched, if lightly, even the woman who was "sheltered" and "happily married," like me. True, to be sheltered and happily married were considered handicaps to realistic thinking. And there was among us a certain indifference to The Vote. I myself seem to have resented, mildly, the proposal to add the vote to all my other obligations, of which I felt I had already a plenty. We laughed appreciatively at the joke of one exasperated sister crying out that "if there is any little old thing a man can do without a woman's help I say let him do it!" And the washerwoman growled "*I* ain't goin' to vote—got enough to do without."

But our consciences were uneasy. Perhaps we *ought* to desire the suffrage; perhaps our elevating influence *was* required in politics. Just here I read a piece by a man which said: "Nine out of ten women who clamor for the vote do so because they think they can run the country better than men." This swung me back again. No, I said to the man in the magazine, not so large a proportion as nine out of ten women are fools—"damn fools," I should have said except that I was raised at a time when your damns (if a woman) remained suppressed desires. No, no; and I reiterated loyally that axiom about the grand success our men had made in public affairs ever since they first undertook to run them. After all, I said to myself, dismissing the man in the magazine, I daresay our simple little feminine ways would never do in politics—be just a monkey wrench in the machinery— Anyway, as the washerwoman says, we have enough to do without. I, for one, have all the rights I want, I said, and more duties than I want, and less time to myself every year I live. I don't *want* the ballot, get away with you! Plenty women felt this way, and our puzzled good American menfolks stood by more ready, I do believe, to give us the suffrage than we to receive it.

Into this aloof and frivoling atmosphere came to us and spoke in the little Chapel room a distinguished beautiful person, Susan B. Anthony, and with her Mrs. Catt. In an evening, in an hour of earnest enlightening speech, those two changed my mind forever. I was ashamed. I was converted. I had been blessed, for no deserving of my own, with all the rights I wanted from my birth. No man of all my kin or connections had ever imposed upon me or coerced me, or wished to. So, being happy and free, and fortunate, I would let misfortune go hang! So, I would go on picking roses in the garden while I wreathed a foolish roundelay about my already possessed rights! I repudiated such egotism as soon as I came to see it.

I doubt if any group in history on obtaining the ballot ever before set to work so industriously as we to educate themselves for their new duties. In California, at least, the women organized state-wide for the study of the forms of government, the technique of elections and political campaigns, the composition of legislatures and courts, and all the machinery of municipal, county, and state government. The work we did in clubs and meetings, the reading and study we undertook, the efficiency of our leaders who marshaled and directed us, that was to our credit. I have seldom seen it noted or heard any praise for such a novel approach to the exercise of citizenship.

The hourglass corset, somewhat modified, still standardized the silhouette in my young days. "Uncorsetted" was a term of reproach, ladies did not spill around so immodestly, especially if fat. I, however, was a wisp, my weight a scant ninety pounds, and I got by without corsets, the very idea of which I detested. But with what a price did I purchase my freedom! No freak, I understood perfectly that it was necessary to *look* as though I had on a corset; and I accomplished it by fashionable seams, whalebones in all of them, firm linings, uncompromising fit, and reinforcements underneath by means of corded, stiffened waists, thick and elaborate. This waist, an *ersatz* garment, had to "hold up the skirts," too, the dress skirt and enough petticoats (some to the knee and some to the floor) to keep you warm in winter and assure that you did not "show through" in summer. People used to excuse the corset itself by yarning that it held up the petticoats, but I never could understand the mechanics of that. My underwaists, however, with rows of buttons round and round, did hold up my petticoats or I would know the reason why. One of them that I invented ran down into a sort of hip-yoke and carried three rows of white china buttons, on which hung by appropriate buttonholes at least three of my skirts, the bands lying one above the other like shingles on a roof ("avoiding constriction and distributing the weight"). Skirts were indeed a sad problem, to busy and sensible women. We had to have so many of them on, and for cold weather the long ones were liable to be of dark heavy wool, perhaps quilted besides, and the short under ones red flannel—red being celebrated as a warm color. The layers of starched-muslin summer ones, ruffled and embroidered (and "shimmies," too), were almost as heavy and made lots of washing. But it had to be.

Our dresses were fitted, lined, and buckrammed, touched the floor always, and half of them trailed. I have seen girl students with trails on the Stanford Quadrangles sweeping the pavement, the process assisted by "brush braid" sewed on to the bottom of the dress skirts. I walked around the Seventeen-Mile Drive at Monterey in an afternoon dress, holding up its modest train in one hand. No, I never wore a hoop skirt; that was before my time. And I never wore a bustle either; I considered them vulgar.

For many years nobody asked: "Why don't we take off some of our petticoats? Why don't we hang our dresses upon our shoulders instead of our 'stomachs'? Why don't we cut them off a few inches at the bottom?" But the worms turned at last; and Jenness-Miller, among others, arose. She reduced underskirts and turned the dress into a one-piece garment, neat and comfortable, and clearing the ground. "Dress Reform," among the busy and sensible, was on. Bloomers came coyly forward, thick full dark woolen things, very bunglesome where they banded below the knee, used exclusively for bicycling and athletics. One did not have bloomers as a garment by itself— like pants; they were an element in a complete costume. My first costume was navy blue serge, full bloomers, lined gored skirt to my ankles, Eton jacket over a wash blouse. Though an ardent reformer, I felt so conspicuous in it that I carried a tennis racket when crossing the campus. Mrs. Gilbert, who knew I was no tennis player, laughed at me. She said it wasn't witnessing to my principles.

When bloomers began to be tolerated without the skirt, or when the skirt over them was daringly shortened to the calf, we clothed our exposure with some kind of a legging, a khaki one buttoning up the side to the knee was stylish. A second time I

walked around the Seventeen-Mile Drive and felt bold and free
in the navy blue serge described above. Whenever people were
in sight on the road I wore the skirt; but when we came to a
long empty stretch and Leslie and I were alone I stepped behind
a rock and took it off and pranced on in my bloomers and leggings carrying the skirt rolled up in a netting bag. And bloomers
took a long time to become respectable—a two-legged garment!
Mrs. Bloomer, a modest Christian lady, had started the idea in
an early day under Victorian restrictions—and these do not
easily come out in the wash. A little later than Mrs. Bloomer,
Dr. Mary Walker bolted the paddock, adopted and wore the
complete costume of a man contumaciously, at a time when it
was against the law for a woman to wear trousers, and the United
States government passed special legislation in the case. Dr.
Mary Walker was allowed to dress like a man in every respect;
but, to avoid confusion, she must add to the outfit always some
one feminine item showing that she was a woman. I saw her
in 1913 in the gallery of the Senate Chamber in Washington, a
small, dapper old lady with white shingled hair, trim black
Prince Albert suit, top hat in hand. Black silk ruffles were
sewed to the wrists of her coat sleeves, in compliance with the law!

One could begin reform with the children anyway. Instead
of being trussed up in bellybands my infants wore the "Gertrude suit"—no bands at all and hung from the shoulders.
"What! No bellybands! Aren't you afraid the baby will burst
when he cries?" But mine never did. Christabel had delightful
little gingham things all in one piece, with legs, and she freely
crawled, and she walked, and she ran, and she climbed, and
turned upside down on the trapeze, whenever she wanted to.
True she had frocks and white petticoats "for nice"; and, in
deference to her own maidenly petitions, I gave her a dress over
her bloomers when she went to school. Even so it seems the
eccentricities of her costume caused her great mortification, a
martyrdom I was not then aware of.

"At school," she now informs me, "Malcolm McGilvray used

to jump up on the fence and walk it all around the schoolyard. And I would jump up after him and walk the fence all around. Then the other girls would get up on the fence and start to walk it. But Mrs. Webster would say, 'No, no; you mustn't do that'— 'Why not?' they'd say, 'you let Christabel do it!' 'Christabel has on black bloomers—you've got on drawers and petticoats.'

"But," says my daughter, "all the time I hated the black bloomers and wished I had on white drawers and petticoat."

Yes, the absurdity and inconvenience of our prevailing fashions, their inappropriateness to new habits and new occupations, more and more got on our nerves. We grumbled. We were restive. We tagged along after "The Fashion," it is true, yet there was mutiny in the air. At Stanford we organized. We had a Dress Reform Club, with meetings, and hoped for accomplishment, locally at first; but perhaps our ideas might radiate out, we might reform the world. After much nebulosity it began to emerge in our discussions that the way to clothe ourselves practically, sanely, and (we specified) beautifully, was to study the laws and requirements involved and work out "standardization." Chaos and folly could be overcome by intelligent "standardization." I mention this discussion and our conclusion and aims because so novel at the time and such a proof of our enterprise and acumen. Said I, in a paper written for the Club, airing the notion of "law," "principle," "standard":

The shoulders must conform to certain laws of grace, the sleeves must have a norm and forever be prevented from swelling up into a balloon or shrinking into a sausage bag; the back must be adaptable to every anatomy; the arrangement over the chest calls for careful study as this is the frame for the face. The waistline is the crux, and let not her who possesses one dogmatize for her who does not. . . . . The treatment about the hips and abdomen calls for the greatest skill, if both comfort and beauty are sought . . . . while the general proportions of the garment, its length and width, length of sleeves, and the cut of the neck opening are all factors of importance. . . . . The structure of lines, curves, protuberances, depressions must be studied and understood, and the inner nature of collars, belts, pockets, tabs, reveres, panels, pleats, gathers, hems, fringes, scallops, and the like must be grasped. We must ask ourselves searching questions . . . .

I should think so, indeed! But nothing daunted us. We hoped that "while a certain flexibility would be necessary to adapt the costume to individual personalities" . . . . "a general type may be thus worked out in which fundamentals shall be unalterable." "We want relief at once" . . . . "by putting through a fairly satisfactory conventionalization suitable to quite a proportion of women and near enough to the present vogue to be easily accepted, and worn even by the timid, we believe we shall attain it."

Yes, we struggled and were agitated. We reformed by bits here and there, and camouflaged our tricks. We reformed our little ones, who could not help themselves. Riding astride came in, and helped. Women's athletics helped. The Club elaborated, with much talk, a Pledge about the length of our dresses; some of the members declined it but most of us signed, and it stated that we would never wear a dress with a skirt longer or shorter than six inches from the floor. Standardization.

Then came the hurricane of war, and fashion's flimsy merry-go-round went to pieces. Our clothes emerged, blinking, but (look about you!) revolutionized.

About the time the children were out of my arms and went to school, some quite unmaternal, quite nondomestic yearnings began to worry me. I desired to sing, thought I could sing if I only knew how, technically. I desired to paint, color made me dance all over—desired to dance, too, wished I had learned as a girl; did dance in Madam Emrich's class and won her praise; she declared I "floated." Desired to do something with my fingers itching to make things; settled on embroidery. Now there is embroidery and embroidery. First I went up to Mrs. Griffin's house with a white table napkin and got her to show me how to do my initial in the corner in white. It was not very exciting. Then I went to Mrs. Hodges, next door on Alvarado, and got her to show me how to do a doily with a green leaf outlined around it; for (I thought) I crave color. It took a good while and when finished appeared a dull thing, entirely useless. I guessed the trouble was my disposition for originality, and I went out and gathered eucalyptus leaves, laid them down in an arrangement on paper, and traced around them with a pencil. My intention was a border design of the leaves hanging in a fringe. But why not draw it instead of tracing? I could not draw, never had a single lesson. What, couldn't draw a eucalyptus leaf? No, could not; but I found them easy to trace around . . . .

These dots stand for a period of floundering, the history of which would not be to edification. In time I was guided by my daemon to enter University art classes and learn to draw, color, and design. I worked thus with enthusiasm and patience for several years, taking the class work in large or small lots as my household and social activities allowed. I enlarged my acquaintance with all forms of art; I studied textiles and stitchery; I met the Deerfield ladies, who carried on vegetable dyeing and the Colonial type of embroidery by means of a "village industry," Margaret Whiting and Ellen and Margaret Miller. With their help and inspiration, and the rules dug out of old housekeeping manuals, I became an amateur dyer in the "vegetable" mode. I colored threads and fabrics with the indigo vat, with the tricky madder, with the tannin barks of willow, oak, sumach, maple, which yield you silver, smoky pearl, clear gold tan, greys, browns, and deep gorgeous blacks, if you have the skill. With all the gay and elusive stitches of the world that ladies have worked with their loving fingers I now worked out my own fancies in my own designs and colors and was happy. My embroidery was exhibited in public. Under the caption of "Original Embroidery" it was to be seen at the San Diego and the San Francisco Expositions of 1915, and from the latter it won a large round silver medal.

About 1912–13 there burst up a geyser in the literary world, the "New Poetry." I mention it not because it had anything to do with Stanford, which it did not, but because for me it "marked an epoch."

As I have indicated earlier in this chronicle, I had from the beginning a sort of flair for verse. At ten I wrote doggerel; at fourteen I sent a poem to *St. Nicholas* (*spurlos gesenkt*). *Our Talk*, family paper of the Browns, published my poems. I contributed passable verse to the college publications and was Class Poet at my Cornell graduation. After that my muse went into retirement for a long time. I wrote no poems. But I always knew I *could*, and happily felt that when I had time I *would*.

Meantime I was not even reading poetry much, if any. Longfellow, Whittier, had never gripped me; Holmes had amused me—"The One-Hoss Shay," "The Last Leaf," and all that. Emerson and Thoreau interested me through their prose. Tennyson? Yes, yes; but I almost knew him by heart. Browning? But how could one read him to oneself after hearing Professor Corson's exquisite inflections reveal the abstruse meanings without comment (except the slight pause, the lifting of the eyes to the class, the significant semi-smile)? Lanier? I did keep on with Lanier quite some time, but he was rather lonely to me. I had an occasional Whitman fit, but it passed. We owned Sill and Moody and read them aloud to each other once in a while. On the whole, poetry lay in a half-forgotten background. I was much absorbed those days in living.

Then a creature from Illinois pranced in with a whoop shouting:

"general william booth enters into heaven!"

Everybody sat up and took notice. Even I, though isolated from literary groups, sat up and took notice. I read this astonishing account of what happened in Heaven when General Booth arrived there in some contemporary periodical and took notice all by myself, discussing it with nobody. But Amy Lowell began to babble and bugle and boom, and Free Verse arrived, and the Imagist fog condensed into an Anthology, and Sandburg published his book of poems on Chicago, beginning (nauseously, I thought) "Hog-butcher of the world," and Harriet Monroe, astutely recognizing A Movement, created an organ for it—*Poetry: A Magazine of Verse*. Then I concluded something was doing and I had better look into it.

My initial reaction to Amy Lowell and to Free Verse was absolutely Philistine, to use a term current in my youth. I just laughed and, I fear, pooh-poohed. But my superciliousness had no effect on Miss Lowell or any of the other performers. They kept right on. I began to be curious. Surely, I ruminated, they are not *fools?* Although it was hard work and entirely uncongenial, I took hold and read as it appeared everything poetical with a thorough and conscientious industry. I intended, if possible, to get their point of view; I was piqued by these solemn antics; my brains were challenged. I could not help laughing (the sense of humor cannot always be controlled) when A. Lowell told in her nonchalant free verse about how she would like to sit straddle of a ridgepole and shingle a roof; I heard she was fat, and I have a vividly pictorial imagination. Besides, you do not shingle a roof that way. Sandburg's *Chicago Poems,* most carefully perused with open mind, yielded me not one ray of pleasure. The lovely poem on Fog—"The fog comes, on little cat feet"—touched me not; it lay, for me, a pebble dirtied in the mud. When I finished the volume I said aloud with conviction, "There is not one spark of beauty in it." Lindsay couldn't help but thrill me, I respected him for sticking to rhyme and meter (even if his meter did caper), but why so vulgar? That is another word we used to have when I was young. Of course no one with a bit of poetic sensitiveness could fail to be startled and charmed with Millay's "Renascence." But it took many readings before I could realize what it was all about.

My education progressed. The New Poetry became not

only intelligible and beautiful to me, but the fresh creative impulse let loose by it in our literature caught me up and swept me along in its rapid current and for more than twenty-five years now has informed and vivified my intellectual life. I own thirty feet of library shelves (I measured them with a yard-stick) devoted to books on modern poetry and critical, his-torical, and technical books *about* poetry. All this time I have read and studied everything I could lay my hands on in that field, and greeted the newer poets as they came along. And I have seen now the waning and dispersing of the Movement so suddenly born in 1912. Amy Lowell, the masterful, is gone; Lindsay is gone; Teasdale is gone; Elinor Wylie is gone; Mar-guerite Wilkinson, that helpful handmaid and no mean poet herself, is gone; Harriet Monroe, the invaluable, is gone; Robin-son is gone. Millay, Frost, Sandburg remain, the gods be praised. But nobody seems young any more. How brief the generations!

So drenched in poetry for so long, I, of course, began to do what I had always expected to do when I had time: I began to write poetry myself. If anybody asks you what is my "hobby," reprove them first for using that silly term, but answer them, "Poetry."

"*Cheer up! The worst is yet to come!*" the slogan of The Pirate Camp, skull and crossbones their banner, the pirates our David, Sid and Billie Adams, Dick Ramsey, Francis Bergstrom, probably Remond Richardson; Leslie and Professor Bergstrom for the grown-up element, and Christabel in her teens the femi-nine to rule the kitchen. They went to Peters Creek; they swam and fished and did athletics under Francis' father, and ate up sugar so fast that Leslie had to bicycle several times to La Honda for more. (It was learned finally that at breakfast they added sugar to their chocolate until the spoon stood up.) They stayed two weeks gamboling in the redwoods; and there was never a camp like it, so they say.

"*Cheer up! The worst is yet to come!*"

XIX

WAR

I DON'T GET reconciled to this war," Mother said soberly. She was a bride when the war of her generation broke in the 'sixties, married in the North and living there, her birthplace and home in South Carolina and four brothers in the Southern army. Aunt Lida was seventeen then. They scraped lint and rolled bandages for the wounded, wore crape for the killed, read the papers for the lists of "casualties," made little kits for the use of the soldiers, and presented them with flags and flowers and cheers to the departing troops: the Volunteers, the Conscripts, Lincoln's "four hundred thousand more." It had all come round again, a dreary iteration. Aunt Lida was not reconciled to the war either. They were old women; they remembered the Past.

And I too was a pacifist, in principle. *Only this once more.* War cannot end until Germany is beaten, and this is the *war to end war*. This I wrote to Aunt Lida in a letter. "So, you see, we *must* fight," I said to her.

First I voted for Wilson because he kept us out of war. Then afterward a large group of our faculty men got up a paper and signed it with their names. They urged the President to declare war on Germany and sent it to the White House. But this was after the newspapers of February 1, 1917. We read our *San Francisco Chronicle* at the breakfast table; the entire country read its daily paper at the breakfast table on February 1, 1917:

"I beg to direct attention" (it is the German Ambassador to the United States speaking for his government) "to the enclosed

313

memoranda . . . . and to give expression at the same time to the expectation that the American Government will warn American vessels against entering the proscribed areas described in the enclosure and warn its nationals not to confide passengers or goods to vessels touching ports in the proscribed areas . . . ."

Then follow two "memorandums." Memorandum 1, that Germany will "forcibly prevent," after February 1, 1917, "in a zone around Great Britain, France, Italy, and in the eastern Mediterranean all navigation, that of neutrals included, from and to England and from and to France . . . . All ships within that zone will be sunk. . . . ."

Memorandum 2: "From February 1, 1917, all sea traffic will be stopped with every available weapon and without further notice in the following blockade zones around Great Britain, France, Italy, and in the eastern Mediterranean . . . ." (zones specified).

"Neutral ships navigating these blockade zones do so at their own risk . . . . Sailing of regular American passenger ships may continue undisturbed IF:

"(a) the port of destination is Falmouth.

"(b) sailing to or coming from that port course is taken via the Scilly Islands and a point 50° N. 20° W.

"(c) the steamers are marked in the following way which must not be allowed to other vessels in American ports." (Then follow directions for painting up the ships so as not to have them bombed by submarines—very explicit and German.) "On ship's hull and superstructure 3 vertical stripes 1 meter wide, each to be painted alternately white and red. Each mast should show a large flag checkered white and red, and the stern the American national flag." Also, meticulously: "Care should be taken that, during dark, national flag and painted marks are easily recognizable from a distance and that boats are well lighted throughout.

"(*d*) one steamer a week only is to sail in each direction 'with arrival at Falmouth on Sunday and departure from Falmouth on Wednesday.'

"(*e*) and the United States Government must guarantee that these permitted steamers carry no contraband 'according to the German contraband list.' "

The nation laid down its daily paper astounded, for it was at that very moment the morning of February 1, 1917. Three months later, on April 7, 1917, the President, backed by the country, proclaimed our entrance into the War.

Instantly the young men were involved, cannon-fodder. Military training was made compulsory in all colleges for all male students. In June 1917 came the universal draft, all men between twenty-one and thirty liable to conscription. But, heaven be praised, David was still in college, not yet twenty-one. Louis in the federal employ as a chemist was advised against enlistment and if drafted would be excused. We seemed quite safe. David, it is true, was not too young to enlist. His chum since their primer days, Billie Adams, enlisted even before we entered the war and went to France in February 1917 with the First Stanford Ambulance Unit. He served until the Armistice with never a scratch and finished his course at the University later. The Second Stanford Ambulance Unit went over in May 1917. Arthur Kimber, David's intimate, who played chess with him in David's bedroom and the 'cello in John Kimber's orchestra where David did the oboe, went with the Second Unit, right out of college. In France he left the ambulance service for aviation and was blown to bits in his plane "in action," September 1918, aged twenty-two.

"Good luck to Arthur Kimber!" wrote Theodore Roosevelt over his own signature May 11, 1917.

Arthur, that nice, musical, chess-playing boy, who with his brothers and his mother were almost as familiar and intimate with us as our relatives, had a unique duty laid upon him. His Corps Commander chose him for the honor of carrying the first American flag officially sent to France with the troops going overseas. It was known and authorized at Washington; Theodore Roosevelt characteristically sent to the proud boy his good-luck letter, and all the Stanford people on the campus and in town were thrilled with patriotic enthusiasm.

"The Friends of France," with the "American League of California," presented the flags and sponsored, on April 24, 1917, the leave-taking of the Second Stanford Ambulance Unit and a group of forty-two ambulance-service volunteers going at this time from the University of California. Twelve thousand persons gathered in San Francisco's Civic Auditorium for the ceremonies.

From here on I make use of Mrs. Kimber's book, *The Story of the First Flag,* in quotation and reference. She was of course present on the occasion and writes a firsthand account.

"The young men were presented with brassards bearing the insignia of the Society, by the "Friends of France," and four American flags—the gift of the "American League of California," to be taken "by the volunteers under service and with the authority of the War Department to the battle fronts of Europe—were . . . . dedicated." 2500 Berkeley students, 1500 of them uniformed cadets, a thousand Stanford men, detachments from the United States Army and Navy, marched in procession from the Ferry up Market Street. Cheers from the sidewalks. Speeches at the mass meeting in the Auditorium. Cheers bursting the Auditorium. Thousands singing national anthems— "Indisputable evidence" says Mrs. Kimber mildly, "that public feeling had been aroused." "The audience felt that behind the ceremonies lay a great idea—the idea of Liberty! The flags, the strains of 'America,' of 'The Marseillaise,' and of 'The Star-Spangled Banner' were but symbols of that idea. And the sixty-three young men on the platform—young Americans about to leave their homes and their country on a mission of mercy, to serve Humanity by succoring those who shed their blood for Humanity—they, too, were symbols of Liberty, and they were about to take up their service—in France! . . . . In France where the world had seen the ideal of democracy nourished and made strong . . . . and civilization attain to perfect flowering . . . . France, upholding before the world honor and justice and giving the world Beauty. . . . . We were thrilled not only with pride in America—who, breaking at last her long and patient silence, has so noble spoken—but with pride in seeing our nation standing by the side of France, valiant, resolute, invincible . . . ."

The French consul-general was introduced: "the great audience rose . . . . and shouted its acclaim of the representative of France . . . . homage cried across land and sea to the anguished but proud mother of the bravest men and women on earth."

It was a University occasion, a California occasion, an expression of our corner of the United States of America in the first days of our War. Dr. Barrows of the University of California presided; Mayor Rolph of the City of San Francisco spoke, Dr. Wilbur, president of Stanford, spoke, Mrs. Herbert Hoover spoke (Mr. Hoover abroad administering the Commission for Relief in Belgium), young men representing the two colleges and the volunteers, representatives of the clergy and of the Army spoke. And the President of the Friends of France said "The soul of America is triumphant . . . . on the 2d of April, through the immortal words of our President, the nation spoke, and the heart of every true American found peace."

The brassards were pinned upon the sleeves of the volunteers by Mrs. Hoover, and Père Thiery of the French Church pronounced their benediction—"O God, whose ways are inscrutable . . . . thou knowest how to bring good out of evil . . . ." It was not hard to bless young volunteers going out for ambulance service and not to kill. "Then to the music of fife and drum the banners of the Allies were carried up the aisles by

Boy Scouts; the martyr nations and the champion nations side by side—Belgium and Serbia beside France and England, Italy, Japan, Portugal." The four flags were presented to the volunteers by Professor Gayley of the University of California, and the Rev. Walter Cambridge made the following dedicatory prayer:

O Almighty God, who has made of one blood all nations of men, and ordained that in Thy service all shall be free, we give Thee thanks for the freedom which our fathers wrought out in righteousness and preserved to us with their blood; the freedom of which they made the flag of our country the symbol. Grant us now Thy favor, as we bless in Thy name these emblems of our liberty. Unfurled in foreign lands, may they witness there that our faltering and neglect are ended, and so mightily renew the courage of those who are our allies in the service of humanity. And to this end, accept us, O Lord, as in the presence of these colors we renew our solemn purpose to preserve for ourselves and for our children the spirit of those who founded our institutions, as we dedicate ourselves to the effort which is to make our flag everywhere respected as the symbol of power devoted to the service of righteousness and justice and freedom. Grant this, we pray Thee, in the name of Christ. Amen.

These four flags so solemnly presented to the college boys were officially designated by the Secretary of War as the first flags to be sanctioned by the government to represent the United States overseas, and the Stanford flag was the first of the four to arrive "at the front." As the First Stanford Ambulance Unit was already in France, having volunteered and gone over in February, it was decided that to them was due the honor of receiving the First Flag, now in the care of the Second Ambulance Unit. Instead of waiting until the Second Unit got off, it was arranged that the flag should be sent over at once by an advance guard, Arthur Kimber, a Second Unit volunteer, being appointed to the post.

His mother accompanying him, Arthur went immediately to New York, the precious flag "wrapped in its black case" never leaving his side. It was a few days before he could sail. The members of the University of California Units meantime came on to New York also for their sailing. A parade of student volunteers was arranged. U.C. and Stanford are enemies by code, and clash every year in November at a mighty football climax. Here was a Stanford man detached from his gang and in possession of an official banner destined for Stanford men in France. "The Berkeley men seemed much interested in me," runs Arthur's letter, "asked many questions regarding where I was staying and when going to sail. I changed the subject. . . . . We went to Fifty-ninth Street and Fifth Avenue where the parade was to start. And then it happened . . . . Suddenly as I was getting my flag ready they rushed on me . . . . 30 or 40 men overpowered me right before everybody, grabbed the flag, put it in a taxi and rushed it off . . . . I fought my way clear and rushed for the taxi. It was speeding up Central Park Drive with the Stanford flag . . . . I jumped on the running board of a fine car—I don't know whose. The man was dumbfounded but I ordered him on . . . . we picked up a policeman and he commanded the driver to open his throttle. I guess the cop thought a murder had been committed." They caught the Berkeley car, "and believe me the U.C. man was scared when the angry cop asked me if I wanted him arrested." So Arthur and the flag and the U.C. boys drove meekly back together and took their proper places in the parade.

Until the sailing the flag was sheltered in the chancel of the Old Trinity Church, by invitation of the rector. On Sunday, May 13, "the presence of the flag gave to the service a solemn and impressive atmosphere. Hundreds of people knelt before the consecrated emblem and prayed for the great cause to which the flag was dedicated. Some wept, others kissed the folds of the flag and went out." On May 14, 1917, Arthur parted from his mother and alone set sail with the flag on the steamship "St. Louis."

On June 4 at Tréveray the Presentation took place. Arthur's letter describes it: "What a relief! The flag has been presented! . . . . Two French regiments were to be present. And right now let me say that never before has such an honor been con-

ferred on any American force in France—not only to carry the
First Official Flag, but to have such a welcome from the French
Army . . . . Lieutenant Boudrez, Mr. Fishoff and I, in the
staff car . . . . were driven by a splendid French army chauffeur who kept up a constant speed of 35 to 40 miles an hour
around corners and through villages . . . . The complete ambulance unit"—the First Stanford Unit—"crowded into five of the
ambulances, followed us." The First Unit had Alan Nichols
in it, an intimate student friend of Arthur's, who soon lost his
life in the service.

Arrived at the field Arthur was given instructions how to
proceed, and he says he was mighty glad of instructions when
the moment of the ceremony came and he was trying to recall
the little speech he had made up the night before "sitting for 3
hours in Alan's ambulance, and finally turned in, at eleven
o'clock, having got things in some shape."

"The field of review was on top of a high hill overlooking
the valley and village, and with a wonderful outlook in all directions. As we approached we could see company after company
of French soldiers maneuvering into position. They all wore
the steel helmets and had the bayonets in place.

"First the Colonel reviewed the troops by riding up and
down in front of them. Then he took his place just in front and
I marched to position with a French guard of honor, and the
staff officers and guards took their places in our rear. Right in
front of them were Alan Nichols, 'Doc' Speers (to be official
color bearer after the presentation) and Walter Snook. Nichols
and Snook are now escorts to the colors. Behind them were the
French flags and regimental standards with their guards of
honor, and behind them the band. The Stanford boys lined up
in back of them. To either side were the two regiments and the
two mounted officers. At a signal from the Colonel I started my
speech . . . ." The good boy continues with his speech, "as
near as I can remember it," so that his mother and brothers may
know just what he said. It is a good speech, straightforward

and modest. I am sure his mother loved it. He says at the end, addressing the men of the First Stanford Unit: "I feel greatly honored to have been selected to carry this flag to you, and I assure you that it is with a very deep feeling of pride and relief that I complete my mission and hand the flag over to Colonel Colon, who will present it.

"My Colonel, here is the flag."

The Colonel, says Arthur, then made a very eloquent address and presented the flag to Roland Speers, now its official bearer. The band played the "Star Spangled Banner" and ended with the "Marseillaise"—they had played the "Marseillaise" before while the troops were marching into position. "One of the Stanford boys afterward told me that the Stanford men were just on the verge of crying, and that tears came into his eyes during the ceremony and speeches, but when the band struck up our national air right in back of them shivers went down his body. And other men said they felt the same."

On July 6, 1917, this flag was honored again, the Croix de Guerre pinned to its folds by the General at a grand review of troops in token of the French Government's appreciation of the services rendered by the Stanford Unit carrying it.

On December 3, 1917, Arthur in Paris got his "wings" from the tailor, "silvery white, with a shield in the middle, and a gold 'U.S.' on the shield. The whole is on a black mounting. They also gave me a plain gold-colored Eagle in Paris today. This is fastened with a pin, but the wings are sewed on the coat just over the heart."

"*The flag is safe.* Walt Malm is carrying it back to the United States and to Stanford."

The flag is at Stanford, shrined in the Memorial Church. During the war a big red banner with an increasing number of gold stars hung drooping from the transept gallery rail, and the flag stood in the chancel by the altar. Arthur, as I have said, was bombed in his plane, and his mother became a gold-star mother.

What could pacifism do in face of such idealism, such beauty, such young exaltation? Do you think those who "kissed the folds of the flag and went out" were pacifists! (*Old women muttered "I am not reconciled to this war."*) The pacifists in those days were mouse-squeaks, a few people jailed and forgotten, while the dragons' teeth went on being sowed. Now they have sprung up. And now I am old like my mother and have lived through the war of my generation. If there is another before I enter into a peaceful eternity I hope for the privilege of going to jail for refusing to fight it.

It was hard on David in his senior year, his mates melting off to war, Billie Adams and Sid and James, Whittier Wellman, Knight Jordan, Dick Ramsey, Kimber; the University depleted of students and faculty, women and men too, for Stanford sent its women's units also to the front. The campus was deadly dull. Nobody cared about college work, and the general opinion was that this generation of youth, having tasted blood, would never again return to such tame routines. We held David to his studies. We insisted that he stay on and graduate. He himself, saying little, felt, miserably, how useless he would be at "the Front." This boy, it was discovered in his early child-hood, had the exceptional ear and musical sensitiveness called "absolute pitch"; he loved music, was a fine pianist. He excelled in certain abstract performances of the brain. He was studying economics; statistics fascinated him. He could beat the whole University in chess and held the rank of chess champion. Once at the Chess Club he did a double checkmate and had all the fellows in the Club standing around looking at the board and saying "how pretty!" He had not an "enemy" in the world. Nobody could imagine David shooting a man or gutting him with a bayonet; he could not even be angry with him; there was not a grain of ill-will, much less violence, in him. Besides, he was tortured by noise and confusion, couldn't get him into a factory or mill to show it to him when he was little because

the noise of the machinery hurt his ears and he did not care
how it worked anyway. How could this boy learn to handle a
weapon who could hardly manage a corkscrew, and endure a
cannonade who flinched at the sudden bang of a door, or live
drenched in blood who was unnerved for a day (to his great
disgust) by a cut on his finger? We began to hear about "shell-
shock" from the first of the war; we could not avoid knowing
what David's senseless fate would be.

But he with all other male students went into military training in 1917. I saw him, a corporal in uniform at parade,
serious and dutiful; far from alight and winged as when quivering with joy at the "Otun," as when whirling through the last
phrases of the "Moonlight Sonata." He looked quite the routine soldier—*hay*-foot, *straw*-foot! He graduated in June 1918,
and we had been a year at war. All his special mates were in it
long ago. The entire country was signing pledges not to use flour
and butter in the kitchens, obeying Mr. Hoover—(a little boy
complained "First there was *Mother,* then there was *God,* and
now there's *Mr. Hoover!*") Nothing further could be done to
procrastinate David, and a career in the Quartermaster's department was considered—an ignominious, but, it was said, a necessary assignment. Superior officers even called it "honorable."
As we had Camp Fremont over against us (the sign posted on
our back fence: *"Military Reservation Keep Out"*), there were
plenty of officers about. I consulted one of them, a kindly gentleman, about David's ears and other handicaps. He was dubious
as to what could be done—if it were flat feet, now, or color-
blindness. Perhaps my son could be of use in a new invention
they were working on for an under-water detector of a distant
submarine; acute hearing would be required for that . . . .
perhaps . . . . He would see about it. Took name and address.

There was then for David a wretched summer interim during
which he lodged briefly at the Y.M.C.A. in San Francisco and his
stranger roommate stole his suitcase with contents; during
which he pressed his pants and burned a perfect flatiron shape,

dark brown, on the seat of them; during which he nearly enlisted, expecting, for one day, a place as an officer's secretary, but
the officer was transferred and he was left nowhere; during
which he had a dreadful attack of influenza.

But he got well, Leslie took him on vacation to Tahoe, and,
the government now evolving the S.A.T.C.—Student Army
Training Corps—he enlisted at last in regular fashion. *"Now
you can put a service flag in the window,"* he said. He was sent
off at once with a batch going to a camp near Waco, Texas. We
did not know why he was assigned to Waco, Texas, instead of to
Camp Fremont over the back fence. The troops left on October
11; he was encamped in Texas mud and rain and cold for a
dreary month, undergoing training. On November 11, the
Armistice. The men in the Officers Training Camps were offered
immediate honorable discharge or continuance in training to
receive their commissions in January. David came straight
home.

"David, what was the general feeling among the boys at the
Armistice? Did most of them want to stay on and complete
their training?"

"Naw! Most all of them voted to go home. We didn't want
commissions; we were in it to beat the Kaiser."

What to do with that excellent all-wool serge khaki uniform
and the warm excellent, all-wool trench coat? It was like the
old Indian bones Father abandoned with utter distaste; David
would have nothing more to do with them. I tried to be thrifty
and have them dyed civilian so he would wear them; tried to
present them to the poor; was at a loss, and did not care much
for them myself. I hung them in a storage closet; the moths ate
them; and I cut the remains up into strips for rag carpet. They
were the best possible material, and we needed the carpet
upstairs.

XX

EMERITUS

THE TIME CAME when, to our surprise, we were "emeritus." Our health was excellent, faculties seemed to be unimpaired; but we were emeritus, a mere routine situation, yet disconcerting. I say "we," although technically the honorable title belongs only to my husband, because a married woman necessarily says "we"; it is in the nature of the case.

Our children were married, well-placed, grandchildren coming on. There was not a thing we could not leave; nothing was anywhere required of us. So we went to Europe. We rented our house and disappeared from our haunts for fifteen months. We went to Rome, Florence, Pisa, Siena, Perugia, Assisi; dabbled our fingers in the blue Mediterranean, stared at plumed Vesuvius, walked in a tender rain over the empty silent streets of Pompeii. We went to Paris in midwinter, streets full of slushy snow and Frenchmen blowing their noses into big white handkerchiefs as they strode. Again to Paris in May and June—ah, Paris were Paradise enow!

The Louvre was heated; woolen stockings, heavy shoes, and galoshes were not required to offset the shivers that ran up your spine from the primeval cold of the stone floors of other treasure houses. Leslie did well enough in those frigid galleries and churches, but he could not equal me and my fortitude. I was elate and drugged by an emotion of Beauty that excluded weariness and cold. I rested on the little rush-bottomed chair in Chartres Cathedral gazing at the rose windows, silently striving, in a trance of enchantment, to possess their glory. Hours I spent in the Uffizi reaching for Botticelli's floating loveliness. I walked the long halls of the galleries and gently stepped about the still cathedrals, a devout and "passionate pilgrim" if ever such could exist in this our present world.

In the Italian spring we took a walk in the fields and saw laburnum dripping gold against the sky, and large blue forget-me-nots and clumps of jonquils growing in the fresh green grass. At Paestum we perched on the crumbling masonry quite solitary among the roofless temple columns except for small grey lizards darting over the grey stones and a cat, prowling, desirous to have the crumbs of our lunch. We saw asphodels growing there on the lonely plain near the sea, and remembered Persephone.

We walked together in the hills of the Alps, and through a clean solemn pine forest, and heard the musical different notes of cowbells far off. Sheepbells I bought in Lugano to take home, for their pretty tinkling music.

We charabanced in France. Once when I sat in front beside the formal, silent chauffeur the dogs dashed out at us over and over again at every gate and crossroad; suddenly, as he swerved to avoid a cur for the fortieth time, the driver remarked quietly to himself "*Toujours le chien.*" It amused me—so literary!

We went to Fontainbleau with a party. The French guide between explanations chatted a little in English. "Do you understand my English?" he asked. We praised his English, justly, and he said he had learned it in the war. "I was at the battle of the Somme; I was lying wounded in my arm, suffering greatly; it was my *elbow*" (a graphic touch!), "and two of those English soldiers came along and they picked me up, one on each side of me, and they said 'Oh cheer up! Come along with us.'" He turned half away with a sort of rapt look on his face as though he had an eternal possession in the memory of that moment. "Oh," he said, smiling at us, "you know you don't forget those things. I shall never forget as long as I live. They just

DR. O. L. ELLIOTT

came along—I might have lost my life!" And afterward he was nursed in the English hospital, and after the war ended "I got some boo-oks and studied the grammar myself."

At Mont San Michel swallows were flying around in the high air among the roofs and pinnacles. They made a continual thin crying, or calling, restless and mysterious. One thought of the souls of the dead. At night I waked in our dim chamber, a thousand stone steps above the white muffle of the tide on the rocks. We put on some garments, stole down the crooked stairway, found the bolted door, and let ourselves out upon a paved lane. It was half-past three, with a gibbous moon. We passed along silently, and on the left was a stone wall, one or two small secret staircases breaking it, and on the right a narrow sunken garden where a marble Virgin glimmered in the half-light. We stopped at the open platform of the bastion and leaned on the sea wall to look upward to the Abbey's shadowy mass rising against the East, dark and high. A cool light wind brushed past us silently. There was not a human sound, and only the soft blowing of boughs in the little wood at the base of the ramparts. We stood quiet, gazing. After a long still pause a fainting pallor exquisitely edged the massive silhouette of the church and, inexpressibly subtle, we saw the first-dawn tenderly unfold its wings.

We lived in London for a time, a quaint city, full of flavor. The waitress, a motherly middle-aged woman, hovered over our breakfast table; she brought us cereal, coffee, toast, muffins, eggs, ham, and marmalade. "What," she exclaimed reproachfully (upon our refusal), *"no kipper?"*

At Grantchester, where we went on account of Rupert Brooke and Byron's Pool, we were directed the way to the old mill by a tottering ancient. When I asked about the mill, he came down from his seat by a shed wall, took his pipe from his mouth, and told me very clearly and carefully. He said there would be "fower housen" and that we should turn in at a little "spinney." I could have hugged him for his stubbly face, his pipe, and those

antique words. I remarked in parting that it was a pleasant day.
"Lovely!" he replied.

We boated on the Thames, and passing under the low pointed
arch of a brick bridge saw nests of mud swallows in the groins
of the roof; and we saw white swans on the water and a black
ruffled swan with a coral bill. There were beds of reeds with
tall bluish stems and tawny grey tips rising at the edge of the
olive-green water. Little scared ducks took wing and kicked up
splashes as they flew.

We jaunted to Iffley because Margaret Whiting had told us
to; saw the legendary old yews in the churchyard, the tiny
church where six paces around inside brought us back to the
door again. The vicar had written out and posted a contemporary notice dated June 1926: "The vicar regrets that lately a
few ladies when visiting the church have not conformed to the
Scriptural precept of having the head covered. He sincerely
hopes that this irregularity will now cease." (We were amused
in Italy, where the women habitually went bareheaded, to see
them whip out their hankerchiefs and lay them on top of their
heads when they entered a church.) Iffley was indeed punc-
tilious. Another notice, long and circumstantial, was affixed to
the door giving directions to worshippers. They were not to
linger outside, because every moment in the House of God is
precious; not to look about to see who is or who is not there;
not to speak to anyone in the church, and not to speak to anyone
going out; not to loiter outside. Do nothing to disturb the solemn communion with your God.

Notices abroad so intrigued me that I got to copying them in
my record book. In San Marco, Venice, you are informed in
laborious English that "It is severely prohibited to spoil the
mosaic-works. The violators will be denounced to the judiciary
authority." In England, "You are requested not to lean or sit
on this fence," and again, politely, "Kindly do not enter this
wood." But the British can also be brusque: "Don't spit. 40

shillings"; "All Dogs found trespassing in this estate and in pursuit of livestock will be shot." Yet I felt that the English temperament was for a fair, logical, perhaps discursive, proposition, rather than to dictate. Sometimes long-winded, their notices evidenced both legal earnestness and a humane goodwill. For instance: "Passengers must keep their seats when riding on the outsides of buses to avoid danger when passing under railway bridges and the overhanging branches of trees. Smokers are requested to occupy the rear seats." A Penrith hotel informs you: "Pursuant to the licensing Acts of 1910 and 1921, intoxicating liquors are permitted to be sold and supplied in these premises between the hours of 3 and 5 p. m. on Tuesday Market Day (except Christmas Day) for the accomodation of persons attending the public market."

In the York Museum a written yellowed notice on a very dusty card, dated five years back when I copied it, set forth a curator's grievance, and one could but sympathize with him. It was tacked to an architectural fragment.

NOTICE

Some thoughtless person of an inquisitive turn of mind, in order to find out what might be underneath the lead covering of this stone, has taken his knife and cut the corner off; the result being that the neat appearance of a good piece of work is spoiled. Perhaps if this irresponsible and destructive person should see this notice, it may interest him to know that it has come to the Curator's knowledge who has laid the matter before the Keeper of the Museum. Any further offense will eventuate in the Society taking drastic measures against the offender.

[*Signed*] W. HARVEY BROOK
Hon. Cur. Med. Antiq.

As you enter Christchurch Meadow, Oxford, there is a conspicuous tall post and upon it a notice or, in fact, a Table of Instructions, directed to the custodians of the park but significant for the public also, whose behavior is unmistakably indicated:

Christchurch Meadow

The Meadow keepers and constables are hereby instructed to prevent the entrance into the Meadow of all beggars, all persons in ragged or very dirty clothes, persons of improper character or who are not decent in appearance and behavior, and to prevent indecent, rude or disorderly conduct of every description.

To allow no handcarts, wheelbarrows, bathchairs, or perambulators (unless they have previous permission from the Very Reverend the Dean), no hawkers or persons carrying parcels or bundles so as to obstruct the walks.

To prevent the flying of kites, throwing stones, throwing balls, bowling hoops, shooting arrows, firing guns or pistols, or playing games attended with danger or inconvenience to passersby. Also fishing in the waters, catching birds, or birdnesting, or cycling.

To prevent all persons cutting names on, breaking or injuring the seats, shrubs, plants, trees or turf.

To prevent the fastening of boats or rafts to the iron palisading or river wall and to prevent encroachments of every kind by the river side.

After our fifteen months we came home, resumed our house on the hill, looked about us. We found everything in surprising equilibrium, considering we *had* been gone fifteen months . . . .

"And so to bed?" Here I should give a doubtful shrug— who can recognize his own bedtime? Perhaps my husband has become an "Elder Statesman"—yet the term "grand old man" is usually substituted, meaning something quite different. Assemblages of women invite me to address them and relate my experiences in "the early days"; they honor me with a boutonniere of white flowers tied with a white ribbon; a pretty young woman with a painted face and scarlet finger nails busily pins it upon my unresisting front exactly where she knows it ought to go. She smiles at me condescendingly, with respect, as she backs away. People call Leslie "Sir," and if my sons and their wives lived in the neighborhood I should certainly be "Madam Elliott"! The young grasp my elbow to assist me into the car, and I have to violently shake loose from their hold upon me when I cross the street in traffic.

It does not become age to retaliate; let our claws be furrily sheathed. We can afford it. We have come through without hanging ourselves from the bedpost or putting a bullet through our brains because they were muddled. *"J'ai vecu!"* said the man when challenged to state what he had done in the French Revolution.

But if we keep our wits (I've kept mine) we must be allowed our good-natured reflections upon the world about us, our chimney-corner soliloquies. My own are not voluminous and concern rather the future, and the hope for the future, than animadversions on the present and regrets and nostalgia for the past. I thank the Lord a baby is born every minute, or more likely every second; do not hold me to statistics for it does not matter. They come along all the time, in legions, like Sandburg's grass.

> "I am the grass
> Let me work—"

and the grass, ever coming on after all rebuffs, after all uprootings, conquers all.

Youth, I suppose, must amuse itself. Tinting toenails and appearing three-quarters naked at inappropriate places may be only high spirits instead of a return to the habits of the primitives. I understand the ancient Britons were but partially clothed and tattooed themselves with "woad," a sort of handsome blue dye. Yet their after-history proved them anything but frivolous.

Youth is our only hold on life. Willy-nilly we have bequeathed our own to these new boys and girls, and I presume they are no worse than we were. But different and new. I say take the stone off the child's head. And that is what has indeed happened. This present generation growing up to so amaze us, for our approval or condemnation—for they cannot be ignored—this is the first generation in the history of mankind that has been allowed its head, undictated to. Always The Past, gently or roughly, but always inexorably, the authority and prestige and power of the past has molded the pliant new life as it came. We thought we had to. We never ceased to con-scientiously "bring up" our children—as one would help up a dandelion toward the sun with his fingers. But now, and doubt-less willy-nilly, too, we have for the first time a free generation, young people who have been given their liberty.

"Of course! That is just what is the matter with them!" shouts the condemner.

But I say liberty is our only chance for Life. Freedom brings license, brings its own abuse; liberty is always a risk. But, for Life, that is the price we pay.

<hr />

Father's tall black "Commentaries" stand in a row on a top shelf of my library; Mother's rocking chair stands in my bed-room; the portrait of my grandmother is in my study. Seneca Lake, the glens and woods of Hector, the hills and chequered fields, church bells of Burdett sounding across the pasture lot, the humming of the Golden Bee, are in my heart. Childhood and age reach round and touch, and we have come full circle.